Python, Java, SQL and JavaScript

The Ultimate Crash Course for Beginners to Master the 4 Most In-Demand Programming Languages, Stand Out from the Crowd and Find High-Paying Jobs

Philip Robbins

© **Copyright 2024 - All rights reserved.**

The content contained within this book may not be reproduced, duplicated or transmitted without direct written permission from the author or the publisher.

Under no circumstances will any blame or legal responsibility be held against the publisher, or author, for any damages, reparation, or monetary loss due to the information contained within this book. Either directly or indirectly.

Legal Notice:

This book is copyright protected. This book is only for personal use. You cannot amend, distribute, sell, use, quote or paraphrase any part, or the content within this book, without the consent of the author or publisher.

Disclaimer Notice:

Please note that the information contained within this document is for educational and entertainment purposes only. All effort has been executed to present accurate, up to date, and reliable, complete information. No warranties of any kind are declared or implied. Readers acknowledge that the author is not engaging in the rendering of legal, financial, medical or professional advice. The content within this book has been derived from various sources. Please consult a licensed professional before attempting any techniques outlined in this book.

By reading this document, the reader agrees that under no circumstances is the author responsible for any losses, direct or indirect, which are incurred as a result of the use of the information contained within this document, including, but not limited to, — errors, omissions, or inaccuracies.

Table of Contents

PYTHON PROGRAMMING — 14

INTRODUCTION — 15

What Is Python? — 15
Who Am I? — 16
How Can This Book Help You? — 17

CHAPTER 1: INTRODUCTION TO PYTHON — 18

History of Python — 18
Applications of Python — 19
Different Versions of Python — 20
Why You Should Learn Python — 21
How to Install Python — 23

CHAPTER 2: PYCHARM AND IDLE — 26

Why is Python Interpreter Good? — 26
How to Use the Python IDLE Shell? — 26
How to Use IDLE to Open Python Files? — 27
How to Change these Files? — 28
IDE (Integrated Development Environment) — 28
PyCharm — 29
Python Style Guide — 32

CHAPTER 3: PYTHON FOUNDATIONS — 34

Why are Input Values Required? — 34
Understanding the input() Function — 34
Comments in Python — 38
Reserved Keywords — 39
Operators in Python — 40
Augmented Assignment Operators — 44
Exercises — 45

CHAPTER 4: PYTHON VARIABLES — 46

What are Variables in Python? — 46
How to Name Variables — 48
How to Define Variables — 48
How to Determine the Memory Address of a Variable — 49
Local and Global Variables — 50

CHAPTER 5: DATA TYPES IN PYTHON — 52

What exactly are Data Types? — 52
Different Data Types — 52
Strings — 53
String Formatting — 56
String Manipulation Techniques — 56
Integers — 58
Floating—Point numbers — 59
Boolean Data Type — 60

CHAPTER 6: ADVANCED DATA STRUCTURES IN PYTHON — 61

Lists — 61
Tuples — 68
Dictionaries — 71
Exercises — 72

CHAPTER 7: CONDITIONALS AND LOOPS — 73

Comparison Operators — 73
Control Flow Statements — 75
If/Else Conditional Statements — 76
If Elif Else — 78
For Loops — 78
While Loop — 79
Break and Continue — 80
Exercises — 82

CHAPTER 8: FUNCTIONS AND MODULES — 83

FUNCTION PARAMETERS	86
ARGUMENTS OF A FUNCTION	87
DEFAULT VALUES	89
SCOPE	90
MODULES	92
MODULES AND BUILT-IN FUNCTIONS	93
STRING FUNCTIONS	95
EXERCISES	97

CHAPTER 9: OBJECT ORIENTED PROGRAMMING (OOP) — 98

WHAT IS OOP?	98
HOW DO I CREATE CLASSES?	99
HOW DO I CREATE OBJECTS?	99
INHERITANCE	102
EXERCISES	105

CHAPTER 10: FILES IN PYTHON — 106

FILE PATHS	106
CREATING NEW FOLDERS	107
FUNCTIONS TO MANAGE FILES	107

CHAPTER 11: EXCEPTION HANDLING — 111

'TRY' AND 'EXCEPT'	112
DIFFERENT TYPES OF ERRORS	112

CHAPTER 12: ADVANCED PROGRAMMING — 114

PIP PACKAGE MANAGER	114
VIRTUAL ENVIRONMENT	115
THE SYS MODULE	116
UNIT TESTING	117
SCRAPY	117
REQUESTS	117
PYGAME	118
BEAUTIFUL SOUP	118
PILLOW	118

TENSORFLOW	119
SCIKIT-LEARN	119
PANDAS	119
MATPLOTLIB	120
TWISTED	120
GITHUB FOR PROGRAMMERS	121

CONCLUSION 122

PROGRAMMER FEATURES	122
WHAT NEXT?	124

JAVA PROGRAMMING 125

INTRODUCTION 126

CHAPTER 1: SETTING UP YOUR JAVA ENVIRONMENT 128

THE BASICS OF JAVA INSTALLATION	128
UNDERSTANDING AND INSTALLING PACKAGE MANAGERS: MAVEN, GRADLE, AND BEYOND	130
FIRST STEPS: WRITING AND RUNNING YOUR FIRST JAVA PROGRAM	132
COMMON ISSUES AND TROUBLESHOOTING	134

CHAPTER 2: JAVA FUNDAMENTALS 137

DATA TYPES, VARIABLES, AND CONSTANTS: THE BUILDING BLOCKS	137
CONTROL FLOW: DECISIONS AND LOOPS	139
JAVA'S OBJECT-ORIENTED PARADIGM: A GENTLE INTRODUCTION	143

CHAPTER 3: DIVING INTO OBJECT-ORIENTED PROGRAMMING 146

CLASSES AND OBJECTS: THE BLUEPRINT OF JAVA	146
CONSTRUCTORS: GIVING LIFE TO OBJECTS	148
METHODS: ADDING BEHAVIOR TO OBJECTS	151

CHAPTER 4: ADVANCING WITH OBJECT-ORIENTED CONCEPTS   154

UNDERSTANDING INHERITANCE: LEVERAGING EXISTING CODE   154
POLYMORPHISM: FLEXIBILITY IN ACTION   157
ENCAPSULATION: SHIELDING YOUR DATA   159
ABSTRACTION: HIDING COMPLEXITY   161

CHAPTER 5: GENERIC PROGRAMMING   164

THE NEED FOR GENERICS   164
UNDERSTANDING AND CREATING GENERIC CLASSES   166
BOUNDED TYPE PARAMETERS   168
WILDCARDS IN GENERICS   169

CHAPTER 6: FUNCTIONAL PROGRAMMING IN JAVA   171

AN INTRODUCTION TO LAMBDA EXPRESSIONS   171
STREAMS: PROCESSING COLLECTIONS MORE ELEGANTLY   173
COMMON STREAM OPERATIONS: FILTERING, MAPPING, AND COLLECTING   175

CHAPTER 7: JAVA FEATURES OVERVIEW   180

EXCEPTION HANDLING: DEALING WITH THE UNEXPECTED   180
JAVA COLLECTIONS: LISTS, SETS, AND MAPS   182
CONCURRENCY AND MULTI-THREADING: HARNESSING THE POWER OF MODERN PROCESSORS   184

CHAPTER 8: ADVANCED JAVA CONCEPTS   186

MODULES: ORGANIZING AND SCALING YOUR JAVA PROJECTS   186
ANNOTATIONS: ADDING METADATA TO YOUR CODE   188
JAVA I/O: INTERACTING WITH EXTERNAL DATA   191

CHAPTER 9: REAL-WORLD JAVA DEVELOPMENT   194

BUILDING A CRUD APPLICATION: FROM START TO FINISH   194

CONNECTING JAVA WITH DATABASES   197
BEST PRACTICES: WRITING CLEAN, MAINTAINABLE CODE   199

CHAPTER 10: ADDRESSING FRUSTRATIONS AND OVERCOMING CHALLENGES 202

COMMON MISTAKES AND HOW TO AVOID THEM   202
OVERCOMING IMPOSTOR SYNDROME IN THE TECH WORLD   205
RESOURCES AND COMMUNITIES TO SUPPORT YOUR LEARNING JOURNEY 207

CHAPTER 11: FUTURE OF JAVA AND BEYOND   210

KEEPING UP WITH JAVA'S EVOLUTION   210
EXPLORING THE JAVA ECOSYSTEM: FRAMEWORKS AND TOOLS   213
THE ROAD AHEAD: FURTHERING YOUR JAVA CAREER   219

GLOSSARY OF COMMON JAVA TERMS   223

CONCLUSION   225

SQL FOR BEGINNERS   227

INTRODUCTION   228

CHAPTER 1: RELATIONAL DATABASES AND SQL   229

ADVANTAGES OF RELATIONAL DATABASES   229
WHAT IS SQL?   230
ADVANTAGES OF SQL   230

CHAPTER 2: BASIC SQL SYNTAX AND COMMANDS   232

CREATE   232
INSERT INTO   233
SELECT   233
UPDATE   234
DELETE   235

DROP	236

CHAPTER 3:   SQL DATA TYPES   237

BASIC SQL SYNTAX	237
DATA TYPES	237

CHAPTER 4:   SQL DATA STRUCTURES   242

HOW TO USE DATA STRUCTURES	242
HOW TO SELECT DATA STRUCTURES	242
STACK DATA STRUCTURE	243
TREE DATA STRUCTURE	244
LINKED LIST DATA STRUCTURE	246

CHAPTER 5:   WORKING WITH TABLES   248

CREATING TABLES	248
ALTERING TABLES	250
INSERTING DATA	251
UPDATING TABLE	252
DELETING DATA	252

CHAPTER 6:   BASIC AND ADVANCED QUERY TECHNIQUES   253

JOIN	253
GROUP BY	253
HAVING	254
UNION	254
ORDER BY	255
ORDER BY DESC	256
INTERSECT	257
MINUS	257

CHAPTER 7:   ADVANCED SQL TECHNIQUES AND OPTIMIZATION   259

JOINING TABLES AND WORKING WITH MULTIPLE DATA SOURCES	259

SUBQUERIES AND TEMPORARY TABLES	262
GROUPING AND AGGREGATING DATA	263
ADVANCED DATA FILTERING AND SORTING TECHNIQUES	265
STORED PROCEDURES AND FUNCTIONS	266
INDEXING AND PERFORMANCE OPTIMIZATION	268

CHAPTER 8: INTEGRATIONS WITH OTHER DATA MANAGEMENT TOOLS 272

WHAT IS DATA MANAGEMENT?	272
DATA MANAGEMENT FUNCTIONS	272
APPROACH TO DATA MANAGEMENT	272
SQL DATA MANAGEMENT TOOLS	273
IMPORTING AND EXPORTING DATA TO AND FROM OTHER FORMATS	275

CHAPTER 9: WORKING WITH DATA IN A DISTRIBUTED ENVIRONMENT 278

WHAT IS A DISTRIBUTED ENVIRONMENT?	278
HOW IS DATA PROCESSED IN DISTRIBUTED DATABASE?	280
LAYER FOR THE COLLECTION AND PREPARATION OF DATA	280
LAYER FOR DATA SECURITY	280
LAYER FOR THE DATA STORAGE	280
LAYER FOR PROCESSING OF DATA	281
DATA VISUALIZATION LAYER	281
ADVANTAGES OF THE DISTRIBUTED DATABASE	281

CHAPTER 10: BUILDING DATA PIPELINES AND AUTOMATING DATA PROCESSES 283

WHAT ARE DATA PIPELINES AND THEIR USES?	283
COMPONENTS OF A DATA PIPELINE	283
AUTOMATING DATA PROCESSES IN SQL	286
USING SQL IN DATA ANALYSIS AND BUSINESS INTELLIGENCE	287
SECURITY AND PRIVACY CONSIDERATIONS IN SQL	288

JAVASCRIPT PROGRAMMING 291

INTRODUCTION	292

WHY JAVASCRIPT	**293**
HISTORY OF JAVASCRIPT	**295**
FEATURES OF JAVASCRIPT	**295**
APPLICATIONS OF JAVASCRIPT	**296**
LIMITATIONS OF JAVASCRIPT	**297**
WHAT MAKES JAVASCRIPT A LIGHTWEIGHT PROGRAMMING LANGUAGE?	**297**
IS JAVASCRIPT INTERPRETED, COMPILED, OR BOTH?	**298**

CHAPTER 1: JAVASCRIPT SYNTAX AND DATA TYPES 299

STRING	**299**
NUMBER	**300**
BIGINT	**301**
BOOLEAN	**301**
OBJECT	**302**
SYMBOL	**303**
UNDEFINED	**304**
NULL	**305**
TYPEOF	**306**
JAVASCRIPT DATA TYPES – RECAP	**307**

CHAPTER 2: VARIABLES AND OPERATORS 308

WHAT IS AN OPERATOR?	**308**
JAVASCRIPT ASSIGNMENT OPERATORS	**308**
JAVASCRIPT ARITHMETIC OPERATORS	**309**
JAVASCRIPT COMPARISON OPERATORS	**311**
JAVASCRIPT LOGICAL OPERATORS	**313**
JAVASCRIPT BITWISE OPERATOR	**314**
JAVASCRIPT STRING OPERATORS	**314**

CHAPTER 3: CONDITIONAL STATEMENTS 315

IF-ELSE	**315**
IF STATEMENT	**315**
JAVASCRIPT IF ELSE STATEMENT	**315**
JAVASCRIPT IF ELSE IF STATEMENT	**316**

CHAPTER 4: LOOPS 318

FOR LOOP   318
WHILE LOOP   318
DO-WHILE LOOP   319
FOR-IN LOOP   319

CHAPTER 5:   FUNCTIONS   321

INTRODUCTION TO JAVASCRIPT FUNCTIONS   321
DECLARE A FUNCTION   321
CALLING A FUNCTION   322
PARAMETERS VS ARGUMENTS   322
RETURNING A VALUE   322
THE ARGUMENTS OBJECT   324
FUNCTION HOISTING   325

CHAPTER 6:   OBJECTS   326

OVERVIEW OF OBJECTS IN JAVASCRIPT   326
CREATING OBJECTS   327
ACCESSING AND MODIFYING OBJECT PROPERTIES   328
WORKING WITH OBJECT METHODS   329
OBJECT ITERATION AND MANIPULATION   330
WORKING WITH BUILT-IN OBJECTS   332
EXERCISES   334

CHAPTER 7:   CLOSURES   335

WHAT IS A CLOSURE IN JAVASCRIPT?   335
JAVASCRIPT CLOSURE   336
JAVASCRIPT CLOSURES AND LOOPS   337
ES6 LET KEYWORD   337
IIFE AND CLOSURES   338
MOVING FORWARD WITH JAVASCRIPT CLOSURES   339

CHAPTER 8:   PROTOTYPES   340

PROTOTYPE CHAIN   341
CREATING AND USING PROTOTYPES   342

CHAPTER 9: THE DOCUMENT OBJECT MODEL (DOM) — 344

THE ORIGINAL LEGACY DOM — 345
THE W3C — 347
THE IE4 DOM — 348

CHAPTER 10: EVENT HANDLING — 351

CLICK EVENT — 351
MOUSEOVER EVENT — 352
FOCUS EVENT — 352
KEYDOWN EVENT — 353
LOAD EVENT — 354

CHAPTER 11: ASYNCHRONOUS PROGRAMMING — 355

ASYNCHRONOUS VS. SYNCHRONOUS COMMUNICATION — 355
WHAT ARE JAVASCRIPT CALLBACKS? — 356
PROMISES IN JAVASCRIPT — 356
JAVASCRIPT'S ASYNC/AWAIT — 357

CHAPTER 12: JAVASCRIPT FRAMEWORK AND LIBRARIES — 358

COMPARING LIBRARIES AND FRAMEWORKS — 358
JAVASCRIPT LIBRARIES — 360
JAVASCRIPT FRAMEWORKS — 361
REACT — 361
ANGULAR — 365
NODE.JS — 368
NPM — 370
WEBPACK — 373
BABEL — 375

CONCLUSION — 377

Python Programming

Introduction

Computers can be categorized as machines with no inherent intelligence, but they have drastically helped to advance our world in countless ways. With computers, our world runs much more efficiently and error-free—we tell them what to do, and they deliver flawless results. Computer programmers are the people who communicate with computers in what are called programming languages, and they have been doing so for many years. These programming languages vary based on their working systems, just as human language varies based on region.

One of these computer programming languages is called Python, and in the computer realm, this is a quite popular (and easy to learn) high-level programming language. This book will intuitively teach you Python. Even if you have no experience with any programming language, you will be able to grasp the basics of Python and put them to use.

What Is Python?

Python is a high-level programming language that is popular within the programming community. It is simple, versatile, and contains an extensive library of third-party frameworks. It is also considered to be one of the most popular modern programming languages, being highly accessible for beginners. You can even use it to create software in your programming domain of choice.

Accredited universities such as Stanford teach Python to computer science graduates as an introductory language. Many online courses that explore programming basics also use Python as the default language. As you can see, it's very prevalent and therefore highly useful to learn. For these reasons, I am happy that you have chosen this book to help you learn Python quickly and intuitively.

Who Am I?

If you search the Internet, you are likely to find thousands of resources available for learning Python. And while this is great, it can also be overwhelming—therefore, many beginners can get frustrated because they do not have concise instructions with a clear walkthrough.

My name is Philip Robbins, and I am determined to offer a clear pathway for beginners to excel. I have more than twenty years of experience working in the field of software development using Python, and I am an expert Python programmer. My love for programming started a decade ago when I avidly played video games. It all started with my enthusiasm to mod a Pokémon game that I was playing. My will to successfully change a small bit of code to feel accomplished sparked excitement to understand programming logic and variables at a young age. With some modding experience, I was able to understand how programs work and spent time experimenting with different programming languages.

Fast forward a few years, and I started creating small scripts that could automate workflow. However, I had still not chosen a particular programming language, and this made it challenging to be an actual software program developer. All of the programming languages I had tried, such as C and Pearl, were challenging to implement and almost made me quit programming due to massive frustration many times. Fortunately, during those turbulent times I discovered Python in its initial stages. Python first began as a hobby project by one developer, so its initial form was not very clean. Once it gained in popularity, however, fellow developers began to notice the open-source project. This spurred them to add their contributions as well. Thus, they effectively modeled it into the efficient programming language it is today.

Within a few months of learning Python basics, I began implementing my pre-existing code into Python. I was astounded by the code's portability as well as its lack of clutter. Once I learned how Python worked, there was no turning back. I began writing my software and publishing them using different stores. Even though my main job was to create web applications, I successfully created several other side projects in various domains with the help of Python.

Now that I am proficient in Python, I am interested in helping people who are struggling to learn this coding language. Even when I was first modding games in the beginning stages, I always had a passion for quickly assisting people in learning programming. I use layman's terms to explain complex topics, and this has helped many of my friends and colleagues understand them better. My passion for programming and teaching has compelled me to write this book to help beginners who are new to Python.

How Can This Book Help You?

Though Python programming looks easy to implement, in truth it is not. If you have a thorough understanding of the several foundational topics Python contains and how you can utilize them to solve problems, this is incredibly helpful. As such, this book provides you with the theoretical knowledge you need to know to understand the foundations and practicality of the programming language you are trying to use.

To get the most out of this book, we recommend cognitive learning techniques. These will enhance your experience with this material.

- Use cognitive memory techniques such as Memory Palace to keenly remember the data. However, there is a difference between simply mugging up the required information in your brain versus formally storing it when using cognitive techniques.
- Use mind maps to map different concepts to quickly implement them in your projects. Mind maps are cognitive learning tools that use visual excellence via a short diagram to remember large amounts of data easily.
- Use the passive recall technique to quickly review all of the topics you have learned in this book. Passive recall can also help strengthen your programming foundations.
- Don't just use the code given in this book. Instead, reimplement your code using similar strategies. Using the simple copy-and-paste technique will not help you in creating your code.
- Use the Feynman technique to explain all of the basic programming concepts you have learned in this book to someone unaware of the subject. You have a strong knowledge of the core foundations if you can explain concepts in simple terms.

As a programming language, Python expects you to be as innovative as possible. Therefore, if you treat programming with Python like solving a puzzle, then you will intuitively discover ways to trick your brain into creating complex code logic for addressing real-world problems. This book helps you to become as effective as possible with Python programming.

Chapter 1: Introduction to Python

Python is a powerful programming language that is easy to learn, has a strong foundation, and can support multiparadigm workflows. As a result, it is an excellent starting point for beginners who want to delve into programming. Python's popularity stems primarily from its lack of clutter and boilerplate code.

For example, writing a simple snake game in C or C++ usually requires 300 lines of code. In contrast, with Python you can limit the number of lines of code to less than 200. This significant difference in terms of implementation contributed to Python becoming the most popular open-source language in the world. Python quickly became the waypoint for the open-source revolution, with so many enthusiastic programmers and developers writing thousands of libraries for various computer fields.

History of Python

Guido van Rossum, who created Python, made it as a side project over the Christmas break. Using what he learned working with the ABC programming language, he made an interpreted programming language that is easy to understand and use. He first used Python to impress hackers in an online community with his knowledge of how Unix works.

But after getting feedback from his fellow programmers, he worked on it for a few months to make it better. So, he made a programming language that was easy and quick to understand. Guido van Rossum has been called the "benevolent dictator" of the Python community because of what he has done for the Python project. Open-source developers can be given this high award.

Python has always been one of the 10 most popular programming languages, according to TIOBE rankings, ever since it came out. Python's simple way of solving problems has helped it beat other programming languages, like Pearl, and become one of the easier ones for beginners to learn.

Python is based on the idea that there is only one way to solve a problem, which is different from the idea behind programming languages like Pearl, which is that there are many ways to solve a problem. So, Python gave the programming community the discipline it needed and made software development grow by a factor of ten.

Look at the Python Applications below to see how important Python was to programmers around the world.

Applications of Python

Python made its mark in many areas of science and technology today.

1. Web Domain

Python has had most of its early effect as a programming language on web technology. While Java was the most popular thing on the web, Python wasn't as popular. Over time, Python has become popular among web developers thanks to third-party frameworks like Django and Tornado.

In the twenty years since then, Python has become one of the most popular scripting languages for websites, second only to JavaScript. Python is a programming language that is used by big companies like Google, Facebook, and Netflix. A well-known web framework called Django can also help programmers write backend code for several APIs.

Python is also popular for automating tasks, so it is often used to make bots like Pinflux.

2. Scientific Computing

Python is popular with scientists because it is free for anyone to use. Also, programs like NumPy and SciPy make it easier for computer scientists to do experiments with less code. Since Python is also better at mathematical calculations and software, Scientists have no choice but to use it these days.

3. Machine Learning and AI

AI and machine learning are now two technologies that can be used together to give more jobs to developers. There are a lot of third-party libraries for Python, like TensorFlow, that are all about implementing Machine Learning algorithms.

Python is also very good at adapting to technologies like Deep Learning and Natural Language Processing. This makes it one of the main candidates to become a better language for making AI-related technology.

4. Linux and the Management of Databases

As businesses around the world grow, there is a big need for developers who can manage databases and internal systems well. Developers need to know enough about different operating systems, like Linux, and they also need to know enough about Python to automate other procedures that are needed to test how well methods work on an internal network.

5. Penetration Testing and Hacking

Python is also used by hackers with both good and bad intentions. For example, white-hat hackers use Python tools that are widely used to do penetration testing. On the other hand, hackers with bad intentions use Python scripting to make exploits that automatically steal sensitive information from their targets.

Python's ability to be used in almost any area of computer programming has led to the development of several other high-level programming languages, like Go, Groovy, and Swift. Python spread the idea that programming should be as simple as possible.

Different Versions of Python

When Python came out at the start of the 1990s, it wasn't as good as it is now. Rossum built the library without any help from anyone else, so it had a lot of bugs and mistakes. But because Python was so popular right away in the programming community, hundreds of independent developers helped Rossum make a much bigger project in the two years after the first version came out.

Python was also able to get a lot of smart people to check and change the code because it was open source. Because of this, the Python core programming team has put out two main versions, Python 2 and Python 3, for developers all over the world in the last 20 years.

In 2022, Python 2 is still used by a lot of programmers, even though Python core developers no longer support it. Choosing which version to use depends on what you are doing.

Python 2

Python 2 is now an old version that came out in the year 2000. Still, it has been the most used version of Python for more than 20 years. Python 2 is easier to use and has a lot more frameworks and libraries from outside sources that can be used for development.

Even though Python 2.7 will no longer get official updates after 2021, it is still the best version for many software domains. But it's hard to move all of the frameworks and libraries from Python 2 to Python 3, so many companies still use Python 2 as their default version.

Python 3

Python 3.9 is the most recent version of the programming language that developers can use. Python 3 is faster and gives developers many more classes for working with the core library. Compared to Python 2, it is also easy to keep up with.

Which one Should I Choose?

Which version of Python you use should depend on what kind of software you are making. For example, a lot of data scientists use Python 3, while developers who work with legacy software use Python 2 to connect components.

Note:
All the Python code in this book is written in Python 3, since it makes more sense for beginners to start with a newer version.

Why You Should Learn Python

Python started to become more popular in the early 1990s, when companies all over the world started to use the internet's power to make complex web applications. Traditional programming languages like C and C+ were hard to learn and made it hard for programmers to write good code quickly. During this time, Python helped many companies make libraries that worked well with the C and C++ libraries they already had. Also, programmers started using Python to quickly deploy code because it was easier to work with than other high-level languages.

By learning about some of Python's many benefits, you can see how powerful and easy it can be for developers with different backgrounds in computer science.

It Is an Interpreted Language

Instead of using a compiler to run instructions like other programming languages do, Python uses a new piece of software called an interpreter. Instead of taking a lot of time to run a program with a compiler, the interpreter uses modern computer techniques to parse the code before the program is run. This dynamic parse time can cut down on the time you have to wait while the program is running. Python also uses parts of natural language to get rid of unproductive ways of coding that can slow down production. Because of how it is set up, it is also easy to automate programming in Python, which is why system developers and Linux administrators like it so much.

It is Open Source

One of the first things that led to the open-source revolution was Python. Because Python is open source, you can change any code and share it on your own. Open-source culture also makes it easier for programmers all over the world to share their knowledge and resources to make libraries and frameworks that can help developers make new projects.

As a beginner, having one-click access to both complex and simple projects can help you understand how programming works and make it easy to make new, creative projects.

It Supports Multiple Paradigms

To write and run code, different programming languages use different programming paradigms. Java, on the other hand, uses an object-oriented paradigm, while C uses a functional paradigm. A programming paradigm changes how developers work and how they try to solve a problem.

Python supports multiple paradigms, like the structured, functional, and object-oriented paradigms. This makes it a good choice for programmers who want to solve problems in different ways.

It uses a Garbage Collection Mechanism

Managing memory is an important skill for application developers to have. High-level languages such as Java and C use complex data management techniques. Even though these mechanisms work perfectly, it takes a lot of time to keep them in good shape. In Python, on the other hand, memory is handled by garbage collectors. You can easily use the data and variables that this strategy no longer uses.

It Is Easy to Understand

One of the many reasons developers like Python is that it is easy to read. All of the code is easy to understand, which makes it easy to keep up. When Python code is easier to read, its quality goes up, and when the quality goes up, it takes less time to fix bugs in the code.

Portability

Python can also run on any operating system, which makes it easy for developers to use it in different ways with just a few hours of work. Users only need to install the interpreter on their system for Python programs to work.

For instance, let's say a programmer writes a program for Linux that makes it easy to automate SQL database management. Then, anyone who has access to the code can place it on Windows or Mac machines by changing a few parts of it.

It Has Great Custom Libraries

If you want a programming language to be widely used, it needs to have great libraries. Developers can play around with a lot of these libraries in Python.

Aside from these custom libraries, programmers can also make interesting software with the standard libraries that the Python core development team gives them.

It Supports Component Integration

Python makes it easy for programmers to add new code to code that has already been written. Also, its advanced integration of components makes it a good choice for making advanced customization options for different software applications.

Component integration keeps developers busy by adding new features to older software so it can run on newer operating systems.

It Has a Great Community

The Python community is very helpful and can help new programmers quickly solve any problems they run into while writing code. Aside from Python forums, resources and well-written guides from a variety of experienced programmers can help developers get past any problems.

Since there are a lot of open-source Python projects on GitHub, a hobbyist programmer can just look at the code to see how complex logic is implemented in software.

How to Install Python

To write Python code, you must install an interpreter on your system. Without this interpreter, no developer would be able to write or run Python programs. Python can be put on any modern operating system because it can be moved around. In this section, we'll talk about how to install Python on Linux, Mac, and Windows.

How do I Install Python in Linux?

Since most programmers use Linux as their main operating system, we'll start by installing Python on your local machine using Linux. Linux is a free operating system that most programmers and businesses use. Because of this, Python is already on many Linux distributions.

To see if Python is installed on your Linux system, use the CTRL+ALT+N command to open a new command terminal.

When the new command terminal opens, type the following command into it.

Terminal Code:
```
$ python3
```
If Python is installed on your system, the license information for the version of Python that is installed will show up in your terminal.

If you get the output "command not found," on the other hand, it means that Python is not installed on your system. Since Python is not installed, you can now use the package managers for Linux to install Python for different distros.

Before installing any software on Linux, you must first update all the tools on Linux and make sure there are no conflict errors that could stop Python installation.

Terminal Code:
```
$ sudo apt-get upgrade
```

You can use the code above to update package files on a Linux system that is based on Debian.

Use the following Pacman command to upgrade packages on an Arch-based system.

Terminal Code:
`$ sudo pacman -S`

After upgrading the packages, you can use the commands below to install Python on your Linux system.

Terminal code for Debian systems:

`$ sudo apt-get install python3`

Terminal code for Arch systems:

`$ pacman -u python3`

Look at the official Python documentation to install in other Linux distributions like Gentoo and kali.

How do I Install Python on macOS?

macOS is the operating system that Apple makes by default. Python 2 is often installed as native software because it is built with UNIX support.

Make sure you open a new terminal from Settings > Utilities > Terminal to see if macOS is installed on your Apple-supported hardware.

Enter the following command once a new terminal has been opened.

Terminal Code:
`$ python3`

If you don't see a Python version message, it means that Python is not installed on your system. To install Python from scratch, use homebrew.

Terminal Code:
`$ brew install python3`

How do I Install Python on Windows?

Windows is the most used operating system in the world, based on the number of people who use it. Many people and programmers use Windows because it is easy to use, and there are many ways for Python programmers to quickly get their code into Windows.

To install Python on your Windows system, you must first download an executable package from the official Python website. Once the package is downloaded, you can install the software by double-clicking on it. For Python code development to work on some Windows systems, you may need to change the environment variables in the Control panel.

Once everything is set up as needed, open a command prompt window to see if the Python interpreter is correctly installed.

Command Prompt Code:

```
>> python —version
```

If the command tells you what version of Python is installed, then Python is set up correctly on your system. If not, you might have to copy and paste the error into Google or use Python forums to figure out what's wrong.

Chapter 2: PyCharm and IDLE

Once you've installed Python, you'll need a development environment on your system to write programs. IDLE stands for "Integrated Development and Learning Environment." Even though you can work with the basic IDLE that comes with a basic Python installation, developers are encouraged to use IDEs (Integrated Development Environments) like PyCharm for better software development workflow. IDEs make developers more productive and make it easier for them to find bugs in code that has already been turned into software.

Why is Python Interpreter Good?

The Python interpreter is great because it is flexible and has more features than traditional compilers. For example, compared to compilers, a Python interpreter makes you wait less. Compilers run the code after it has been written and check for mistakes. The interpreter, on the other hand, checks the code as it is being written and lets the programmer know if there is a problem before the code is run. Real-time error reporting is a good way for beginners to learn how to code while they are doing it.

When you install Python on your computer, it also installs the IDLE. To start the IDLE, you can type "Python" in the terminal interface. The REPL mechanism (Read-Eval-Print Loop) is used by IDLE to show the output on the computer screen. REPL is a basic method that Python interpreters use to check the lines that have been written and parse them so that they can be shown on the screen. This is done based on the input and output that are given.

Python IDLE can be a great tool for people who are just starting to learn how to code. Even though most enterprise software development is done on IDEs like PyCharm, learning some basic commands for Python IDLE can help you understand how Python interpretation works.

How to Use the Python IDLE Shell?

Once Python is installed, open a terminal or command prompt and type the following command to start the IDLE.

Command:
```
$ python
```

As shown below, when you press Enter or Return, a new shell will open.
>>>
You can test how Python IDLE works on your system by using some of the basic math or Print commands.

Program Code:
```
>>> print ("This is a sample to check that the IDLE works")
```
Output:
```
This is a sample to check that the IDLE works
```
When the Enter button is pressed, the program goes into REPL mode, and the text between the double quotes is shown on the computer screen. This is because IDLE knew that the shell window used the print() method to show strings.

You can also use math operations to test the IDLE workflow.

Program Code:
```
>>> 8 + 3
```
Output:
```
11
```

Exercise:
Use the IDLE window to check the results of other math operations, like multiplication and division.

Note:
It's important to remember that as soon as you close the terminal window, all of your code will be lost. So, even if we use an IDLE, we need to make sure that all of our code is put into a Python file.

How to Use IDLE to Open Python Files?

IDLE makes it simple to open and read Python files with a .py extension on the terminal. Keep in mind that this command will only function if you are in the same directory as the Python file.

Program Code:
```
$ python mysample.py
```
The prior command will open the previously written code for the programmers to read.

- IDLE can automatically highlight unique syntax components.
- IDLE assists developers in completing code by providing hints.
- IDLE can easily indent code.

To use any Python files on your IDLE shell, use the GUI file option and click the 'Open' button. However, advanced programmers advise using the path to open Python files if you are not in the same directory.

How to Change these Files?

Once the files are open in IDLE, you can begin editing the code in the file with your keyboard. Because IDLE provides line numbers, developers can easily manipulate any non-indented code. Once the file has been edited, press the F5 key to run it on your terminal code.

If there are no errors, the output will be displayed; otherwise, the traceback errors will be displayed.

While not as efficient as other advanced IDEs on the market, Python IDLE serves as an excellent debugging tool. It has several debugging features, including the ability to place endpoints, catch exceptions, and parse code to quickly debug the code. However, it is not ideal and may cause issues if your Project library grows.

Regardless of how little it offers, IDLE is possibly the best developer tool for complete beginners.

Exercise:

Develop a new program in Python IDLE to add two numbers and debug it with breakpoints. If you are unfamiliar with any programming components, you are free to use any Internet resources to solve this simple problem.

IDE (Integrated Development Environment)

Python IDLE is frequently not recommended for real-world application development due to its inability to handle highly demanding projects. Developers are instead asked to manage and develop their code in specialized development environments known as IDEs. Furthermore, IDEs provide programmers with tight integration capabilities with various libraries.

IDE characteristics

1. Simple Integration Into Libraries & Frameworks

One of the important features of IDEs is that they make it simple to integrate libraries and frameworks into software applications. IDLE requires you to assign them individually each time you use them, whereas IDEs do the hard work for you by autocompleting various import statements. Many IDEs also support direct git repository integration.

2. Integration of Object Oriented Design

Many Python programmers who create applications employ an object-oriented paradigm. Unfortunately, Python IDLE does not include any tools to help developers create applications while adhering to object-oriented principles. All modern IDEs include components such as class hierarchy diagrams to help developers get their projects started with better programming logic.

3. Syntax Highlighting

Syntax highlighting assists programmers in increasing productivity and avoiding simple, obvious errors. For example, you cannot use reserved keywords like 'if' to name variables. The IDE automatically detects this error and assists developers in understanding it through syntax highlighting.

4. Code Completion

All modern IDEs use advanced artificial intelligence and machine learning techniques to complete code for developers automatically. The IDEs gather a lot of information from the packages you use, so they can suggest different variables or methods based on your input and the logic you're writing. Even though auto-completion is a useful feature, you should never rely entirely on it because it can occasionally disrupt program execution and cause errors.

5. Version Control

Version control is a major source of frustration for developers. For example, if you use private libraries and frameworks in your application, they may occasionally be updated, causing your application to fail. As a developer, you must be aware of these changes and implement new code execution for all applications to function properly. The version control mechanism enables developers to easily update their core applications without causing any disruptions to previously written code. IDEs support direct version control with websites like GitHub.

IDEs can also provide advanced debugging features for developers in addition to these features. For example, the most popular Python IDEs for independent developers and organizations are PyCharm and Eclipse. We will use PyCharm as our default IDE in this book because it is much more efficient than Eclipse and much easier to set up.

PyCharm

PyCharm is a Python-only IDE produced by JetBrains, a pioneer in software tool development. Initially, the JetBrains team created PyCharm to manage their IDEs for other programming languages. However, due to its portability, the JetBrains team later released it as a standalone product for users worldwide. PyCharm is available for all major operating systems and comes in two flavors: community and professional.

The community version is open-source, free software that anyone can use to write Python code. It does, however, have some limitations, particularly in terms of version control and third-party library integration.

The professional version is a paid IDE that offers advanced functionality and numerous integration options to developers. For example, using the professional version of PyCharm IDE, developers can easily create web or data science applications.

What Features does PyCharm Provide?

PyCharm is well-known for its unique features for enthusiastic Python developers, as well as its high-quality integration capabilities.

1. Code Editor

PyCharm's code editor is among the best in the industry. When working with new projects in this editor, you will be astounded by the code completion abilities. Furthermore, JetBrains has used several advanced machine learning models to make the IDE intelligent enough to understand even the most complex programming blocks and provide useful suggestions.

While working as a developer, the PyCharm editor can also be customized for a better viewing experience. Light and dark themes are available to users, allowing you to change the theme based on your mood.

2. Code Navigation

PyCharm's complex and comprehensive file organization system makes it simple for programmers to manage files. Bookmarks and lens mode, for example, can assist Python programmers in effectively managing their essential programming blocks and code logic.

3. Refactoring

PyCharm includes advanced refactoring features that allow developers to easily change the names of files, classes, and methods without breaking the program. When you use IDLE to refactor your code, it immediately breaks the code because the default Python IDLE is not intelligent enough to distinguish between new and old names.

When it comes to updating their code or migrating to a much better third-party library for one of their software components, most Python developers use Advanced refactoring capabilities.

4. Web Technology Integration

The majority of Python developers work in the web domain, which accounts for a sizable portion of the software industry. PyCharm simplifies the integration of developers' software with Python web frameworks such as Django. PyCharm is also intelligent enough to understand HTML, CSS, and JavaScript code, which are commonly used by web developers to create web services.

All of these features make it simple for Python web developers to integrate existing web code into a Python framework.

5. **Integration With Scientific Libraries**

PyCharm is also well-known for its strong support for scientific and advanced mathematical libraries like SciPy and NumPy. While it will never completely replace your data integration and cleaning setup, it will assist you in developing a basic pseudo logic for all of your data science projects.

6. **Software Testing**

PyCharm can execute high-level unit testing strategies for even the most complex and large projects with numerous members. It also includes advanced debugging tools and remote configuration capabilities for using the Alpha and beta testing workflows.

How to Use PyCharm?

With enough information about PyCharm, you should be convinced that it is a necessary development tool for your local system. This section contains the information you need to install PyCharm and understand how to use it to better manage your Python projects.

Step–1: Install PyCharm

PyCharm can be installed on almost any operating system.

To begin, obtain the installation package from the official website or one of the numerous package managers.

Navigate to the JetBrains official website and click the downloads tab in the upper right corner. Now, depending on your operating system, download the executable or dmg file and double-click it to follow the instructions on the screen.

To download a professional version of the software, you must first provide payment information to download a trial version. When the trial period expires, you will be charged and will be able to use the professional version without issue.

Note:

For the PyCharm IDE to install successfully on your system, Python must be installed. This is because it detects the Python path and installs the software's core libraries automatically.

Step–2: Create New Projects

After installing the software, launch the PyCharm IDE from your applications or the Desktop icon. When you open PyCharm, a new popup will appear, allowing you to start a new project from scratch. You can open a new project using the button in the upper left corner of the software interface using the "File" option. Other options include importing and exporting existing projects or quickly saving current working projects.

When you first open a Python project, you will be prompted to choose which Python interpreter you want to use for all programming procedures. If you don't know where to look for the Python interpreter, choose 'virtualenv,' which will automatically search the system and find one for you.

Step—3: Using PyCharm to Organize

Creating new folders and resources for your Program files is essential once you begin creating projects with PyCharm.

To create a new folder on your project interface, simply select the new --> folder option. You can include any Python scripts or assets used in your software in this section.

When you create a new file in a separate folder, a file with the.py extension is created. As a result, if you want to create different class files or templates, you must do so explicitly while creating a file in your folder.

Step—4: Advanced Features in PyCharm

Once the code is written and integrated, you can use the built-in IDLE interface or the PyCharm unique output interface to run it quickly.

All code you write will be automatically saved in real time, so you won't have to worry about losing any critical project data due to a bad network connection or power outage. To save a copy of a project on your local system, simply press Ctrl S or Cmd S.

When the program is finished, press Shift + F10 to run and compile the code with the help of an interpreter.

Using the Ctrl F or Cmd F commands, you can search for any method, variable, or snippet in your project. Simply use this shortcut and enter the information you're looking for.

Once the Python code has been imported and deployed to the required operating systems, you must begin setting up a debugging project environment to constantly clear bugs on your system. To place breakpoints and solve logical problems without messing up the entire code logic or breaking the core program, press Shift + F9.

Python Style Guide

Python programming grew in popularity among programmers due to the programming philosophy it supported and continues to support. Python aimed to be simple, whereas other high-level programming languages aimed to be more complex. Pearl is a great example of how this philosophy was applied and how it complicated many things for an average programmer.

Python core developers encouraged early Python adopters to adhere to a simple set of well-known principles known as "The Zen of Python" to write code that both works and looks good. Even after twenty years, these principles are still relevant for Python programmers, and every Python programmer should be aware of them.

Enter the Python code below on the terminal to read all of these principles.

Terminal Code:

```
$ import this
```

We will go over some fundamental principles to better understand the philosophy that Python promotes to developers.

Beautiful Is Better Than Ugly.

All Python programmers are encouraged to write semantically symmetrical code that is also visually appealing. Beautiful code must be well-structured; thus, programmers must write conditionals without complicating the code. Many lines of code can be made more visually appealing by employing indentation techniques. Beautifying code improves readability and can help to reduce runtime.

Explicit Is Better Than Implicit.

For whatever reason, many developers try to conceal their programming logic, making it difficult for other programmers to understand. Python opposes this routine and encourages developers to write explicit code logic that is understandable by all. This is also one of the reasons why open-source Python frameworks and libraries are more popular.

Simple Is Better Than Complex.

Your primary goal as a Python programmer should be to write simple code. Simplifying your code logic can help you improve your programming language skills. Your ability to write less complex code improves as you gain experience.

Complex Is Better Than Complicated.

As with any software, there are times when you need to write complex code that solves multiple problems at once. When working on complex code, avoid making it too complicated. Using exceptions and files effectively can assist you in quickly reducing complicated code that may later turn into annoying bugs.

There Should Be Only One Approach.

Unlike its predecessor languages, C and C++, Python advocates for consistency. As a Python programmer, you only need to use one logic for all of the instances in your program. Uniformity provides flexibility and makes it easier to maintain the code.

Chapter 3: Python Foundations

Python programmers must ensure that input is provided directly from the user and output is provided based on the inputs to have dynamic applications. The Python interpreter and all functions in your program can access the user's input values.

We will provide a few example programs in this chapter to help you understand how to improve the user experience of the software you have created based on input and output operations.

Why are Input Values Required?

Application survival is dependent on input values. Everything runs on the user's input values, from web applications to the most recent metaverse applications. When you log in to Facebook, for example, you must enter your email address and password. These are inputs, and your account will be authenticated only if the information provided is correct.

Face data points are used as input in advanced applications such as facial recognition technology. Nowadays, every real-world application requests and collects user input data to provide a better user experience.

Use Case:

Assume you created a Python application for a mature audience that cannot be used by anyone under the age of 18.

For the above scenario, we can use conditional input verification by asking the user to enter their age. If the user is over the age of 18, the application will become available to him or her. However, if the user is under the age of 18, the application will be inaccessible. Python evaluates whether or not someone can access your software based on inputs from all supported data types. This is just one example from the real world. Numerous applications can be performed by utilizing input from your end users.

Understanding the input() Function

When you call the input() function in the middle of a Python program, the interpreter will pause and wait for the user to enter the values using one of their input devices, such as a keyboard, mouse, or mobile touchscreen.

Typically, the user will provide input in response to the prompt. To create real-world applications, you must first create a good prompt GUI. This chapter will look at the text command prompts available to developers.

After entering the values, the user must press the "Enter" button on their system for the interpreter to resume and parse the logical programming statements used.

Example:
```
sample = input ("Which country are you from? ")
print (sample + " is a beautiful country!")
```

When the above program is run and executed, the user will first see an output prompt, as shown below.

Output:
```
Which country are you from?
```

At this point, the user has to enter an answer. Let's suppose we write "United States of America":

```
Which country are you from? United States of America
United States of America is a beautiful country!
```

You can experiment by changing the input above to another country to see what happens.

Output:
```
Which country are you from? France
France is a beautiful country!
```

How to Write User Prompts?

It is recommended to use better prompts to get the user's attention when using the input() function and attempting to receive inputs from the user.

Remember not to include any extraneous information in the text. Make the prompt as straightforward as possible.

Prompt Code:
```
example = input("Which is your favorite hockey team? ")
print ("So you are a " + example + " fan. Hurray!")
```

Output:
```
Which is your favorite football team? Boston Bruins
So you are a Boston Bruins fan. Hurray!
```

You can also use the input() function to prompt the user by displaying multiple lines of strings.

We use the print() function to display text on the screen from the beginning of the book. The only recommended method for printing to a computer screen is print().

Any input you pass to the print() function will be converted to a string literal and displayed on the screen. While you are not required to be aware of the print() function's arguments, learning some parameters that can help you format your code is recommended.

What are String Literals?

String literals are advanced characters that can assist you in quickly formatting your data. For example, \n is a common string literal that can assist you in entering data from a new line.

Program Code:
```
prompt = "This is a simple question to find out what you
         like."
prompt += "\n So, please say your favorite food: "
example = input(prompt)
print (example + " is delicious")
```

Output:
```
This is a simple question to find out what you like.
So, please say your favorite food: Pasta
Pasta is delicious
```

Other popular string literals that can help you output data with a new tab or without whitespaces and separators are \t, \b, and \d.

What is an End Statement?

The print() function also accepts an end argument, which can be used to append any string data to the end of your string literals, as shown below.

Program Code:
```
print("Italy is a beautiful country. ", end = "Do you
        agree? ")
print("Yes, I do!")
```

Output:
```
Italy is a beautiful country. Do you agree? Yes, I do!
```

In the above example, "Do you agree?" is the appended text

Numerical Values as Input

So far we have seen how the input() function is used to capture user input as a string. When expecting numerical input, such as integers (int) or floating-point numbers (float), the string obtained from input() must be converted to the respective numerical type. This is achieved using int() for integers and float() for floating-point numbers.

We'll delve deeper into the specifics of int and float data types in the "Data Types" section.

Practical Example for 'int':

Let's say we want to write a program that asks the user for their and then prints a message indicating what the age was the previous year. Since age is typically counted in whole years, we use int for this purpose.

```
# Ask the user for their age
age_str = input("Enter your age: ")

# Convert the string input to an integer
age = int(age_str)

# Compute age last year
age_last = age - 1

# Print the age
print("Last year you were", age_last, "years old.")
```

Output:
```
Enter your age: 50
Last year you were 49 years old.
```

Typing "int(age_str)" we are converting the string to an integer. Notice that we could also have directly written the following:

```
age = int(input("Enter your age: "))
```

To compute the quantity "age - 1" the "age" variable must be an integer. Without the conversion, the code would not work:

```
age_str = input("Enter your age: ")
age_last = age - 1
print("Last year you were", age_last, "years old.")
```

Output:
```
Enter your age: 50
ERROR!
Traceback (most recent call last):
NameError: name 'age' is not defined
```

Practical Example for 'float':

Suppose we want to calculate the area of a circle. The user will input the radius, which might be a decimal number, so we use float.

```
# Ask the user for the radius of a circle
radius = float(input("Enter the radius of the circle: "))

# Calculate the area (using 3.14 as an approximation of Pi)
area = 3.14 * radius * radius

# Print the area
print("The area of the circle is:", area)
```

Output:
```
Enter the radius of the circle: 21
The area of the circle is: 1384.74
```
Here, we directly convert the radius from a string to a float for calculation. The float() function allows us to handle decimal numbers, making it suitable for scenarios where precision is needed.

Comments in Python

When programming teams work on complex and time-consuming projects, a lot of information must be exchanged between team members for the project's essence to be understood. Comments allow programmers to pass information without disrupting the program's flow.

When a programmer uses comments, the Python interpreter ignores the comments and moves on to the next line. However, because Python has a large number of open-source projects, comments assist developers in understanding how to integrate third-party libraries and frameworks into their code.

Comments make the code more readable and easier to understand. While it may appear that some programmers do not need to remember the code logic they have written, you would be surprised at how often programmers forget the code logic they have written. Having specific insights into how you wrote the code logic will be very useful for future reference.

Python allows programmers to use two types of comments in their code.

Comments on a Single Line

Single-line comments are the most commonly used type of comment by Python programmers because they can be easily written between the lines of code. To use single-line comments, use the '#' symbol. Anything that comes after this symbol will be ignored by the interpreter.

Program Code:
```
# This is an example of a single-line comment followed by a
        print of a hash symbol
print ("This is an example.")
```

Output:
```
This is an example.
```
Because a single-line comment was used, the interpreter ignored it and only executed the print statement.

Why are Single-Line Comments Important?

Single-line comments are commonly used in the middle of code to assist other programmers in understanding how the program logic works and to detail the functions of the implemented variables.

Comments in Multiple Lines

While it is possible to write three or four lines of continuous comments using single-line comments, it is not recommended because Python provides a better way to annotate multi-line comments. Python programmers can use string literals to create multi-line comments, as shown below.

Program Code:
```
'''
This is a comment
In Python
with 4 lines
Author: Python Best '''
print ("This is an example.")
```

Output:
```
This is an example.
```

When you run the above program, only the print statement is executed, just like single-line comments.

Why Are Multiline Comments Important?

Multiline comments are frequently used by programmers to define license details or to explain comprehensive information about various packages and methods with various implementation examples. The code can be effectively understood by the programmers who are reading it.

Reserved Keywords

Reserved keywords are programming language default keywords that programmers cannot use as identifiers while writing code. Identifiers are commonly used to name variables, classes, and functions.

The interpreter will throw an error if you use a reserved keyword in your program. For example, using 'for' for one of your variables will not work because 'for' is typically used in Python programming to define a specific type of loop structure.

There are 33 reserved keywords that you are not permitted to use in your programs. As a Python programmer, it is critical to avoid making unnecessary mistakes when working on complex projects.

Exercise:

Using the Python terminal, try to find the reserved keywords in Python to become familiar with the Python commands we discussed previously.

Operators in Python

In mathematics, operators are first used to form mathematical expressions. The first programmers used these operators and the basic programming components to easily assign and manipulate values.

Operators are commonly used by computer programmers to combine literal and form statements or expressions.

Example:

$2x + 3z = 34$

Here, 2x, 3z, and 34 are literals, and + and = are operators that are applied to these literals to form an expression.

Operators can be combined with any number of literal values to form complex expressions that can aid programmers in the implementation of difficult algorithms.

Example:
```
a = 18
b = 20
print(a + b)
```

Output:
```
38
```

a and b are the operands, whereas = and + are operators that are used.

Different Types of Operators

Different types of operators can be used by programmers to implement various types of programming logic. The most commonly used operators are arithmetic operators, which assist programmers in applying mathematical logic to various literals, such as variables, in their code.

The arithmetic operators that a Python programmer needs to know to write better programming structures are addition, subtraction, multiplication, and division.

1. Addition

To add two literals to a program, use the addition operator. These literals can be variables or lists, and they can sometimes be data of two different data types. The Python interpreter is smart enough to recognize two different data types and return a result to the programmer. The addition operation is represented by the symbol '+'.

Program Code:
```
x = 26
y = 15
z = x + y
```

```
# + is the addition operator
print(z)
```

When the program runs using an IDE or IDLE, the interpreter will add the two variable values and assign them to the variable 'z', as specified by the developer.

Output:
41

2. Subtraction Operator

The subtraction operator is used to subtract two literals. These literals can be variables or lists, and they can sometimes be data of two different data types. - is the symbol for the subtraction operation.

Program Code:
```
x = 26
y = 15
z = x - y
# - is the subtraction operator
print(z)
```

When the program is executed using an IDE or IDLE, the interpreter will find the difference between the two variable values and input it into 'z' as specified by the developer.

Output:
11

3. Multiplication Operator

The multiplication operator computes the product of two literals. These literals can be variables or lists, and they can sometimes be data of two different data types. The symbol * represents a multiplication operation.

Program Code:
```
x = 6
y = 4
z = x * y
# * is the multiplication operator
print(z)
```

When the program runs in an IDE or IDLE, the interpreter will find the product of the two variable values and enter it into the 'z' variable as specified by the developer.

Output:
24

4. Division Operator

In a program, the division operator is used to find the division quotient of two literals. The quotient can also be calculated using floating-point numbers, and the division symbol "/" is used.

Program Code:
```
x = 8
y = 4
z = x / y
# / is the division operator
print(z)
```

When the program runs in an IDE or IDLE, the interpreter will find the quotient of the two variable values and enter it into the 'z' variable as specified by the developer.

Output:
```
2.0
```

5. Modulus

Modulus is typically used to calculate the remainder of a division operation. The modulus operator can be used to implement a wide range of programming logic, and % is the modulus operation symbol.

Program Code:
```
x = 9
y = 4
z = x % y
# % is the modulus operator
print(z)
```

When the program is executed using an IDE or IDLE, the interpreter will find the remainder of the two variable values and input them into 'z' as specified by the developer.

Output:
```
1
```

The quotient, in this case, is 2.25, but the remainder is 1, as shown in the program output. You can use floor division operations instead of displaying floating-point numbers as a quotient for division operations.

6. Floor Division

Floor division is an alternative arithmetic operator that developers frequently use when they are not concerned with the precision of the result. The nearest integer for the quotient obtained after a division operation is usually displayed by this operator.

"//" is the symbol for a floor division operator.

Program Code:
```
x = 9
y = 4
z = x // y
# This is the floor division operator
print (z)
```
Output:
2

The above program has a Quotient of 2.25. However, because we are using the floor division operator, the program has returned the nearest integer.

7. Bitwise Operators

Bitwise operators are advanced operators that developers frequently use to perform special features such as compression, encryption, and error detection.

Bitwise operators of various types are used in all high-level programming languages.

AND (&)

OR (|)

XOR (^)

NOT (~)

All these bitwise operators follow the same principles as logical operators in mathematics.

Operator Precedence

Because there are different operators and mathematical expressions are formed by combining them, dealing with advanced mathematical expressions to create real-world applications can quickly become complex. Operator precedence provides programmers with clear objectives for prioritizing which operators perform a mathematical operation.

If a developer fails to follow operator precedence rules, the values may change completely, resulting in application crashes.

Operator Precedence Rules in Python:

In any mathematical expression you deal with in Python, precedence takes precedence. As a result, if operators are enclosed by parenthesis, the interpreter will address them first and then move on to the others.

Bitwise operators are usually given second precedence.

The mathematical operators used for multiplication and division are given the highest priority. The operators that must be preferred in the same order are *, /, %, and //.

The remaining arithmetic operations, such as addition and subtraction, take precedence. These operators are represented by the symbols + and -.

Comparison and logical operators have final operator precedence.

Augmented Assignment Operators

Augmented assignment operators provide a shorthand way to update the value of a variable based on its current value. These operators combine an arithmetic or bitwise operation with an assignment operation. They can make your code more concise and potentially easier to read.

Here's a list of common augmented assignment operators and their equivalent long-form operations:

Augmented Assignment Operator	Equivalent Long-Form Operation	Description
a += b	a = a + b	Addition
a -= b	a = a - b	Subtraction
a *= b	a = a * b	Multiplication
a /= b	a = a / b	Division
a %= b	a = a % b	Modulus
a //= b	a = a // b	Floor Division
a **= b	a = a ** b	Exponentiation
a &= b	a = a & b	Bitwise AND
a |= b	a = a | b	Bitwise OR

Example:
```
# Using += for incrementing a value
count = 10
count += 5   # This is the same as count = count + 5
print(count)   # Output: 15

# Using *= for squaring a value
num = 6
num *= num   # This is the same as num = num * num
print(num)   # Output: 36
```

Exercises

1. Create a program that asks the user for two numbers and performs addition, subtraction, multiplication, and division operations using these numbers. Print the results of each operation.

2. Write a program that asks the user to input two numbers and then performs both a modulus and floor division operation on those numbers. Print the results of both operations to the screen.

3. Write a program that asks the user to input a temperature in Fahrenheit. Convert the temperature to Celsius using the formula C = (F - 32) * 5/9. Display the result in Celsius.

4. Write a program that asks the user to input their age in years, computes their age in seconds (assume 365 days per year, 24 hours per day, 60 minutes per hour, 60 seconds per minute) and displays the result.

5. Create a program that asks the user to enter the original price of an item, enter the discount percentage and finally calculate and display the price after the discount.

Chapter 4: Python Variables

To function properly, Python programs require basic components like variables and operators. These elements, including variables and operators, are simple for novice programmers to comprehend and apply, allowing them to develop algorithms necessary for creating sophisticated software.

What are Variables in Python?

Variables are a way to store and handle data in a Python program. They allow both users and the software to interact with the data. Without data, software applications are useless and serve no purpose for end-users.

Variables are used in Python to store data in a specific computer memory location, allowing the software to upload or download data. The concept of variables was first used in Algebra and has been a fundamental part of high-level programming languages since their inception.

For example, in the mathematical equation $2x + 3y$, the variables x and y can be assigned values, which can then be used to change the output of the equation. In programming, variables with unchanging values are referred to as constants. To understand how variables work in Python, it's important to understand the execution of Python programs, which can be demonstrated through a print statement.

In the same way, by using variables, you can modify the output of a program by supplying literal values. Variables are replaceable, while values that shouldn't be replaced are often referred to as constants in programming.

To grasp how variables function, one needs to comprehend the execution process of Python programs. A print statement will help illustrate this.

Example:

Program Code:
```
print("This is a sentence.")
```

Output:
```
This is a sentence.
```

The code instantly displays the output once the print statement is executed. But there is much more happening behind the scenes.

What happens?

- The program reads each line and matches it with the libraries it has access to.

- An interpreter performs this matching process, using high parsing abilities to identify each character in the program, match variable details, and retrieve information from memory locations to validate the program's logic.
- Despite complex parsing, the program will raise errors if the interpreter cannot find defined methods or variables.
- In the above example, the interpreter recognizes the print statement as a core library method in Python and outputs any string literals in parenthesis.

If you understand the explanation, it is now time to learn about variables in Python.

Program Code:
```
program = "This is a sentence."
print (program)
```

Output:
```
This is a sentence.
```

What Happened?
- At the onset of the program execution, the interpreter will typically parse every line of code given by the programmer.
- Instead of just encountering a print statement followed by text, the interpreter now sees a special identifier referred to as a variable named 'program.' The interpreter checks prior code and discovers that the variable is defined with text and saved at a specific memory location.
- Subsequently, the interpreter will display the variable on the screen as directed by the programmer by retrieving the information defined within the variable.
- This is the fundamental process by which variables work, even in complicated code logic.

Variables can change instantly when they are substituted. A Python programmer needs to be aware of this because dynamic programs frequently alter variables according to user inputs and replace them even as the program operates in real time.

Program Code:
```
sample = "My first example"
print(sample)
sample = "My second example"
print(sample)
```

Output:
```
My first example
My second example
```
Since we know that the Python interpreter parses the code line by line sequentially, the first statement in the previous example is printed with the first variable value provided, and the second print statement is printed with the second variable value provided.

How to Name Variables

When creating variables, all Python programmers must follow the Python community's default guidelines. Failure to follow these conditions will result in difficult-to-ignore errors or, in rare cases, application crash. Using a specific guideline when developing programs can also help to improve readability.

Rules to keep in mind:

Python guidelines specify that variable names can only contain numbers, alphabetical characters, and an underscore. So, for example, 'sample1' can be used as a variable name, whereas '$sample1' cannot because it begins with the unsupported symbol $.

Python programmers can't begin a variable name with a number. For example, 'sample1' is a valid variable naming format, whereas '1sample' is not.

Python programmers can't use reserved words assigned to various Python programming routines. Currently, developers cannot use 33 reserved keywords as identifiers when developing real-world Python applications. For example, the keyword 'for' is reserved.

While this is not a hard and fast rule, it is always preferable to use a simple variable naming method for improved readability. Using complex or confusing variable names can make your code appear sloppy. While this is a good practice for other high-level languages such as C, C++, and Pearl, Python does not support it.

How to Define Variables

All variables defined in the Python programming language begin with the assignment operator (=) to assign a value to the variable.

Syntax Format:

Name_of_the_variable = Value_of_the_variable

Example:
```
example = 123
# This is a variable with an integer data type
example1 = "USA"
# This is a variable with a string data type
```
In this case, "example" is the name of the variable we created, and 123 is the variable value we assigned to it when it was created.

Consider the variable-defining method above, where we did not explicitly mention any variable data type because Python is intelligent enough to understand variable data types on its own.

How to Determine the Memory Address of a Variable

All variables are kept in a separate memory location. The Python interpreter will pull the information from this memory location whenever you call the variable name. When you ask the Python interpreter to replace a variable, it will simply take the previously placed variable value and replace it with the new variable value. The old variable value will be deleted or saved for future use cases using a garbage mechanism.

Pointers are commonly used in programming languages such as C to quickly determine and pull information about a variable's memory location. Python, on the other hand, does not support pointers because it is often difficult to implement and requires many compilation skills that the interpreter is usually unaware of. Instead, Python developers can use the built-in id() function to quickly obtain the variable's memory address.

Program Code:
```
# First, let's create a variable with an integer data type
sample = 32
# Now let's call its memory address using the built-in
         function id()
address = id(sample)
print(address)
```

Output:
1x10744488x

In this case, 1x10744488x is the variable's hexadecimal memory location.

Using the method below, you can now replace the variable and see if the id() has changed.

Program Code:
```
# Let's assign a value to the variable 'sample' and print
         its address
```

```
sample = 64
print(id(sample))
# Now we replace the variable value with a new one
sample = 78
# This will again print the output of the memory location
        address
print(id(sample))
```

Output:

1x10744488x
1x10744488x

Although the memory location did not change, a small print verification (print(sample)) is sufficient to see that the variable value has changed.

Local and Global Variables

Variables can be both local and global, depending on your programming logic. Local variables, in theory, can only be used in the methods or classes that you specify. Global variables, on the other hand, can be used in any part of the program without issue. When you call a local variable outside of a function, the Python interpreter will usually throw an error.

Program Code:

```
# This is an example of a local variable within a function
def mysample():
    x = "This is a sentence"
    print(x)
mysample()
```

Output:

This is a sentence

In this example, the variable is defined as a local variable within a function. As a result, whenever you call it from within a function, it will throw a traceback error, as shown below.

Program Code:

```
# This is an example of a function with a local variable
def sample():
    x = "This is a sentence"
    print(x)
# This is another function
def secondsample():
    print(example)

sample()
secondsample()
```

Output:
```
This is a sentence
NameError: name 'x' is not defined
```

Global variables, on the other hand, can be used to initiate variables for the entire program.

Program Code:
```
# Let's create a global variable
x = "This is a sentence"

# Let's initialize two methods
def method1():
    print(x)

def method2():
    print(x)

# Let's call them
method1()
method2()
```

Output:
```
This is a sentence
This is a sentence
```

Since both functions can access global variables, two print statements are displayed on the computer screen.

It is entirely up to you to decide which type of variables to use. Many programmers rely heavily on local variables to make their applications run faster. Global variables, on the other hand, can be used if you don't want to be overwhelmed with memory management.

Chapter 5: Data Types in Python

Python programmers use a wide range of data types to build cross-platform applications. As a result, a Python programmer must understand the significance of data types in software development.

What exactly are Data Types?

To be more specific, data types are a set of predefined values that programmers use when creating variables. It is also important to remember that because Python is not a statically typed language, it is not necessary to explicitly define variable data types. All statically typed languages, such as C and C++, typically require programmers to define variable data types.

While Python programmers are not required to define them to create programs, understanding the various available data types is still necessary for developing complex programs that can interact with users efficiently.

Here's an example of a statically typed language and how variables are defined.

Program Code:
```
int years = 12;
```
In this case, int is the defined data type, years is the variable's name, and 12 is the value supplied to be stored in the age variable.

Python, on the other hand, defines a variable without explicitly defining the variable type, as illustrated below.

Program Code:
```
years = 12
```
years and value are provided here. However, the data type is not defined because the Python interpreter understands that the value provided is an integer.

Different Data Types

Before we get into the various data types that Python supports, let's talk about the basic programming fragments that developers use to create logical statements while programming.

Let's see a simple expression and statement. To make logical statements in a programming language, three main components are used.

Data identifiers

To store data, programming components such as variables, lists, and tuples are created.

For example:

a = 24

a is a variable in this programming fragment that was created to store sequential data.

Literals

These are the values assigned to any data fragments created by a program.

For example:

a = 24

In this programming fragment, **24** is the literal assigned to the newly created data fragment.

Operators

Operators implement mathematical operations while developing code for real-world applications.

For example:

a = 24

The assignment operator = is used in the preceding code. Other arithmetic operators, such as +, -, *, and /, are well-known for producing logical Python code.

We'll go over some of the most common data types used by Python programmers in their applications.

Strings

Strings are data types that are commonly used to represent a large amount of text. String data types, for example, can be used to represent text in a program by linking them with single quotes. When a string data type is created, an 'str' object with a sequence of characters is created.

Text messages are the most common way for humans to communicate with one another. As a result, strings are the most important data types for developers to understand to create meaningful software. It is also critical to represent data in strings because computers only understand binary data. As a result, using ASCII and Unicode encoding mechanisms is critical.

Python 3 introduced an advanced encoding mechanism for understanding foreign languages such as Chinese, Japanese, and Korean, making Strings indispensable for software development.

In what way are strings represented?

```
z = 'This is my sentence'
print (z)
```

Output:
```
This is my sentence
```

Everything between the single quotation marks is a string data type. The variable 'z' is used to define this string data. The number of bits a variable occupies usually determines its memory location and size when it has a string data type. A string data type's number of characters is directly proportional to its bit count.

In the previous example, 'This is my sample' has 17 characters, including whitespaces.

As a Python programmer, you have several other options for defining strings. When working on real-world projects, use a single type whenever possible for consistency.

Program Code:
```
# Double quotes to define strings
a = "This is my sentence"
print(a)

# Three single quotes to define strings
b = '''This is my sentence'''
print(b)

# Three double quotes to define strings
c = """This is my sentence
 but with more than one line """
print(c)
```

Output:
```
This is my sentence
This is my sentence
This is my sentence
 but with more than one line
```

In the previous example, we defined three methods for defining strings. Special characters, symbols, and new tab lines can also be used between quotes. Python also supports escape sequences, which are used by all programming languages. For example, '\n' is a popular escape sequence used by programmers to create new lines.

How do I Access Characters in Strings?

Because strings are the most commonly used data types in Python, the core library includes several built-in functions for interacting with string data. To access characters in a string, you must first know the index numbers. Index numbers typically begin with 0 rather than 1. Negative indexing and slicing operations can also be used to access a portion of a string.

Example:
```
# We first create a string to access its characters
s = 'PYTHON'

# We print the whole string
print ('Whole string =', s)

# We print the first character
print ('1st character =', s[0])

# We print the last character using negative indexing
print ('Last character =', s[-1])

# We print the last character using positive indexing
print ('Again, Last character =', s[5])

# We print the first 2 characters (index 0 to 1)
print ('Sliced character =', s[0:2])
```

Output:
```
Whole string = PYTHON
1st character = P
Last character = N
Again, Last character = N
Sliced character = PY
```

Because all string data types are immutable, it is impossible to replace characters in a literal string. As a result, attempting to replace string characters will result in a Type error.

Program Code:
```
s = 'PYTHON'
s[1] = 'c'
print(s)
```

Output:
```
TypeError: 'str' object does not support item assignment
```

String Formatting

With the modulus (%) operator, Python makes it simple to format your string. It is known as *string formatting operator*.

Program Code:
```
print ("Today I have eaten %d apples" %3)
```

Output:
```
Today I have eaten 3 apples
```
You can use %d to format integers. You can also use %s to format your text.

String Manipulation Techniques

Because strings are the most commonly used data type, the Python core library provides several manipulation techniques for programmers to use. Understanding string manipulation techniques will help you quickly extract data from a large pool of data. These techniques are more widely known among data scientists.

1. Concatenate

Concatenation is the joining of two distinct entities. Using the arithmetic operator '+,' two strings can be joined together using this procedure. If you want to improve string readability, simply use whitespaces between the two strings.

Program Code:
```
example = 'Today is' + 'a wonderful day'
print (example)
```

Output:
```
Today isa wonderful day
```
Remember that whitespaces are not allowed when concatenating. While concatenating, you must add whitespaces on your own, as shown below.

Program Code:
```
example = 'Today is' + ' ' + 'a wonderful day'
print (example)
```

Output:
```
Today is a wonderful day
```

2. Multiply

When you use the String multiply technique, your string value is continuously repeated. The * operator can be used to multiply string content.

Program Code:
```
example = 'Yes '* 4
print(example)
```

Output:
```
Yes Yes Yes Yes
```

3. Appending

You can use this operation to add any string to the end of another string by using the arithmetic operator +=. Keep in mind that the appended string will only be added at the end of the string, not in the middle.

Program Code:
```
example = "Today is a beautiful day "
example += "to start learning Python!"
print (example)
```

Output:
```
Today is a beautiful day to start learning Python!
```

4. Length

In addition to string operations, you can use prebuilt functions in the core library to perform additional tasks in your code. The 'length()' function, for example, returns the number of characters in a string.

Blank Space will be added as a character in the string as well.

Program Code:
```
example = 'Tomorrow it will be sunny'
print(len(example))
```

Output:
```
25
```

5. Find

When you use strings as your primary data type, there will be times when you need to find a specific part of the string. To solve this problem, you can use the built-in find() function. The output will provide an index for the position the first time the input is found so you can verify.

When you use the find() function in Python, the interpreter will only return positive indexes.

Program Code:
```
example = 'Tomorrow it will be sunny'
sample = example.find('it')
print(sample)
```

Output:
9

If the substring is not found, the interpreter will return a value of -1.

Program Code:
```
example = 'Tomorrow it will be sunny'
sample = example.find('hi')
print(sample)
```

Output:
-1

6. Lower and upper case

lower() and higher() functions can be used to convert characters in a string to completely lower or upper case.

Program Code:
```
example = "Asia is the biggest continent"
sample = example.lower()
print(sample)
```

Output:
asia is the biggest continent

Program Code:
```
example = "Asia is the biggest continent"
sample = example.upper()
print(sample)
```

Output:
ASIA IS THE BIGGEST CONTINENT

7. Title

To convert string format to camel case format, use the title() function.

Program Code:
```
example = "Asia is the biggest continent"
sample = example.title()
print(sample)
```

Output:
Asia Is The Biggest Continent

Integers

In Python, integers are special data types that allow you to include integer numbers in your code. To perform arithmetic operations or to provide information about a statistical value, numerical values are required.

When a Python interpreter encounters a data value of the integer type, it creates an int object with the value provided. Because int object values are not immutable, they can be replaced whenever the developer desires.

'int' data types are used by developers to create a variety of complex features in their software. Integers are commonly used to represent the pixel density value of an image or video file.

A developer needs to understand the unary operators (+,-), which can be used to represent positive and negative integers, respectively. The unary operator does not need to be specified for positive integers (+), but it must be included for negative integers.

Program Code:
```
x = 13
y = -92
print(x)
print(y)
```

Output:
```
13
-92
```

Python can handle numbers with up to ten digits. While most real-world applications do not cause bottlenecks due to larger numerical values, it's better to be sure that no huge integers are involved.

Floating–Point numbers

Not all numerical values are integers. You may occasionally need to work with data with a decimal value. Python ensures that developers deal with this data using floating-point numbers. With floating-point numbers, you can work with decimal values up to ten decimal points long.

Program Code:
```
x = 3.121212
y = 58.4545
print(x)
print(y)
```

Output:
```
3.121212
58.4545
```

Floating-point numbers can also be used to represent data in hexadecimal notation.

Program Code:
```
x = float.hex(15.2698)
print(x)
```

Output:
0x1.e8a2339c0ebeep+3

Floating-point data types are also commonly used by Python programmers to represent complex and exponential numbers.

Boolean Data Type

Booleans are special data types that are typically used to represent a True or False value when comparing two different values.

Program Code:
```
A = 21
B = 55
print (A > B)
```
Output:
```
False
```
Because the value of A is not greater than the value of B in the preceding example, the output is False. When dealing with logical operations, Boolean data types come in handy.

Chapter 6: Advanced Data Structures in Python

Python programmers frequently deal with large amounts of data, so using variables all the time is not a good idea. Data Scientists, in particular, who frequently deal with large amounts of data, may become overwhelmed by the volume of dynamic data they must deal with. As a result, when working on complex and data-intensive projects, it is critical to use the lists option provided by Python's core library. These are similar to data structures such as arrays found in core programming languages such as C and C++.

Understanding the various data structures provided by Python, as well as learning techniques to add or modify data using these data structures, is a must for any Python programmer.

Lists

Lists are Python data types that allow you to add different data types sequentially. Lists have all of the same properties as variables. They can be easily replaced, passed, or manipulated with the help of the Python core library's methods.

In Python, lists are typically represented as follows:

[22, 23, 24]

The list elements here are 22, 23, and 24. It is also important to understand that all list elements are of integer data type and are not explicitly defined because the Python interpreter can detect their data type.

In the above format, lists begin and end with a square bracket. A comma will be used to separate all of the elements in the list. It's also worth noting that if the elements in a list are of the string data type, they're usually surrounded by quotes. All of the elements in a list are also referred to as items.

Example:

[Alaska, California, Alabama]

Alaska, California, and Alabama are referred to as list elements in this context. As an example, all of the lists can be assigned to a variable. When you print the variable, the list will be printed like any other data type.

Program Code:
```
x = ['Alaska', 'California', 'Alabama']
print(x)
```
Output:
```
['Alaska', 'California', 'Alabama']
```

Empty List

If a Python list has no elements, it is referred to as an empty list. An empty list is also known as a null list. It's usually written as [].

Program Code:
```
# This is an empty list
emptylist = []
```

List Indexing

Python makes it simple to manipulate or replace the elements of a list, specifically through the use of indexes. Indexes typically begin with 0 and provide Python programmers with numerous functions, such as "slicing" and "searching," to ensure that their programs run smoothly.

Assume we have a list that we have previously used. We will print each element on the computer screen using the indexes.

Program Code:
```
myList = ['California', 'Alaska', 'Alabama']
print(myList[0])
print(myList[1])
print(myList[2])
```
Output:
```
'California'
'Alaska'
'Alabama'
```

In the previous example, when the Python interpreter detects 0 as an index, it prints the first element. As the index rises, so does the position on the list.

The items in the list can also be called as shown below, along with a string literal.

Program Code:
```
myList = ['California', 'Alaska', 'Alabama']
print(myList [1] + ' is a wonderful state')
```
Output:
```
Alaska is a wonderful state
```

If you provide an index value that is greater than the number of list elements present, an index error will be returned.

Program Code:
```
myList = ['California', 'Alaska', 'Alabama']
print(myList [3])
```

Output:
```
IndexError: list index out of range
```

Note: It is also important to remember that the floating-point number cannot be used as an index value.

Program Code:
```
myList = ['California', 'Alaska', 'Alabama']
print(myList [2.2])
```

Output:
```
TypeError: list indices must be integers or slices, not
         float
```

As shown below, all lists can have other lists as elements. Child lists are all the lists contained within a list.

Program Code:
```
x = [[5,123,4],56,32,14]
print(x)
```

Output:
```
[[5, 123, 4], 56, 32, 14]
```

You can call the elements in the child list using the 'list [][]' format.

Program Code:
```
x = [[5,123,4],56,32,14]
print(x[0][1])
```

Output:
```
123
```

In the previous example, the second element of the nested list is 123, which is displayed as output. The elements of a list can also be referred to using the negative index. Typically, -1 denotes the last index, whereas -2 denotes the element preceding the last element.

Program Code:
```
myList = ['California', 'Alaska', 'Alabama']
print(myList [-1])
```

Output:
```
Alabama
```

You've already learned about how lists are represented. In the following section, we will discuss some of the functions that can be manipulated using a list data structure.

Slicing Using Lists

Slicing lists allows programmers to avoid dealing with an overwhelming number of elements contained within a list. By slicing, you can focus only on the part of a list that is relevant to your program logic.

Syntax:

Listname[start of the index : end of the index]

A colon is typically used to separate the beginning and ending indexes of the list that you want to slice.

Program Code:
```
myList = [23,34,78,94,54]
print(myList[1:3]) # 2nd and 3rd elements (index 1 and 2)
```

Output:
```
[34, 78]
```

You do not need to enter the list's beginning or end when slicing the list elements. If it is not entered, the interpreter will assume it is the first or last element in the list.

Program Code:
```
myList = [23,34,78,94,54]
print(myList[:3])
```

Output:
```
[23, 34, 78]
```

Because the slice value before the semicolon was not provided in the previous example, the interpreter assumed it came from the first element.

Program Code:
```
myList = [23,34,78,94,54]
print(myList[3:])
```

Output:
```
[94, 54]
```

In this example, the interpreter has assumed that the value following the semicolon represents the end of the list. If neither value is provided, the entire list is returned, as shown below.

Program Code:
```
myList = [23,34,78,94,54]
print(myList[:])
```

Output:
```
[23, 34, 78, 94, 54]
```
Get list length

To quickly determine the length of a list, use the built-in len() function.

Program Code:
```
myList = [23,34,78,94,54]
print(len(myList))
```

Output:
```
5
```

Changing Values of a List

As shown below, you can easily change the values inside a list using the assignment operator.

Program Code:
```
myList = [23,34,78,94,54]
myList [3] = 58
print(myList)
```

Output:
```
[23, 34, 78, 58, 54]
```

You can also replace a list value with an already existing list value, as shown below.

Program Code:
```
myList = [23,34,78,94,54]
myList [3] = myList[2]
print(myList)
```

Output:
```
[23, 34, 78, 78, 54]
```

Concatenating Lists

The Arithmetic operator '+' can be used to easily combine two lists.

Program Code:
```
myList = [23,34,78,94,54]
x = [1,2,3]
print(myList + x)
```

Output:
```
[23, 34, 78, 94, 54, 1, 2, 3]
```

Replication of a List

Using the '*' operator, you can quickly multiply list elements with this function.

Program Code:
```
print([1,2,3] * 4)
```

Output:
[1, 2, 3, 1, 2, 3, 1, 2, 3, 1, 2, 3]

Element Deletion

Using the 'del' statement, you can easily remove an element from a list.

Program Code:
```
myList = [12,13,14,15,16,17]
del(myList [2])
print(myList)
```

Output:
[12, 13, 15, 16, 17]

Using the operators "in" and "not in"

Using the logical operators 'in' and 'not in,' Python makes it simple to determine whether a list element is present or not in a list. As a result, this function returns either a True or False Boolean value.

Program Code:
```
colors = ['yellow', 'orange', 'blue']
x = 'orange' in colors
print(x)
```

Output:
True

index()

Using the index() list function, you can quickly determine the index position of a list element.

Program Code:
```
x = [12, 45, 78]
print(x.index(45))
```

Output:
1

If you provide a list element that does not exist within a list, you will receive a type error.

Program Code:
```
x = [12, 45, 78]
print(x.index(49))
```
Output:
```
ValueError: 49 is not in list
```

insert()

You can insert a new element to the list at any position in the list by using the insert() function.

Syntax:

insert(index position, 'item')

Program Code:
```
x = [12, 45, 78]
x.insert(2,11)
print(x)
```
Output:
```
[12, 45, 11, 78]
```
The third element is moved to the fourth position and the new element is added to the third

sort()

Python developers can easily arrange all the elements in a list using either ascending or descending order by using the sort() function.

Program Code:
```
x = [78, 12, 45]
x.sort()
print(x)
```
Output:
```
[12, 45, 78]
```
If you use strings in the list, the list will be sorted alphabetically.

Program Code:
```
x = ['yellow', 'blue', 'orange', 'grey']
x.sort()
print(x)
```
Output:
```
['blue', 'grey', 'orange', 'yellow']
```

Tuples

Even though lists are popular data structures that Python programmers frequently use in their applications, they have several implementation issues. Because all lists created with Python are mutual objects, they are simple to replace, delete, or manipulate.

As a software developer, you may be required to keep immutable lists that cannot be altered in any way. That's why tuples exist. Within Tuples, it is not possible to change initiated elements in any way. When you try to change the content of a tuple, you will get a "Type Error" message.

Program Code:
```
# Let's create a tuple using Python
t = ('Cat', 'Tree', 'Apple')
print(t)
```

Output:
```
('Cat', 'Tree', 'Apple')
```

In the previous example, we simply initiated a tuple and used a print function to display it on the screen. Tuples, unlike lists, are not represented with square brackets, but rather with parenthesis to distinguish them from lists.

To understand how tuples work, try changing one of the elements in the preceding example and printing the tuple to see what happens.

Program Code:
```
t = ('Cat', 'Tree', 'Apple')
print(t)

# Trying to replace an element in the tuple...
t[2] = 'Mango'
print(t)
```

Output:
```
('Cat', 'Tree', 'Apple')
TypeError: 'tuple' object does not support item assignment
```

In the previous example, if a tuple element is changed, the interpreter will throw an error. This demonstrates that all tuple elements are immutable and cannot be replaced, deleted, or added.

Tuples Concatenation

Tuples, like the many list operations we've seen, can be used to work on specific operations. For example, just like lists, you can use Python to add or multiply the elements in a tuple.

Program Code:
```
tuple1 = (17,18,19)
tuple2 = (16,19,28)
# Adding two tuples
print(tuple1 + tuple2)
```

Output:
(17, 18, 19, 16, 19, 28)

The Addition operator is used to concatenate two tuples in the preceding example. Similarly, you can use the multiplication operator to quickly increase the elements in your tuple. We can also nest tuples within tuples. This is commonly referred to as nesting tuples.

Program Code:
```
X = (1,2,3)
Y = ('Orange','Apple','Banana')
Z = (X,Y)
print(Z)
```

Output:
((1, 2, 3), ('Orange', 'Apple', 'Banana'))

Two tuples are nested within another tuple in the previous example.

Replication

When working with lists, you can use the * operator to repeat the values.

Program Code:
```
T = (4,5,6) * 4
print(T)
```

Output:
(4, 5, 6, 4, 5, 6, 4, 5, 6, 4, 5, 6)

As previously stated, changing the values of tuples is impossible because they are designed to be immutable. Here is what happens if we try to swap one value for another.

Program Code:
```
T = (45,78,89)
T[2] = 15
print(T)
```

Output:
TypeError: 'tuple' object does not support item assignment

Slicing With Tuples

The slicing technique, which uses indexes to extract a portion of the tuple, makes it simple to slice a portion of the tuple.

Program Code:
```
t = (24,25,26,27,28,29,30)
print(t[2:4] )
```

Output:
```
(26, 27)
```

Tuple Deletion

It is not possible to delete a specific element from a tuple, but it is possible to delete the entire tuple using the command below. This is true for any type of variable.

Program Code:
```
t = (24,25,26,27,28,29,30)
del t
print(t)
```

Output:
```
NameError: name 't' is not defined
```

Dictionaries

Dictionaries are special data structures that Python provides to store values as pairs rather than single values as lists and tuples do. The "key: value" pair is used by dictionaries to ensure that the data provided is more optimized and works better. Dictionaries are also represented by curly brackets, which distinguishes them from lists and tuples.

How Do I Create a Dictionary?

As previously stated, dictionaries are defined using key: value pairs separated by commas. The elements will be placed in sequential order and must be separated.

Syntax:

Dictionary_sample = { key: value , key: value ………) }

As a developer, you can add an unlimited number of key:value pairs to a dictionary.

Example:
```
Capitals = {'France': 'Paris', 'Spain': 'Madrid', 'Italy':
      'Rome'}
print(Capitals)
```

Output:
{'France': 'Paris', 'Spain': 'Madrid', 'Italy': 'Rome'}

You can also build a nested dictionary. A nested dictionary is a dictionary within a dictionary:

```
Capitals = {'France': 'Paris', 'Spain': 'Madrid', 'Italy':
      'Rome', 'Australia': {'Melbourne', 'Sydney'}}
print(Capitals)
```

Output:
{'France': 'Paris', 'Spain': 'Madrid', 'Italy': 'Rome',
      'Australia': {'Sydney', 'Melbourne'}}

The last key: pair value in the second example has a dictionary with two key:pair values.

Exercises

1. List exercise: Create a list of 5 numbers and then print the sum and average of the numbers.

2. Create a tuple of 5 names and then print the first and last name.

3. Create a dictionary with 5 key-value pairs and then print the value of the third key.

4. Create a list with 5 fruits (e.g. apples, bananas, etc.). Ask the user to input a fruit. Check if the fruit is in the list. If the fruit is in the list, display a message saying "The fruit is in the list." If the fruit is not in the list, display a message saying "The fruit is not in the list."

5. Create a list with 3 colors. Then ask the user to give a color as input. If the color is in the list, display a message saying so. Otherwise, append the color given by the user to the end of the list and print the updated list

Chapter 7: Conditionals and Loops

Any computer program must make decisions for real-world applications. A mobile application with advanced software, for example, will use your inputs to display whatever you want. While using a mobile or web application, the user makes decisions. The program must be intelligent enough to provide a relevant interface based on the user's selection. This dynamic thinking is very similar to human thinking.

When writing in Python, you must be aware of conditionals and loops to ensure that your programs mimic these conditions. These are high-level programming structures that can make your Python programs more effective.

Conditionals and loops can also help you reduce the execution time of your programs, making them run faster. A Python programmer who wants to work with well-known teams should be aware of these techniques, as they are also prerequisite requirements for more advanced topics such as Functions and Modules, which we will discuss further.

Comparison Operators

To practically understand conditionals and loops, you must be aware of the various comparison operators supported by Python as a programming language.

Comparison operators, also known as relational operators, typically compare two operands to each other and return a Boolean value, either True or False.

Note: 'True' and 'False' are special Boolean values supported by Python to assist programs in making relevant decisions. Boolean values are the basic logic gates present within microprocessors.

1. **Less than (<) operator**

This operator determines whether the left operand value is less than the right operand value.

Program Code:
```
print(12 < 19)
```
Output:
```
True
```

Program Code:
```
print(87 < 36)
```
Output:
```
False
```
If you look at the two examples above, you'll notice that the first has a 'True' output because 12 is less than 19, while the second has a 'False' output because 87 is not less than 36.

With a less-than operator, you can apply the same principle to floating-point values.

Program Code:
```
a = 9.5 < 10.26
print(a)
```
Output:
```
True
```
To compare strings in ASCII format, you can also use the "less than" operator.

Program Code:
```
a = 'Banana' < 'banana'
print(a)
```
Output:
```
True
```
Because the ASCII value of lowercase letters is usually higher than that of uppercase letters, the Boolean value in the previous example is True.

Exercise:

Determine the ASCII sum for the word 'banana' mentioned above.

These relational operators can also be applied to other data structures, such as tuples. Before comparing, however, ensure that all of the values in a tuple are of the same data type.

Program Code:
```
print((15,18,98) < (25,48,18,19))
```
Output:
```
True
```
If the tuples have different data types, an error message will appear on the terminal.

Program Code:
```
print((20,30,40) < ('three',4,5))
```

Output:
```
TypeError: '<' not supported between instances of 'int' and
          'str'
```

2. Greater than (>) operator

A *greater than* operator is typically used to determine whether the left operand value is greater than the right operand value.

Program Code:
```
print(32 > 56)
```

Output:
```
False
```

The Boolean value in the first example is False because the right operand value 32 is less than 56.

The same relational operator can also be used with floating-point values and other data types, such as tuples.

3. Equal (== operator)

An *equal* operator determines whether the values of the right and left operands are equal. If the operand values are the same, the Boolean value is True. Otherwise, it's False.

Program Code:
```
print(5 == 5)
```

Output:
```
True
```

Program Code:
```
print(12 == 21)
```

Output:
```
False
```

Control Flow Statements

With a solid understanding of comparison operators under your belt, you are now ready to learn about the various control statements that are required of all Python developers. Control flow statements are commonly used by programmers to write simple code for beginners.

Sequential Structure

All of your program's steps will typically be executed linearly in a sequential structure. As a result, many programs have a sequential structure to avoid writing complex code. However, sequential code requires a high level of skill from programmers because developing programming logic linearly can be difficult.

Example:
```
a = 6
print (a, "is a perfect number")
```

Output:
```
6 is a perfect number
```

In the previous example, the Python interpreter parsed the code line by line to produce an output.

Conditional Structure

The conditional structure is a well-known programming structure that is used to execute only a portion of the program while ignoring the remaining logical code based on the conditional statements.

Only partial statements are executed in a conditional structure, which allows Python interpreters to save time by not parsing the entire code.

If and if-else conditional structures are two well-known conditional branches used by Python programmers.

Looping Structure

Looping structures are useful when you want to repeat the same statement or programming logic in a program based on logical conclusions. The Python interpreter allows you to repeat a programming step until the condition is met.

To make the most of the looping structure, developers must write both loop-starting and loop-terminating logic. While and for loops are two common looping structures that Python programmers can use in their code.

If/Else Conditional Statements

To perform specific operations, conditional statements rely on fundamental decision-making. If the condition is not met, the conditional logic will skip that particular block.

Python includes a basic if/else statement for choosing between two blocks using a logical statement.

Syntax:

if condition:

  execute statement

else:

  execute statement

Program Code:
```
x = 31
if x % 4 == 0:
    print("This number is divisible by 4")
else:
    print("This number is not divisible by 4")
```
Output:
```
This number is not divisible by 4
```
Explanation:
- To begin, we must define a variable that will be used when we set up our condition for the if/else conditional.
- Indentation is required for the code that is eventually executed after the if (else) statement.
- Advanced programs use automatic input methods to get values from users.
- After storing the variable, the interpreter will parse the condition used by the if block.
- The Python interpreter will perform a remainder operation to see if the number is divisible by 4.
- If it is divisible by 4, the block immediately following the if statement should have been executed.
- Because the condition is false, the interpreter will skip the if block and instead execute the statements in the else block, which will result in the output.

Let's see an example of a condition that fulfills the if block.

Program Code:
```
x = 32
if x % 4 == 0:
    print("This number is divisible by 4")
else:
    print("This number is not divisible by 4")
```
Output:
```
This number is divisible by 4
```
If the condition is satisfied the print statement in the if block is executed, and the else block is skipped by the interpreter.

If Elif Else

Using multiple conditional expressions in a single program block allows you to make better use of conditionals.

Program Code:
```
n = 15
if n % 3 == 0:
    print("Number divisible by 3")
elif n % 4 == 0:
    print("Number divisible by 4")
else:
    print("Number not divisible by 3 and 4")
```

Output:
```
Number divisible by 3
```

In the previous example, the Python interpreter must check three conditions. When the Python interpreter determines that the first condition is true, it prints it and ignores the other two.

If any two statements are true, only the first one in the sequence of the code will be printed.

For Loops

Looping structures, like conditionals, are building blocks for Python software. Instead of constantly checking a condition, you can loop it using a for or while loop.

A for loop can be used with any data structure, including lists, tuples, and dictionaries.

Syntax:

for i in object:

  { Enter the body of a loop here }

When a condition is specified, the for loop can loop through all the items of the data structure.

Example:
```
v = [45,89,56]
out = 0
for val in v:
    out = out + val
print ("Sum of the 3 elements of the vector v:", out)
```

Output:
```
Sum of the 3 elements of the vector v: 190
```

In the previous example, instead of performing arithmetic operations on each element of the list, we simply used a for loop to automate this procedure.

While Loop

While the for loop is great for automating tasks, it can be difficult to write logical code since there is no way to apply a condition to the loop. This is where a while loop comes in handy.

A while loop will be provided before looping, with the condition being checked each time the loop occurs.

Syntax:

while condition

   {Enter the statement for a while loop here}

Example:
```
a = 0
b = 1
N = int(input("Enter number: "))
while b <= N:
    a = a + b
    b = b + 1
print ("The sum of numbers from 1 to", N, "is", a)
```

Output:
```
Enter number: 10
The sum of numbers from 1 to 10 is 55
```

Conditionals and loops can be nested to create more complex programs.

Break and Continue

Loops can complete a large amount of complex programming logic in a short period. While they are useful in many situations, they can consume a lot of run-time memory, causing programs to crash unexpectedly.

To solve this problem, Python provides two programming components known as break and continue.

Break Statement

When the Python interpreter encounters a 'break' in a program, it immediately ends the loop and moves on to the line following the loop. Any time the 'break' occurs inside a loop, the loop will end and the next statements will be executed.

Syntax:

break

Example Program:
```
M = 10
j = 1
while j <= M:
    if j %2 == 0:
        print(j, "is divisible by 2 ")
    if j % 3 == 0:
        print(j, "is divisible by 3 ")
        break
    j = j + 1
```

Output:
```
2 is divisible by 2
3 is divisible by 3
```

When the interpreter reads the break statement in the previous example, the program will end. What would the output be without the 'break'? (hint: all the numbers <= 10 that are divisible by 2 and 3...).

Continue Statement?

When the Python interpreter encounters 'continue' in a program, it immediately ends the loop and moves on to the next iteration. Keep in mind that this statement will not completely end the loop. Proceeding to the next logical statement in a loop will only save time and processing energy.

Example Program:
```
for letter in 'Productivity':
    if letter == 't':
        continue
    print('Letter now:', letter)
```

Output:
```
Letter now: P
Letter now: r
Letter now: o
Letter now: d
Letter now: u
Letter now: c
Letter now: i
Letter now: v
Letter now: i
Letter now: y
```

Exercises

1. Write a program that asks the user for an integer and calculates the factorial of the given number. Use a for loop to accomplish this task.

2. Write a program that counts the number of vowels (a, e, i, o, u) of a string given as input from the user. Loop the string and check if the current character is a vowel.

3. Create some code to produce a random number between 1 and 100. The program should then ask the user to guess the number and say each time if it's too high or too low until the user has entered the correct number. Use a while loop to accomplish this task. (Hint: import the library 'random' typing 'import random' and then use the function 'random.randint(1, 100)').

4. Write a program that prints the first n even numbers. Ask the user for the value of n. Use a for loop to generate the numbers, and an if statement to determine if the current number is even.

5. Write a program that prints the first n Fibonacci numbers. The Fibonacci sequence is a series of numbers in which each number is the sum of the two preceding ones. The first two numbers in the series are 0 and 1. Use a for loop to generate the numbers and break the loop when n numbers have been printed.

Chapter 8: Functions and Modules

Python supports a variety of programming paradigms. The functional programming paradigm is the most widely used programming paradigm for developers to write code in. Functional programming is adaptable and simple to use for simple projects that require fewer developers to complete the code. Because of the faster implementation of various programming components, the functional paradigm is also considered versatile.

Creating programs with functions may be difficult because you must always call the function within the program. With the help of a few examples, you can learn functional programming and create complex programs with less code.

A Real-World Example:

Functions were first used in mathematics to solve complex problems in discrete mathematics. Later, programmers began implementing this concept to reuse previously written code without rewriting it.

Let's use a simple mobile app to demonstrate how functions work in real-world applications.

Picsart is a popular mobile photo editing app that offers a variety of filters and tools for image manipulation. For example, the crop tool makes it simple for users to crop their images. Now, when Picsart developers write code, they typically use a variety of libraries, frameworks, and functions. Cropping, for example, necessitates its function due to the numerous complex tasks involved in dividing pixels and providing output to the user.

Assume the developers wanted to update the application to include video cropping support. For programmers, there are currently two options.
1. They can design a cropping function from the ground up.
2. They can use the photo cropping function and add additional functionalities.

Many developers prefer option two because it is simpler and saves time. However, as previously stated, creating functions is not as simple. It requires a great deal of complex logic to connect the functions to the core application framework and other third-party libraries.

Types of Functions

System functions and user-defined functions are the two main types of functions.

The core Python library provides system functions, which are frequently used by developers to perform common tasks. 'print,' for example, is a system function that displays a literal string literal on the screen.

Developers, on the other hand, create user-defined functions specifically for their software. Users can also integrate third-party libraries' user-defined functions into their code.

Regardless of the type of code you use, keep in mind that the primary goal of using functions as a programmer is to solve problems with less reusable code.

How do they Work?

The philosophy behind the use of functions in programming is similar to that of mathematical functions. The developer will first define a function with complex code logic and a name that can be called from anywhere in the program using unique programming components known as parameters. The developers then explicitly define what type of parameters the user can provide for fewer crashes.

If the function is not called, users will be unable to use the code logic that the developer created. Function calling is frequently displayed in the front end via buttons, tabs, and other graphical user interfaces. While it may be as simple as a tap for the end user, a function will be called programmatically for a software component to function properly.

How should you Define your Functions?

There is no need to define the default system functions because they are built. You can only call them. Even though programmers can modify system functions, doing so is not recommended because they are typically complex, and messing with them will break your code.

Python developers who want to create game-changing software, on the other hand, can use the "def" keyword to create functions.

A simple example is provided to help you understand function declaration in Python more quickly.

Program Code:
```
# Function to print a welcome message
def welcome():
    print ("Good morning, I Hope you are fine.")
welcome()
```

Output:
Good morning, I Hope you are fine.

Explanation:
- While this is a simple program, its workflow is similar to that of more complex programs. When working on real-world projects, the number of steps only increases.
- First, we use the 'def' keyword in line 1 to initialize a function in the program. If the def keyword is not used, the function will not work because the interpreter will not understand that it is a function.
- The name of the function is defined alongside def. The function is called "welcome" in this case. The same rules apply to naming functions as they do to variables.
- The body of the function is everything that comes after the comment. Variables, functions, and constants can all be part of a function body. The main core logic of the function is usually defined in this body.
- The body of the function is usually preceded by a comment or docstring. We used a comment in this example. When you use two single quotes to provide information about a function, this is referred to as a docstring.

If you are using multiple lines to provide information, then you can use three single quotes.

Example:
```
# This is an example of a function that we are using for
      beginners
def myFunction():
    '''
    Author: John
    Function: myFunction
    What does it do? It simply prints
    '''
    print ("Hi! I wish you a wonderful day!")

myFunction()
```

The program's third line defines a print statement that displays content on the screen. You can use as many built-in functions as you want in this area to make your program look more natural for the time being. Even though the data is static, it helps you understand how legacy applications work.

The final line shows how the developer invokes a function. In this case, myFunction() is a function call. There are no parameters between parentheses because this is a simple program. Multiple parameters can be used in complex programs. When the interpreter finds a function call, it immediately searches for the function and does whatever the function requests.

Function Parameters

There were no parameters in the previous example function. That is not the case in real-world applications, as programs are frequently complex and difficult to understand. To use functions, you must first create functions that use parameters and perform tasks.

Assume, based on the previous example, that we have two users for our application, and we need to greet them by calling them by their names.

Program Code:
```
def mysample():
# Function that prints the same welcome message to two
        different users
    print("Hi Sam, I hope you are fine!")
    print("Hi Tom, I hope you are fine!")
mysample()
```

Output:
Hi Sam, I hope you are fine!
Hi Tom, I hope you are fine!"

To begin, create two print statements that use both input/conditionals and print statements to validate the user and display the correct output. This is overly complicated and unnecessary, as parameters can assist you in creating dynamic welcome messages for your users. Not just for two, but for thousands of users, with just a minor change when creating a function.

Consider this example function with a single parameter that can assist you in creating a dynamic message.

Program Code:
```
# This is an example function with a single parameter
def mysample(name):
    print ("Hi " + name + ". " + "How are you doing?")
mysample('Sam')
mysample('Tom')
mysample('John')
mysample('Mike')
```

Output:
Hi Sam. How are you doing?
Hi Tom. How are you doing?
Hi John. How are you doing?
Hi Mike. How are you doing?

Explanation:
- A function named 'mysample' is created, and the parameter 'name' is defined between parenthesis. Because the Python interpreter is intelligent enough to parse any data value provided by the user, you may not need to specify the data type for this parameter.
- The programmer used the arithmetic operator to divide the string after calling the parameter in the print function. As a result, whenever the user enters data, it is placed between the default strings.
- In the following lines, the developer has called the function with the parameter input. For complex applications, the parameter cannot be fixed and must be provided by the user. We used the default parameters in this example. The parameters provided by the developer are Sam, Tom, John, and Mike.

If you want to start creating more advanced functions, you can use Python's argument functionality.

Arguments of a Function

To fully utilize their capabilities, all modern applications use variables for the functions. In the previous example program, we used default arguments for the function parameter. However, for Python developers, always providing parameters by default is not ideal. Users can pass arguments to the function through all parameters. While there are several ways to pass arguments to function parameters, the most common are positional and keyword arguments.

Positional Arguments

When using positional arguments, programmers typically provide the values for the function parameters directly. It may appear to be perplexing, but many programmers use it since it is easier to implement. It is essential to remember the order in which positional arguments are passed.

Program Code:
```
def age(who, years):
    '''
    This function states the age of different people
    '''
    print(who, "is", years, "years old")
age('Mike', 35)
age('Tom', 24)
```

Output:
```
Mike is 35 years old
Tom is 24 years old
```

The arguments for the first instance in the previous example are 'Mike' and 35. Because no data types are specified, the Python interpreter will determine the value type and throw it to the function.

Parameter names are important because there is no direct way to understand the data type that we are using. A name is represented by a literal string, while a number is represented by an integer data type. A comma is typically used to separate all the arguments.

It is easy to make mistakes when using positional arguments, as demonstrated below.

Program Code:
```
def age(who, years):
    print(who, "is", years, "years old")

age(35, 'Mike')
age(24, 'Tom')
```

Output:
```
35 is Mike years old
24 is Tom years old
```

While the function produces an output, it is incorrect because the arguments are for opposite parameters.

Keyword Arguments can be used to define function parameters to solve these minor issues with positional arguments.

Keyword Arguments

With keyword arguments, you can directly pass arguments to the function parameter. Keyword arguments use parameter = value format to give arguments to any function.

Keyword Arguments cause less confusion but take more time to implement and hence are not often used by developers working on complex projects that involve a lot of code.

Program Code:
```
def age(who, years):
    print(who, "is", years, "years old")

age(who = 'Mike', years = 35)
age(years = 24, who = 'Tom')
```

Output:
```
Mike is 35 years old
Tom is 24 years old
```

The format in which keyword arguments are defined here is *parameter = argument*. In *who = 'Mike'*, for example, *who* is the parameter and *Mike* is the argument.

Default Values

Not all values in a Python or other programming language program must be dynamic. Default values, also known as 'constants,' are sometimes used by developers when passing arguments to a function. Using default values for parameters is completely optional for programmers.

However, defining default values is recommended because it reduces boilerplate code and offers better data management if the project is complex. Boilerplate code is unnecessary, but it must be written by developers for the interpreter to function properly. While Python is clutter-free in comparison to other high-level languages, some changes to the code, such as defining default values, are required to improve code readability.

Program Code:
```
def age(who, years = 35):
    print(who, "is", years, "years old")

age('Mike')
age('Tom')
```

Output:
```
Mike is 35 years old
Tom is 35 years old
```

Because we have already defined a parameter value in the previous example, function calling becomes easier and takes less time.

It is important to remember that even if you have given the default value, the Python interpreter will end up replacing the argument if it is defined again.

Program Code:
```
def age(who, years = 35):
    print(who, "is", years, "years old")

age('Mike')
age('Tom', 24)
```

Output:
```
Mike is 35 years old
Tom is 24 years old
```

Even though the default value is 35, the argument for Tom is given as 24. In this case, the Python interpreter replaces it with the new argument value.

Scope

Scope is critical for developers to understand the various types of functions available and to find ways to use them without difficulty. Functions, like variables, have a local scope and a global scope, as previously explained.

Local scope variables are all variables created within a function that can only be used within it. By contrast, any variable that can be used is referred to as a global scope variable.

Remember that a function can have both local and global variables. As a result, all variables used in the function should be either local or global.

Why is Scope Crucial?

The scope functionality is mostly used to maintain the garbage mechanism more effectively. To increase the program's speed, all variables that have been replaced or have not been used in a long time are usually destroyed. While they can be recreated when the function is called, the process still consumes runtime.

Instead, when a variable with global scope is created, it will probably be called multiple times. Therefore, having a global scope is useful to avoid the need to reinitialize variables. Regardless of the software you are creating, using scope whenever possible can help you increase your efficiency while working on complex projects.

Local and Global Scope

Rule–1: Local Scope Variables Cannot Be Used in a Global Scope

Program Code:
```
def mysample():
    x = 12
mysample()
print(x)
```

Output:
```
NameError: name 'x' is not defined
```

The previous example declares a variable with a local scope and a value of 12. When we call the function and attempt to print the variable value from the global scope, we get a traceback error because local variables, unlike global variables, can only be called within a function.

Program Code:
```
def mysample():
    x = 12
    print(x)
mysample()
```

Output:
12

Because the function is called from the local scope, the program runs without error and prints the local variable to the computer screen using the print statement.

Rule—2: Regardless of their scope, all local functions can use all variables.

Program Code:
```
x = 23
def mysample():
    y = 45
    print(x)
mysample()
print(x)
# print(y) would produce an error
```

Output:
23
23

When the variable is called from the local and global scopes, the value of the variable 'x' is printed.

Rule—3: Local variables that are used by one function can't be used by another.

Program Code:
```
def f1():
    x = 12
    print(x)
f1()

def f2():
    print(x)
f2()
```

Output:
24
NameError: name 'x' is not defined

Because it is a variable from the local function, the 'print' function works for the first time. The variable value, on the other hand, causes a traceback error for the second time because the function 'f2' can't access the variable of the function 'f1'.

It should be noted that variables in both the local and global scopes can have the same name without confusing the interpreter. However, for better programming practice and to avoid confusion, it is recommended that local and global variables be given different names.

Modules

In a programming language, a module is a group of functions. You can use these groups of functions in any software component by simply importing the module and calling the function with your parameters as arguments.

Python imports modules much better than traditional languages like C and C++. Many programmers import modules to use the module's methods and add additional capabilities on top of it.

Syntax:

import { Name of the module }

Example:

```
import math
```

The syntax above will import all the built-in math module functions into your program. As a result, you can now present your arguments for these methods.

What is the function of Import?

Import is a Python library function that copies all the functions in a specific file and links them to the current file. In this way, you can use methods that aren't in the current file. Furthermore, creating modules is useful to avoid writing the same code over and over again.

How do I Create Modules?

While importing modules from third-party libraries saves time, as a developer, you must be aware of the importance of creating modules on your own.

Assume you're developing a web application for a torrent service. It would be beneficial if you wrote a large number of functions to make the application work. To improve organization, it will be better to create a networking module and include all networking-related functions in it. Following that, you can create a module with a GUI and several functions to aid in the creation of a visually appealing application.

To begin creating a Python module, you must first create a text file with the.py extension. After you've created the.py file, you can now add all the functions to it. For example, in the.py module we just created, you could include the following function to multiply two numbers.

File - examplemodule.py

```
def sum(a,b):
# This method computes the sum of two numbers
```

```
c = a + b
return c
# The sum will be the output
```

We will show a sample script that imports the previous function as the module is created.

Program Code:
```
import examplemodule
```

After pressing the enter key, the functions in that module will be available to a Python programmer working on other projects.

Program Code:
```
examplemodule.sum(12,23)
```

Output:
35

The script will automatically detect the 'sum' function, and the sum will be displayed on the computer screen based on the arguments provided.

Modules and Built-In Functions

While creating complex and complicated software applications, developers can make use of several built-in functions and modules. While user-built functions are great for solving complex problems, they are difficult to implement and sometimes unnecessary because built-in functions can do the job.

1. print()

It is the most commonly used built-in function in Python. Everyone, from beginners to experienced programmers, uses the print() statement to display output on the computer screen. As previously stated, the content you want to display on the screen should be placed between the quotes.

2. abs()

It is a built-in function that returns the absolute value of any integer. If a negative integer is given as input, this function will return the positive value.

Program Code:
```
z = -65
print(abs(z))
```

Output:
65

3. round ()

It is a built-in mathematical function that returns the closest integer number to any given floating-point number.

Program Code:
```
x = 12.32
y = 4.23
print(round(x))
print(round(y))
```
Output:
```
12
4
```

4. max()

This built-in Python function returns the highest number among a set of numbers. This function can be applied to any data type, including lists and variables.

Program Code:
```
x = 31
y = 78
z = 36
mymax = max(x,y,z)
print(mymax)
```
Output:
```
78
```

5. min()

This built-in function returns the smallest number among a set of numbers.

Program Code:
```
x = 31
y = 78
z = 36
mymin = min(x,y,z)
print(mymin)
```
Output:
```
31
```

1. sorted()

It sorts all the elements in a list in either ascending or descending order, depending on your preference.

Program Code:
```
t = (5,857,165,43,430,60,753,15)
s = sorted(t)
print(s)
```

Output:
[5, 15, 43, 60, 165, 430, 753, 857]

2. sum()

sum() is a built-in function that takes as input a list or a tuple and adds their elements. All the elements of the list or tuple must have the same numerical data type. For example, if string data types are in the input, the program will fail with a type error.

Program Code:
```
t = (5,857,165,43,430,60,753,15)
s = sum(t)
print(s)
```

Output:
2328

3. len()

This built-in function returns the number of elements of the object in input.

Program Code:
```
t = (5,857,165,43,430,60,753,15)
s = len(t)
print(s)
```

Output:
8

4. type()

This function returns the data type of the object in input. If it is a function, the details about the parameters and arguments will be displayed as well.

Program Code:
```
t = 45.789
print(type(t))
```

Output:
<class 'float'>

String Functions

Strings are data types that require more attention from the programmer than other data types. Dozens of built-in functions in the Python core library have been created for programmers to make the most of data stored using strings.

1. strip()

It deletes the arguments passed to it as a parameter. The arguments will be removed from all instances where they appear.

Program Code:
```
text = "Python"
print(text.strip('hon'))
```

Output:
```
Pyt
```

2. replace()

It replaces one part of a string with another. If there are multiple words in the same string data type, you can specify how many to replace as a parameter.

Program Code:
```
text = "Have a great day!"
print(text.replace('great', 'wonderful'))
```

Output:
```
Have a wonderful day!
```

3. split()

It splits a string when the arguments you provided appear in the input text for the first time.

Program Code:
```
text = "There are three apples in the fridge"
print(text.split(' '))
```

Output:
```
['There', 'are', 'three', 'apples', 'in', 'the', 'fridge']
```

Since the argument we provided is a white space, in this case the output is a list with the words of the original string as elements.

4. join()

With this function, you can insert a separator between the elements of a list, as long as they are characters.

Program Code:
```
country = ['Italy','France','Spain']
x = " ~ "
x = x.join(country)
print(x)
```

Output:
```
Italy ~ France ~ Spain
```

Exercises

1. Create a function that takes two numbers as parameters and returns the result of the sum of both numbers.

2. Create a function that takes a string as a parameter and returns the number of vowels in the string.

3. Create a function that takes two strings as parameters and returns a message indicating if both strings are equal or not.

4. Create a function that takes a number as a parameter and returns a message indicating if the number is positive, negative, or zero.

5. Create a module with a function that takes a list as a parameter and returns the sum of all elements in the list. Import this module into another script and use the function to sum a list of numbers.

Chapter 9: Object Oriented Programming (OOP)

Until now we have discussed functional-oriented programming and provided several examples of code. While the functional programming paradigm is popular among independent developers, it can be difficult to implement when working with a team where many members must effectively communicate using their code.

Even though functional-oriented programming reduces a lot of code clutter, it is still difficult to import modules every time you create a new file. Importing more modules increases the program's run time exponentially.

Because of these issues, many programmers preferred to use Object-Oriented Programming languages such as Java during Python's initial release. But when Python 2 was released, everyone was enthusiastic to learn that Python had begun to support Object-Oriented Programming, transforming it into a multi-paradigm language.

With several examples, this chapter delves deeply into various object-oriented principles.

What Is OOP?

OOP is a popular programming paradigm in which classes and objects are used to organize functions into logical templates.

A class is a collection of data or methods that can be easily accessed using dot notation. Classes are accessible to variables and methods outside the class due to object behavior.

A Real-World Example:

Assume you are developing an application that explains details about various vehicles and models of those vehicles.

A functional programmer would create a function for each vehicle and then another for each model. It may appear simple when there are only a few vehicle models, but as the number of vehicle models grows, code reuse becomes difficult for developers.

In Object Oriented programming, however, the programmer will first create a 'vehicle' class and define various properties and values. The developer will then create a separate class for each type of vehicle. Because of the Object Oriented programming paradigm, the developer can access and call all those properties with a simple dot notation rather than creating functions for each property again.

Object Oriented programming saves time and is useful to reuse code thanks to features like polymorphism and inheritance.

How Do I Create Classes?

Classes are a way to create custom data types and they represent a blueprint from which objects are typically created. Classes include various logical entities such as attributes and methods. Specific rules must be followed when creating classes.

- All classes that are created must be preceded by the keyword 'class.'
- Variables created within a class are nothing more than class attributes.
- All attributes in a class are public and can be used at any time by using the . (dot) operator.

The syntax for class creation:

class ClassName:

Class-level attributes

Definition of the attributes

Initialization method

The self method that we'll discuss

Class methods

Specific methods (functions) of the class

In Python, you can't use reserved keywords for class names. Otherwise, a traceback error will occur, causing the application to crash.

How Do I Create Objects?

In Python programming, an object is an entity that has a state and behavior. Everything within a class can be considered an object. A variable created within a class, for example, can be used as an object. Objects are frequently used by programmers who are unaware of their existence.

What exactly is an object?

Every object is made up of a state. A state usually reflects the properties of an object.

Every object has a behavior. The behavior of an object changes depending on the method in which it is used.

All objects have an identity. Objects use identity to interact with one another. Assume there is a Cat class that describes different cat features and behavior. Objects in that class can be of various types.

The name of the cat is typically used to identify the object

Attributes such as cat age, type, and color can be used to describe the state of an object.

Behaviors of an object include jumping, sleeping, and running in relation to a cat.

How to create an object?

All you have to do to create an object is give it a name. For instance, if the 'Cat' class is defined, we can write:

Program Code:
```
obj = Cat()
```
This will generate an object called 'obj' belonging to the Cat class.

The Self Method

You should be aware of the self method, which is automatically created when a class is created.

The concept of a self method is very similar to that of pointers in other programming languages such as C and C++.

If you want to call the methods, you must provide at least one argument to the self method. Every method that an object invokes is automatically transformed to a self object.

The __init__ Method

The __init__ method is similar to C++ and Java constructors. When a class is started, it runs as a default method. As a result, if you want to create an object with an initial value, you must enter those values into the __init method as a developer.

We'll make an example now by using self and the ___init__ method.

Program Code:
```
# Define a class called "Person" with the "name" attribute
class Person:
    # Define a class attribute shared by all instances of
        the class
    species = "Homo sapiens"

    def __init__(self, name):
```

```
        # Initialize the name attribute as an instance
            attribute
            self.name = name

# Create two instances of the Person class with different
        names
person1 = Person("Alex")
person2 = Person("Sam")

# Print the names of each person
print("Name of person 1:", person1.name)
print("Name of person 2:", person2.name)
# Print the species attribute shared by all instances of
        the class
print("Species:", Person. species)
print(person1.name,'and',person2.name,'are',Person.species)
```

Output:
```
Name of person 1: Alex
Name of person 2: Sam
Species: Homo sapiens
Alex and Sam are Homo sapiens
```

In the previous example, we defined a class as well as instance attributes. There are a few simple rules to keep in mind:

You must provide a class name

You must create at least one attribute

You must provide a self argument and a __init__ method

An object must be instantiated

Following object instantiation, you can create instance attributes that can use the object.

Classes and Objects With Methods

In the previous example, a class attribute is created, followed by a method and the __init__ function. Finally, two objects are instantiated, and they are accessed using dot notation.

Program Code:
```
class Person:
    species = "Homo sapiens"

    def __init__(self, name):
        self.name = name

    # Define a method to say hello
    def say_hello(self):
        return "Hello, my name is " + self.name

person1 = Person("Alex")
person2 = Person("Sam")

# Print the names of each person
print("Name of person 1:", person1.name)
print("Name of person 2:", person2.name)

# Call the say_hello method on each person
print(person1.say_hello())
print(person2.say_hello())
```

Output:
```
Name of person 1: Alex
Name of person 2: Sam
Hello, my name is Alex
Hello, my name is Sam
```

Explanation:

In the above example, a class attribute is created, and then a method is created along with the __init__ function. In the end, the object is instantiated, and the object is accessed by using the dot notation.

Inheritance

One of the most important aspects of Object-Oriented programming is inheritance. Inheritance refers to the process of defining a new class without adding new methods or arguments but rather deriving them from other classes. The new class is commonly referred to as the child class. The parent class is the class from which all methods are inherited.

Real-World Example:

When developing real-world applications, inheritance comes in handy in a variety of situations. Assume you are developing a camera mobile application for iOS.

While creating the application, you may need to create several modules for the various functions it provides. You've noticed that you're reusing code for GUI interfaces after a few months of development because your team is still using function-oriented programming.

You decided to use an object-oriented framework for your project to save time and money. Since you're now using the OOP paradigm, you can reuse the code you've already written for GUI interfaces and link it to the new classes you're creating. This saves time and energy by allowing programmers to add new features without having to rewrite the old ones.

Syntax for Python inheritance:

class BaseClass:

{ Body of base class }

class DerivedClass(BaseClass):

{ Body of derived class }

Please keep in mind that both base and derived classes must follow all the previously described class rules.

Program Code:

```
# Define a base class "Polygon" with a method to return the
        number of edges
class Polygon:
    def __init__(self, num_edges):
        self.num_edges = num_edges

    def edges(self):
        return self.num_edges

# Define a subclass "Rectangle" based on the Polygon class
class Rectangle(Polygon):
    def __init__(self, length, width):
        # Call the __init__ method of the parent class to
        initialize the number of edges
        Polygon.__init__(self, 4)
        self.length = length
        self.width = width
```

```
    # Define a method to calculate the area of the
        rectangle
    def area(self):
        return self.length * self.width

# Create an instance of the Rectangle class
rect = Rectangle(40, 10)

# Print the number of edges and the area of the rectangle
print("Number of edges:", rect.edges())
print("Area:", rect.area())
```

Output:
```
Number of edges: 4
Area: 400
```

Explanation:

In the previous example, we defined the class 'Polygon' first, and then built the second class 'Rectangle' on top of it. A rectangle with dimensions of 40 by 10 is created. When the 'area' method is called, the area of the square is computed. You can create another polygon class in the future by simply writing a method to calculate the area.

With enough knowledge of Object-Oriented Programming, you can create classes and objects that can interact to create software that uses many components and performs multiple tasks. Look at the open-source code hosted on GitHub to learn more about OOP.

Exercises

1. Create a class called Person with a constructor that takes in the person's name, age, and occupation. The class should have methods get_name(), get_age(), and get_occupation() that return the respective values. Create an instance of the class and call the methods to display the values.

2. Create a class called Student that inherits from Person. The class must have a constructor that takes in the name, age, occupation and a list of subjects. The class should have a method get_subjects() that returns the list of subjects. Create an instance of the class and call the methods to display the values.

3. Create a class called Rectangle with a constructor that takes in the width and height. The class should have methods get_area() and get_perimeter() that return the area and perimeter of the rectangle, respectively. Create an instance of the class and call the methods to display the values.

4. Create a class called BankAccount with a constructor that takes in the owner's name, balance, and type of account. The class should have methods get_balance(), deposit(amount), and withdraw(amount) that return the balance, deposit an amount, and withdraw an amount respectively. Create an instance of the class and call the methods to display the values.

5. Create a class called Vehicle with a constructor that takes in the make, model, and year. The class should have methods get_make(), get_model(), and get_year() that return the respective values. Create two classes, Car and Truck, that inherit from Vehicle. The Car class should have an additional method get_type() that returns "Car" and the Truck class should have an additional method get_type() that returns "Truck". Create instances of both classes and call the methods to display the values.

Chapter 10: Files in Python

Python stores data in variables for both static and dynamic data. While variables are ideal for storing data during the execution of a program, they can be difficult to use when the data is sensitive and needs to be reused repeatedly. Variables can self-destruct to clear memory, which is inconvenient for users who want to save or reuse their data for multiple purposes. Python provides files to better interact with data of any size or format. Understanding file operations and implementing them in your programs is essential for creating better software as a Python programmer.

File Paths

Python programmers typically work with multiple files and two parameters. The first is the file name, which makes it easy to find, the second is the file path.

For example, if file.pdf is the name of a file, then "C:/ users/ downloads/file.pdf" is the path format of a file. The file extension in the file name 'file.pdf' is pdf. To manage files, most operating systems employ an efficient file management system.

It is critical to understand file management techniques. For this reason, you must understand the fundamentals of file managers used in the operating systems you are working in. For example, Windows uses file explorer to manage files, whereas Mac systems use Finder. Regardless of the operating system and file manager you use, files are typically organized in a logical hierarchical order using root directories, folders, and subdirectories.

Hierarchical Arrangement of Files

For the program to detect the file location, you must enter the entire path. The entire path of the file is generally written hierarchically to determine the directory, subdirectories, and folders.

For example, in 'C:/users/sample/example.pdf,' C is the system's root directory and sample and users are subdirectories within it. Because there may be multiple files with the same name in different folders, it is critical to use the entire path to determine the file's location.

As a programmer, you should be aware that Windows systems use Backslashes to differentiate between the root directory and subdirectories. Other operating systems, such as Mac and Linux, use forward slashes to distinguish between root and subdirectories.

If you don't want to use back or forward slashes while entering code on the terminal for whatever reason, you can use a function called os.path.join.

Program Code:
os.path.join('C', 'first', 'second')

Output:
'C\first\second'

Current Working Directory

While running complex code, you may need to interact with multiple files in the same directory as a Python programmer. A function called os.getcwd() can be used to help programmers interact with other files in the same directory. When your absolute path is identified, all files in the directory or subdirectory will be shown as output.

Creating New Folders

Several Python programs usually require users to generate files or the application to create files in different directories on its own. A save file for a game, for example, may be generated automatically by the software without any user intervention. All Python programmers must be aware of the importance of creating new folders for the applications they create. To create a new directory, use the os.makedirs() function.

Program Code:
import os
os.makedirs('D: /user/ Python/myfolder')

In the previous example, we first imported the 'os' module containing the system function design. The makedirs() function was then called with a path as the function parameter. "myfolder" is the name of the new folder created in the directory by the above function. You can check by opening your file manager or typing cd into a command prompt.

Please make sure to provide an absolute path to the directory where you want to create a new folder.

Functions to Manage Files

Files are complex and require a plethora of built-in functions to function properly. You can easily manipulate, open, and close files with Python from your IDE or terminal. By default, the Python interpreter can run both .txt and .py extension files.

If you want to work with file types like pdf and jpg, you'll need to install third-party libraries. By experienced Python programmers, these file types are referred to as binary file types.

To begin, we will create a file called example.txt on the path "D:/user/Python/example.txt" to help you understand the concepts of Files. You are free to use your path when creating a file.

This example txt file will be used to describe file functions such as open(), close(), write(), and read().

Assume the example.txt file contains the following:

Content:
```
This is a Python file.
```

How to Open Files

It is quite simple to open files with a Python command. All you need to know is the file's absolute path and how to use the open() function.

Program Code:
```
myfile = open ('D: /user / Python / example.txt ')
# This will open the file
```

The open() function, along with the parameter, is used in the example. The parameter in this example is the path provided to open a file. When a file is opened, the Python interpreter cannot read or write it, but the user can read it using the default viewer in which it was opened.

Before running this statement, make sure you have the necessary software to open the files. For example, if you try to open an mp4 video file and there is no native application that can open it, it will not be a viable solution.

What Happens?

When the interpreter locates the open() function, a new file object is created, and all changes made during this phase must be saved to be reflected in the original file. If the file is not saved, the Python interpreter will ignore all changes.

How to Read Files

When Python opens a file with the open() function, it creates a new object, and the Python interpreter can now easily read the entire file's content with the read() function.

Program Code:
```
filecontent = myfile.read()
# read() will scan all the content present in the file
```

Output:
```
This is a Python file.
```

In the previous example, we used the read() function to send the scanned data from the file to a new variable called 'filecontent'. Depending on the complexity of the file, you can also send the information into files to lists, tuples, or dictionaries.

While the read() function just prints the file content, the readlines() function can be used to organize the content of a file to new lines.

We will use a simple example to demonstrate this Python feature. First, in your working directory, create a new file called 'mynewfile.txt.' After opening the file, enter a few lines, as shown below.

mynewfile.txt:

```
This is an example of a document
We are simply connecting the dots
This information will be used to manipulate text
The Python interpreter is fast
```

Let's now call the readlines() function on the terminal.

Program Code:
```
myfile = open(mynewfile.txt)
# This variable helps us open a new file with the name
        provided
myfile.readlines()
```

Output:
```
['This is an example of a document \n', ' We are simply connecting the dots \n', ' This information will be used to manipulate text  \n', 'Python interpreter is fast']
```

The output included a newline character \n for each line in the file. Numerous advanced file functions can be used when developing real-world applications.

How to Write Content to Files

You can use the write() function to insert new data into any file. The write() function is very similar to the print() function, which is used by programmers to display content on the screen. It displays the contents of the file with the name you specify.

The open() function allows programmers to open the file in write mode. All you need to do is append an argument to let the interpreter know you want to open the file and add your content.

Once you've finished writing into the file, use the close() method to close it and save it in its default location.

Program Code:
```
myfile = open('example.txt', 'w')
#This makes the file open in write mode
myfile.write ('This is how we write on files! \n')
```

```
myfile.close()
```

The output will show the content of the screen as well as the number of characters.

You can also append text as an argument by using 'a'.

Example:
```
myfile = open('example.txt', 'a')
# The file is open in write mode
example.write('This is a new version')
# The above statement will be added to the file provided
myfile.close()
```

To check whether the message has been appended, use the read function, as shown below.

```
myfile = read(example.txt)
print(myfile)
```

You can usually copy, paste, or cut files and folders using the default file manager functions, such as Windows Explorer and Mac Finder. However, in Python you must use a built-in library known as shutil, It creates programming components that can be used to quickly copy, move, or delete files.

To use the shutil library's default functions, you must first import the library.

Chapter 11: Exception Handling

All applications occasionally crash as a result of incorrect user input or an error that occurs. It is possible to inform the user about why the application has crashed. If you can't help them, your software should at the very least detect that the application has collapsed and send the logs to your server to help them find solutions. Giving users a heads-up about errors is the bare minimum that modern application developers can do to improve their user experience.

Exception handling is a computer programming feature that helps developers to write scenarios for which an application may crash and explicitly instruct the user if this occurs.

Do you remember the famous "This application has stopped responding" with a red 'x' mark on Windows systems? It is one of the most well-known exception handling interfaces in any system. While your exceptions do not have to be of the highest quality, they should be adequate for a better end-user experience.

In Python development, writing valid exceptions is considered a sophisticated skill. Exception handling also assists programmers in detecting bugs and logical defects in a program early in the workflow. An exception also saves a significant amount of time during testing and maintenance.

Exception Handling Example:
Go to your profile and try to tweet an image that is larger than 24MB. After loading, the Twitter web or app interface will display a popup informing you that your image cannot be uploaded due to its larger size.

In this case, Twitter developers have built an exception handling interface to help users understand why their images are not being uploaded. Exception handling is an excellent tool for improving the user experience.

All well-known third-party libraries include exception handling methods that you can import and use in your applications.

We will teach you how to handle exceptions using the Divide-by-zero error.

When you divide a number by zero, the value is usually undefined because it is referred to as an infinite value. Similarly, if a user of your application attempts to divide a number by zero, you must display a ZeroDivisionError. This error can be displayed using try and except statements.

'Try' and 'Except'

When creating exception handling tasks, you should be aware of the leading programming components Try and Except. The try block is where developers must specify the likelihood of finding the error in the Python interpreter. The except block, on the other hand, requires information about what to do if a specific error that we defined occurs during program execution.

Program Code:
```
# Try and except block in a function
def divide32(x):
    try:
        A = 32/x
        print(A)
    except ZeroDivisionError:
        print ("I can't divide by 0")

divide32(8)
divide32(0)
divide32(16)
```

Output:
```
4.0
I can't divide by 0
2.0
```

We started with a try and except block that told the interpreter where we could expect an error popup and what information should be displayed if there was one.

Different Types of Errors

Python documentation contains a plethora of system errors. When we discussed the Zero division error in the previous example, you may have noticed a straightforward approach. Different errors have different methods for avoiding them or running applications even when they are present.

Understanding the causes of some system errors can help you understand the fundamentals of debugging your applications.

Value errors

These errors occur when you pass arguments to a function that doesn't accept those data types. A value error can cause your application to crash unexpectedly.

Uploading a pdf file when only image files are permitted is an example of an exception trigger.

Import error

These errors occur when you are unable to import a module directly into your program. They are typically caused by a network connection failure or issues with online package managers.

Example of an Exception Trigger: You are unable to sync your data on your private cloud accounts due to an import error.

OS error

You may occasionally encounter issues because the software is incompatible with your operating system version. These errors frequently occur because the system kernel does not understand what the application is saying. These errors are fairly common when using Linux distributions.

Example of an Exception Trigger: The application crashes because the host is running an unsupported version of an operating system.

Type error

This error typically occurs when a user or developer enters a value for a data type that the application does not yet support.

Name error

When a variable or function that has not yet been defined in the program is called, this error occurs.

Index error

Index errors typically occur when you provide an index that is greater than the list you have created.

Chapter 12: Advanced Programming

Many third-party Python frameworks provide specific functionalities to programmers. It's sufficient to import the base libraries. That's why Python's popularity has skyrocketed. Libraries are great for developers to create real-world applications that ordinary users can use. You should be aware of certain commonly used Python libraries to write valid complex code without having to start from scratch.

The source codes for the majority of these libraries will be available for exploration on websites such as GitHub or Bitbucket.

Pip Package Manager

All operating systems make applications available to their users. Python isn't an operating system, but rather a software interpreter. Any software that is not written in Python can't run using a Python interpreter because the Python interpreter does not understand the source code used by that software.

There are thousands of paid and free Python software downloads available from many sources. A simple Google search for Python software for the domain you are interested in can provide thousands of results. To install this software on your own, you will need at least a basic understanding of executable files.

Python offers package managers to download package files into your operating system to be immediately executed. In this way, you can easily install the software you need. While there are many third-party Python package managers, the default pip is the most common and every Python programmer should be familiar with it.

Why Using Pip

New packages and dependencies can be installed.

There is an index that lists all Python package repositories that are available on pip servers.

Before installing the software, use it to go over the requirements.

Remove all packages and dependencies that you no longer use.

First, check if pip is installed on your system. Pip is usually included with Python.

Terminal Code:
$ pip -version

If it prints out the pip version information details, your system has the package manager installed. If not, you may need to manually download and install it from the official website.

How to Install Packages?

To install packages, you should always use the syntax format shown below.

$ pip install name_of_the_software

For example, if you want to install the "Seaborn" package, the syntax is the following:

$ pip install seaborn

To check the information associated with the content before installing, use the command below:

$ pip show seaborn

This terminal code will return a lot of metadata information, including the Author, Package name and location.

Use the code syntax format below to uninstall any package installed on your system using the pip package manager.

Syntax:

$ pip uninstall nameofthepackage

For example, to uninstall the Seaborn package you previously installed, use the command below:

$ pip uninstall seaborn

You can also search for a package using the code format shown below.

$ pip search name_of_the_package

This will show you all packages from the package index for you to examine and select from.

Virtual Environment

Typically, when you install a package, you are also installing many dependencies. These dependencies may occasionally overlap with other software, causing the package to fail to install. To help developers in creating independent projects, the 'virtualenv' package can be used to create an isolated virtual environment.

First, use the pip package manager to install the 'virtualenv' package.

Installation command:
$ pip install virtualenv

Once the package is installed, you can use the below command to create a new directory using a virtual machine.

`$ virtualenv mydir`

All the packages, files, and software you install will be saved in this new directory, without interfering with any system dependencies or packages. To begin, run the following command to activate the virtual machine.

Terminal Command:

`$ source mydir/bin/activate`

After you've installed all of your packages, deactivate this virtual environment with the following command:

Terminal Command:

`(mydir) $ deactivate`

The sys Module

To master Python it's crucial to understand how a Python interpreter works. An interpreter typically parses every variable, method or literal in the code before executing a logically written program and checking for syntax, type, and index errors. It is important to examine how an interpreter works and stores information required for the use of specific software.

The Sys module in Python makes it simple for developers to check this information.

`import sys`

path

This sys library argument will tell you the default path of the Python interpreter installed on your system:

`print(sys.path)`

argv

This method will return a list of all the existing modules in the system:

`print(sys.argv)`

copyright

This method will show the user the copyright information for the Python interpreter or software:

`print(sys.copyright)`

getrefcount

This method shows how frequently a program uses a variable or object:

`print(sys.getrefcount(myvariable))`

Unit Testing

Before developing, a programmer must ensure that the program follows all Python's guidelines. Even if the logic in your programs is correct, it may cause problems in the future due to practical issues. These bottleneck situations should be avoided to provide a better user experience.

Python allows and encourages programmers to check their code using unit testing frameworks. The framework 'unittest' is installed by default to force programmers to create testing conditions from scratch for their programs.

How Do Unit Tests Work?

You may become overwhelmed when testing their code because the Python documentation does not provide a specific set of rules for conducting unit tests. However, experienced programmers always emphasize that it is best to start testing code for methods first and then expand to other programming components.

Using this methodology, you can test any part of the software.

The tested code can be easily shared with other developers. Furthermore, eventual build and runtime errors during this process will be shared with your team.

You can group tests and call them collections, and then manually organize them to keep these tests up to date.

Other third-party frameworks can be installed by programmers to improve their unit testing skills.

Scrapy

Scrapy is a Python library designed specifically for scraping purposes. Spiders are typically used to scrape data from dynamic websites and search engines. Scrapy is great to create advanced spiders capable of intuitively extracting data from web or mobile pages.

To install Scrapy, enter the following code into any package manager.

Installation command:
```
pip install scrapy
```

Requests

Requests is a Python library used to create HTTP requests for web or mobile applications. You can easily manage requests and responses for all web content that your application uses with Requests.

The web response data is typically in **JSON** format. It is normally difficult to read, but Requests parses the JSON file and displays the information in a readable manner. Scrappers also make use of the requests library to build automation software for major websites.

Use the default pip package to install Requests.

Installation command:

`pip install requests`

Pygame

Python is also used to create games for handheld consoles and mobile devices. Pygame is a popular third-party gaming framework among independent developers worldwide. Pygame includes both multimedia and physics libraries, allowing developers to create 2D and 3D games. Pygame also includes sound, mouse, keyboard, and accelerometer components for creating highly interactive games.

Most Pygame developers create games for Android phones and tablets because the SDL Pygame framework is highly adaptable to these devices.

Use the following command to install Pygame on your local system.

Installation command:

`pip install pygame`

Beautiful Soup

Beautiful Soup is a popular Python scraping library that can retrieve HTML and XML data from a variety of sources with a single click. It can generate an efficient parse tree of the various directories and sub-directories present on the website, allowing users to easily organize the scraped information.

Before scraping, Beautiful Soup understands the most recent technologies, such as HTML 5 elements on a web page. Beautiful Soup is used by several third-party software, including Ahrefs, to handle their premium keyword research tools, which frequently need to scrape data from billions of pages on the internet.

Use pip to install Beautiful Soup on your local system.

Installation command:

`pip install beautifulsoup`

Pillow

Pillow is one of many Python libraries that make image manipulation simple. Image enhancement is required in a variety of computer domains, and Pillow makes it possible by leveraging the legacy PIL project, which was considered a better image manipulation library written in C.

Pillow is a fork of the PIL project, which is no longer being developed. Pillow supports a variety of image formats, including png, jpeg, gif, and ttf. Furthermore, you can use Pillow's built-in methods to perform many photo editing functions, like rotating, resizing, cropping, and changing filters.

Use pip to install the Pillow library on your local system.

Installation command:
`pip install pillow`

Tensorflow

Tensorflow is a well-known Machine Learning library for building advanced neural networks. Many developers also use Tensorflow within Deep Learning frameworks to develop software components that are frequently embedded in Deep Learning applications like facial recognition. Google created Tensorflow to make the development of complex machine learning models easier. However, it was later made open source so that enthusiastic developers could contribute to the project.

Tensorflow can be installed using any package manager, such as pip.

Installation command:
`pip install tensorflow`

Scikit-Learn

Scikit-Learn is a widely used machine learning model creation tool that is similar to TensorFlow. Many developers use it to create data analysis and analytics software. Scikit-Learn makes it simple for developers to incorporate advanced machine learning models into their code, such as clustering, Random forests, and K-means algorithms.

Scikit-Learn also supports complex neural networking algorithms used in scientific research, such as the development of genetic algorithms. To install it use the following command.

Installation command:
`pip install -U scikit-learn`

Pandas

Data analysts are in love with Pandas because it is one of the most popular third-party libraries. While R is more popular among data analysts than Python, Pandas is still a good library for developers who want to create advanced data-analysis models. Pandas makes it simple to import and export huge amounts of data in a variety of formats, including SQL, JSON, and Excel. Furthermore, you can use Pandas with greater precision than other libraries for data cleaning and arrangement, which are high-level data analysis techniques.

Use package managers such as pip to install Pandas on your local system.

Installation command:

```
pip install pandas
```

Matplotlib

Matplotlib is a well-known Python library that is used in conjunction with Scipy to implement high-level mathematical functions in your code. Scipy and Matplotlib can be used together to create multidimensional arrays, which can then be used to write complex code to solve real-world scientific challenges. Many computer scientists rely on these libraries to keep their workflows running smoothly.

Matplotlib displays all acquired data in beautiful graphs to help you better understand the data flow. Tkinter is also used to logically arrange data. While Scipy focuses on scientific and technical computing, Matplotlib focuses on data visualization for enthusiasts and organizations.

Use pip to install Matplotlib on your local system.

Installation command:

```
pip install matplotlib
```

To use some of Matplotlib's advanced functions, make sure Scipy is installed using the command below.

Installation command:

```
pip install scipy
```

Twisted

Developers of web-based Python applications must be familiar with various networking concepts. While the core Python library provides enough resources and methods to write efficient networking code, it is always recommended that you use libraries such as Twisted to create complex code more easily. With a single click, Twisted implements networking protocols such as UDP, TCP, and HTTP. Twisted is the default networking component library for many websites, including Twitch.

Use pip to install Twisted.

Installation command:

```
pip install twisted
```

GitHub for Programmers

GitHub is useful for programmers because it allows them to collaborate with teams remotely. GitHub is based on a peer-to-peer GIT repository, so the changes in your code will be reflected in your teammates' computers as soon as they are connected to the internet.

GitHub provides two versions: free and professional. When you use the free version, your code is accessible to anyone who has a GitHub account. With the pro version, your code will be private, and only members of your team will be able to access it. Furthermore, all private repositories use advanced encryption algorithms to safeguard your data.

Why is GitHub Essential for Python Programmers?

Regardless of the computer domain you work in, you may need to use third-party frameworks and libraries available on GitHub when creating projects. You can use GitHub or one of several third-party clients to instantly interact with local repositories.

Dependencies are used by GitHub and all Git-supported clients to easily sync libraries and modules into your code. The Git server's 'commit' option allows you to make changes to the code.

Use the Python shell to run the following command to create a new repository in your GIT server.

Installation command:
```
$ git config -global root "my project."
```
When you enter the git code into the console, a new project is created, and you can now create folders for your project. To start creating a directory on the root of your project, run the command below.
```
$ mkdir. ("Name of the repository: ")
```
If you don't know anything about the GIT server or project you're working on, type the following command into your console.
```
$ git status
```
This way you are ready to begin developing your open-source project to help other programmers in your domain.

Conclusion

First and foremost, congratulations on finishing a comprehensive Python guide. This book has covered a variety of in-depth Python topics that will help you in writing high-quality code for your projects. However, consistent practice with the fundamentals taught in this book is required to improve. Working on projects or practicing competitive coding will only increase your expertise.

Some features of experienced programmers have contributed to their success in their passionate journey with computers and technology. They usually develop several habits that help them become better programmers. As a beginner, you must understand some of these characteristics and incorporate them into your workflow to increase performance within a topic or a group of topics.

Programmer Features

Foundations first

You must understand the fundamentals as much as possible. Writing code for difficult tasks with a solid foundation becomes much easier over time. To strengthen your foundations, familiarize yourself with the Python style guide, which strives for simplicity. Writing simple code and following the Zen of Python rules will help in the improvement of your fundamental knowledge.

Break problems into smaller parts

As a programmer, you must solve complex and complicated problems. Not all problems can be solved with a single logical step. To solve a problem with better runtime execution, a programmer must break it down into smaller problems. This philosophy can assist programmers in developing software with fewer bugs that requires a minimal unit testing strategy.

Find your specialty

No programmer can be proficient in every computer domain. You should have clear what computer domain you are most interested in as a programmer. Experiment with various computing systems to better understand what computer domain you like. Python, for example, is versatile and can be a great resource for data scientists, web developers, or systems engineers. Don't force yourself to learn a little bit of everything; instead, focus on mastering a single domain.

You will learn from errors

Errors can be demotivating, especially if you're just starting. Anytime you get an error, copy the traceback error and search for it in Google or ChatGPT. You will find several solutions to the problem, and fixing it on your own will help you better understand the fundamentals of Python.

Learn to implement algorithms

To improve your writing skills in terms of programming logic, you should learn sorting and search algorithms. Understanding mathematical concepts will also help in the intuitive approach to complex problems. While competitive programmers typically approach problems differently than software developers, understanding their approach can help you overcome various roadblocks that may arise during the software development process.

Python can be used to implement binary search algorithms, graph algorithms, and complex data structures such as Stacks and Queues. To approach Python from an algorithmic standpoint, we recommend using websites like LeetCode.

Get familiar with GitHub

One of the most important resources to be aware of is GitHub. All open-source code is generally available through git repositories. As a result, if you want to make any changes to these repositories, you must contact the repository owners using GitHub commands like 'push' and 'commit.' All companies looking for developers prefer people with GitHub experience because it allows them to quickly integrate you into their team.

Don't overwork

Even though this is not a technical tip, understanding the slow and steady philosophy employed by experienced developers is critical. Never try to take in too much information at once. **Consistency beats performance** and it is more important in the early stages of your career. As a result, instead of cramming the information in a few days, schedule a few hours of Python studying every day. Participate in programs like 100daysofPython on platforms such as Twitter to keep yourself motivated and consistent.

Be aware of testing procedures

Before developing software to end users, it must be thoroughly tested. Understanding unit testing workflows such as Alpha and beta testing will help you provide more functional software with fewer known bugs. Use a user-reporting strategy to recreate bugs more easily in your working machine and resolve them as soon as possible. Clearing bugs requires experience and, at times, an expert opinion. Don't be afraid to ask for help in forums.

Keep a healthy work-life balance

Regardless of your chosen profession, keeping a balance between work and personal life is important. To get the most out of your work time, especially as a programmer, you must be aware of tasks and time management. If you work as a freelancer, apps like Things and Session can help you manage your tasks effectively. Furthermore, using techniques like the Pomodoro technique can help you clear more bugs in less time.

What Next?

I'm glad you're along for the ride as we learn Python. Programming is enjoyable, and no matter how fast you learn, only practice will make you a great developer. So, using the knowledge you've gained from this book, start working on your projects.

If you're stumped as to what projects to try, here are some project ideas to get you started.

Create a management system for a public library in your community.

Create a suburban metro railway reservation system.

Using the Django library, create a simple website.

Use Pygame to create a classic Python game.

Parse Twitter data to build a bot that automatically retweets popular tweets.

I hope that your growth journey is successful in every way!

Java Programming

Introduction

Welcome to the world of Java programming! This book is your guide on the journey to learning one of the most popular and widely used programming languages. Whether you're an absolute beginner looking to start your coding journey or a seasoned developer looking to expand your skill set, this book aims to provide you with a practical and engaging overview of the Java language. By the end of this book, you'll have the foundational skills needed to start writing your own Java programs.

But before we dive into the specifics of syntax, data types, and classes, I want to take a step back and provide an overview of what the Java language is and why it has become so prevalent. My goal is to give you an understanding of the big picture so you know where your new skills will fit in and why Java is such an important programming language to learn. I'll also explain who this book is designed for and what you can expect to get out of it.

This book is designed to guide you step-by-step from having no previous experience to becoming comfortable with core Java concepts and techniques. You will start by learning how to set up your Java development environment and write simple programs. This foundational understanding will then enable you to explore object-oriented programming concepts, generic programming, functional programming styles, and more - all at your own pace.

To properly set the stage for our learning, it's useful to first understand a bit about Java's history, design philosophies, and place in the current technology landscape. When it was first created in the early 1990s, Java's main goal was to enable easy programming of devices, especially televisions, VCRs, and microwaves. However, this original "Java as a TV language" idea never saw much adoption. Instead, Java rapidly grew to power the web through its use in client-side applets. Early web browsers supported the "<applet>" tag that allowed small Java programs to be dynamically downloaded and run within web pages. This brought much hype around Java's potential to revolutionize online content. However, security issues with untrusted applets soon limited their usefulness. Still, Java found new success in its ability to compile once and run anywhere — a key trait known as "write once, run anywhere" or WORA. By writing Java code that targets the Java Virtual Machine (JVM) instead of a specific CPU/OS, software could easily be deployed across Windows, macOS, and Linux. While Java's initial goals evolved, its platform independence and focus on industrial-strength software engineering practices made it a mainstay for both desktop and server-side development.

With continuous innovation bringing features like Lambdas and modularity, Java remains highly relevant today across the cloud, mobile, and beyond. I hope this high-level overview provides helpful context as we delve into the language.

Who is This Book For? This book is designed for a variety of Java learners. The core audience is Complete beginners with no prior coding experience. If you've never programmed before but want to get started with Java as your first language, you'll find the initial chapters break down concepts very gradually. For students taking introductory Java classes, whether in a college course or online/self-paced program, this book can serve as your main textbook. Professionals wanting to learn Java. You may have experience in other languages but are new to Java. The object-oriented approach will feel familiar, while language-specific details are clearly explained. Experienced programmers are expanding their skills. If you're proficient in Java already but want a structured reference, later chapters on advanced topics will provide value. This book provides a foundation to expand your Java knowledge in whatever direction interests you most. Things I don't focus on heavily here include Java APIs, GUI programming, database integration, advanced OOP, and tools like Eclipse or Maven. But you'll have the basics under your belt to dig into any of those areas on your own once finished!

My goal is for this to be an enjoyable, stress-free learning experience. We'll go step-by-step, and you can work through examples at your own pace, revisiting anything you're not totally clear on. Feel free to experiment as well by tweaking the code to see how changes affect the output. Don't worry about memorizing everything perfectly - the most important things are grasping core concepts and gaining comfort reading and writing code. By guiding you to build full programs from the ground up, I aim to help you start "thinking like a programmer" in addition to learning Java itself. Try to understand how each new piece fits into the bigger picture as the programs grow more complex. Ultimately, I hope that you finish this book excited to continue your programming journey on your own using Java or other languages.

With that introduction complete, let's start our journey into Java programming itself in the next chapter. I'm excited to help guide you through understanding the fundamentals step by step. I wish you the very best of luck on your learning journey and can't wait to see what programs you go on to create!

Chapter 1: Setting Up Your Java Environment

The Basics of Java Installation

Installing Java on your computer is the first step to starting your journey as a Java programmer. In this section, we will cover everything you need to know to download and set up a Java Development Kit (JDK) on Windows, Mac, or Linux. Let's get started!

What is the Java Development Kit (JDK)?

The JDK, or Java Development Kit, is an essential software development package that includes the tools needed to compile and run Java applications. It contains the Java Runtime Environment (JRE), which handles running Java code, as well as additional tools like compilers and debuggers used during development. When installing the JDK, you will have the core functionality required to both write and execute Java programs on your computer.

Choosing a JDK Version

Oracle releases new versions of the JDK regularly, with the latest version at the time of writing being JDK 17. However, you may want to choose an earlier long-term support (LTS) version for a stable development environment, such as JDK 11. Be aware that each version introduces changes and new features, so you should choose one and stick with it until you are comfortable upgrading. Compatibility issues can arise between versions, so it's best to select a version and use it consistently for all of your projects.

Downloading the JDK

Now that you've chosen a JDK version, it's time to download the installer file. Navigate to the Oracle downloads page for your Java development platform of choice. For Windows, you can search for and locate the Windows x64 or Windows i586 installer executable. For macOS, download the PKG installer package. Linux users have tar.gz installers available for their distribution. Be sure to click through all the license agreements before initiating the download.

Installing on Windows

To install the JDK on Windows, simply run the executable installer file you downloaded earlier. Accept all licenses and click through the installation wizard, leaving defaults checked where possible. The only mandatory configuration is to select a destination folder - the default Program Files location is typically fine. Make sure to check the box to add the Java bin folder to your PATH environment variable if prompted. This step makes the Java command accessible from any folder in your command prompt.

Installing on macOS

Like Windows, macOS installation is fairly straightforward. Open the PKG file you downloaded and follow the prompts to continue through installation. The default installation path of /Library/Java/Java Virtual Machines is recommended. When complete, you may need to add the Java bin path to your PATH variable manually by updating your ~/.profile file. Restart any open Terminal sessions for the change to take effect.

Installing on Linux

Linux JDK installation requires extracting the downloaded tar.gz file and setting some environment variables. First, create a folder like /opt/java and extract the tar contents there using tar -xzf filename.tar.gz. Then set JAVA_HOME=/opt/java/JDK-version and add $JAVA_HOME/bin to your PATH. For system-wide changes, modify /etc/profile.d/java.sh. For your user, edit ~/.profile or ~/.bashrc instead before sourcing it. Common Linux paths are /usr/lib/jvm or /usr/local/java.

Verifying Your Installation

To verify that your JDK installation was successful, open a new command prompt or terminal session and run the Java --version command. You should see an output listing the Java version number, VM vendor, and other details. You can also test that the java compiler works by creating a new HelloWorld.java file containing a simple program and running javac HelloWorld.java to compile it. If both commands run without errors, congratulations - you now have a functioning Java environment ready to start programming!

Common Installation Issues

While installation generally goes smoothly, a few common issues can occur. Verify your permissions if they are met with authorization errors. Conflicts between multiple Java versions installed simultaneously can also cause problems - consider uninstalling others. Path errors are frequent on Linux/macOS - double-check path settings. If strange errors occur, try reinstalling the JDK to a fresh folder. Oracle's documentation covers additional troubleshooting advice for specific platforms. Being able to resolve installation problems independently is a big part of learning Java.

Wrapping Up

This covers the essential basics of downloading and installing a Java Development Kit on Windows, Mac, and Linux systems. Having the JDK provides the core tools required to begin programming in Java. In upcoming chapters, we'll discuss using build tools like Maven and Gradle as well as writing our first Java program. However, the installation process is the mandatory first step.

Understanding and Installing Package Managers: Maven, Gradle, and Beyond

Now that you have a JDK installed, it's time to supplement your Java development environment with additional tools. Package managers provide automation, standardization, and ease of use when building Java projects. In this section, we'll look at Maven and Gradle - two of the most popular options - as well as some alternatives beyond the basics.

What is a Build Tool or Package Manager?

A build tool, also referred to as a package manager, facilitates the incremental development process. It automates repetitive but necessary tasks like compiling code, running tests, packaging artifacts into distributable JAR files, and more. Build tools also help manage dependencies on third-party libraries, ensuring consistent builds across different machines. This allows developers to focus on coding rather than manual configuration and setup work.

Maven - The De facto Standard

Maven is likely the most well-known Java build tool due to its first-mover status and adoption in large open-source projects. Maven projects are defined through POM (Project Object Model) files containing declarations of project metadata like groupId, artifactId, version, and dependencies. Maven handles downloading dependencies, compiling code, running tests, and building jars - all based on standardized conventions. The central Maven repository hosts thousands of pre-configured dependencies.

Installing Maven

To install Maven on Windows, download the mvn-version-bin.zip file from their website. Extract to a folder like C:\Program Files\Maven and add it to your PATH. On Linux/Mac, you can use a package manager like apt, brew, or yum instead. Then, run the mvn -version to verify. Maven is configured through settings.xml, which lives in the ~/.m2 folder by default. You may also need to tweak environment variables. Maven projects then use the pom.xml structure.

Gradle - Rising Star Flexibility

Gradle is a newer build tool gaining popularity due to its flexible, convention-over-configuration approach. It uses Groovy and a domain-specific language (DSL) implemented through build. Gradle scripts instead of hardcoded conventions. This grants richer customization than Maven at the cost of a steeper learning curve. The main benefits are multi-project structure, custom tasks, broader language support, and incremental compilation.

Installing Gradle

Download the gradle-version-bin.zip file for your system from gradle.org. Unzip and add the bin folder to your PATH, just like Maven. Windows users can also use Chocolatey or Scoop package managers instead. Then, run the Gradle -version to test. Gradle has its own repository but also supports Maven dependencies. Projects define tasks and plugins through the build. Gradle file.

Ant - The Legacy Grandfather

Ant served as the original automated build system for Java long before Maven or Gradle. It uses XML configuration files named build.xml for defining targets (tasks) and dependencies in a less standardized way than Maven's conventions. Ant is lightweight and flexible but more low-level than modern options. It remains useful for smaller projects due to widespread toolchain support and familiarity among older Java developers.

Build Tools in the Enterprise

Larger organizations frequently adopt enterprise-grade build servers like Jenkins or Bamboo for continuous integration instead of strict command-line tools. These server-based options provide features like version control integration, flexible jobs/pipelines, email notifications, dashboards, and more advanced build automation across teams. JBoss Maven Plugin, Gradle Enterprise Edition, and proprietary build systems round out options for big companies.

Additional Build Tools

Other options include:
- SBT (Simple Build Tool) - Scala's equivalent to Gradle featuring interactive mode
- Leiningen - Clojure's build system, inspired by Maven and SBT
- Buck - A build system from Facebook aiming for high optimization
- Pants - Twitter's build tool for Java/Scala supporting incremental compilation

- Bazel - Google's build system offering significant improvements to compile times

Choosing Your Build Tool

In summary, Maven remains the standard for Java projects due to its wide use and good conventions. Gradle offers richer customization at the cost of complexity. For smaller projects, Maven or Gradle will likely suffice, depending on preferences around conventions versus flexibility. Understanding the options gives the flexibility to choose the best fit or migrate between tools as needed.

First Steps: Writing and Running Your First Java Program

Now that you have your Java Development Kit and build tool configured, it's time to verify everything is working properly by creating your first Java program. Writing "Hello World" is a rite of passage for programmers of all languages, serving as a baseline test to confirm the tools are installed correctly before moving on to more complex code. In this section, we'll walk through developing a simple greeting program from start to finish.

Creating the Source File

To begin, we need to create the Java source code file that will contain our program. Files ending in .java define Java classes and are compiled into bytecode files with a .class extension. In your project directory, create a new text file called HelloWorld.java using your preferred code editor or IDE. Save it so the file path ends with the class name and .java extension, as this naming convention is important.

Writing the Code

A basic Java application needs, at minimum, a class declaration and main method. Inside the HelloWorld.java file, add:

```
public class HelloWorld {
  public static void main(String[] args) {
  }
}
```

This defines a public class called HelloWorld containing a public static void main method that can accept command line arguments. The main method is treated as the entry point where program execution begins.

Printing Output

To display output, we use the System.out.println() method. Add the statement "System.out.println("Hello World!")" inside the main method body:

```java
public class HelloWorld {
  public static void main(String[] args) {
    System.out.println("Hello World!");
  }
}
```

This will print our greeting message to the console when the program runs. The out PrintStream object represents the standard output, and println prints the string plus a new line.

Compiling the Code

Now it's time to compile our Java source code into bytecode using the Javac compiler included in the JDK. Open a command prompt, navigate to the project folder, and enter:

```
javac HelloWorld.java
```

If there are no errors, this will generate a HelloWorld.class file containing the compiled code. The .class extension indicates it is bytecode, not human-readable source code.

Running the Program

To execute our program, use the java command while specifying the fully qualified class name:

```
java HelloWorld
```

If all goes well, you should see "Hello World!" printed on the console. This verifies that the code runs as expected and the environment is configured properly to compile and launch Java applications.

Building with Maven

Let's recreate the above using Maven instead of raw commands. Inside your project folder, create a pom.xml with:

```xml
<project>
  <modelVersion>4.0.0</modelVersion>
  <groupId>com.mycompany.app</groupId>
  <artifactId>my-app</artifactId>
  <version>1.0</version>
  <properties>
    <maven.compiler.source>17</maven.compiler.source>
    <maven.compiler.target>17</maven.compiler.target>
  </properties>
```

```
    <dependencies>
    </dependencies>
</project>
```
Then run mvn compile and mvn exec:java -Dexec.mainClass="HelloWorld" to compile and run, respectively. Maven handles the steps behind the scenes.

Building with Gradle

For Gradle, create a build.gradle file:

```
plugins {
  id 'java'
}
group 'com.my company.app'
version '1.0'
repositories {
  maven central()
}
dependencies {
}
mainClassName = "HelloWorld"
```

Then, run gradle build to compile and gradle run to execute - Gradle provides the same functionality in a more customizable manner.

Testing Your Output

To confirm "Hello World!" is output as expected, you can also redirect the program output to a file using java HelloWorld > output.txt. Then, opening output.txt should contain only that greeting string. This verifies the code compiles and runs correctly on your system before progressing.

Taking the Next Steps

Congratulations, you've now created your very first working Java application! This covers the process of using a text editor or IDE to write code, compiling it with Javac, executing with Java, and automating build flows with Maven and Gradle. With a functioning development environment in place, you're now ready to start practicing and expanding your Java programming knowledge. In future lessons, we'll take what we've learned here and apply it by creating more advanced projects.

Common Issues and Troubleshooting

Now that you've successfully written and run a simple Java program, it's time to discuss some common problems beginners encounter and how to troubleshoot them. No journey in programming is without its bumps, but being able to resolve issues independently is an important skill. In this section, we'll cover typical errors, where to find help, and general debugging strategies.

Classpath and PATH Issues

One frequent cause of errors is improperly configured environment variables. The classpath (Windows) or PATH (Linux/Mac) needs to include the Java bin directory so commands like java and javac are found. Missing or incorrect values here can lead to "file not found" exceptions. Similarly, if multiple JDKs exist, the paths must point to the desired one. Carefully double-check installation documentation.

No Main Method Error

A common first program mistake is neglecting to include a public static void main(String[] args) method in the class. Without it, Java won't know where to start execution and will complain about "no main method". Be sure any runnable Java files define this signature entry point method. The access modifiers and argument types are important.

Compilation Errors

Typos, syntax errors, and missing imports will cause the Javac compiler to fail with messages like "cannot find symbol". Go line by line through error descriptions to spot issues in code. Formatting/indentation errors are also syntax problems. Remember to recompile after fixes. IDEs can help find errors, but manual checking is valuable too.

Runtime Errors

Even if the code compiles, logic errors may cause exceptions at runtime like

- NullPointerException
- ArrayIndexOutOfBounds
- ExceptionInInitializerError

These indicate problems in program flow not caught by the compiler. Use print statements, debugger, or exception handling to trace variables and find the origin. Reproducing in smaller pieces helps isolate issues.

Version Conflicts

Multiple JDK versions, mixed JRE/JDK paths, or old patches can conflict. Common signs are VersionFormatExceptions, UnsupportedClassVersions, or NoClassDefFoundErrors. Uninstall legacy versions, update PATH/classpath, and ensure all tools/code match the installed JDK. Incompatible library versions also cause linkage errors.

Maven/Gradle Problems

Problems in POM/build.gradle files, missing repositories, or dependencies that won't resolve are typically built tool configuration issues. Check syntax, network access, and settings files, and try simplifying. Build logs often provide clues. Repositories may need Maven Central declaration. Versions and conflicts between transitive dependencies also occur.

Common Questions Database

If an error isn't immediately clear, search online. Sites like Stack Overflow maintain searchable databases of common problems and solutions crowdsourced from developers worldwide. Search for the exact error message or describe your issue - chances are someone else encountered it before. The answers often include sample code demonstrating fixes.

Getting Live Help

Online documentation and forums are great, but sometimes, human interaction is needed fast. Consider joining a Java help Discord server for immediate assistance from other beginners/experts. Pose very specific questions with code samples - vague descriptions waste people's time. Be polite, thankful for any help received, and pay it forward by helping others when skills increase.

Debugging Methodically

When self-resolved, problems build problem-solving muscles. Slow down, read errors thoroughly, and simplify code to isolate issues. Add print statements to trace values, enable compiler/debugging flags, and use an IDE debugger. Break problems down - is it compilation, runtime, or environment? Methodically exploring error context empowers independent troubleshooting. Consulting peers should only be a last resort after dedicated debugging effort.

Iterative Learning

Bugs are inevitable, so embrace them as learning opportunities. Keep at it - perseverance is key to programming success. With practice, error handling will become second nature. Remember, even experienced developers consult references and ask for help occasionally. Stay positive - every resolved issue expands your skills for the next challenge ahead. Troubleshooting is a journey, so celebrate each step of progress along the way.

Chapter 2: Java Fundamentals

Data Types, Variables, and Constants: The Building Blocks

Any programming language requires a way to store and manipulate data in memory as a program executes. In Java, the fundamental units for working with data are known as data types, variables, and constants. This chapter will provide an in-depth look at each of these core concepts. By understanding data types, how to declare and assign values to variables, and how to define constants, you will gain the foundational knowledge necessary to begin writing Java programs.

Data Types

In the Java programming language, the term "data type" defines the kind of information that a variable can store. These data types fall into two primary categories: primitive data types and reference data types. While reference data types pertain to objects and classes that delve into the territory of object-oriented programming, for now, our focus will be on the primitive data types. Java offers eight primitive data types, each designed for specific purposes and having its own characteristics. Here's a closer look:

Int

The **int** data type in Java is designed to store integer values, which are whole numbers without a decimal point. The value range for an **int** lies between -2,147,483,648 and 2,147,483,647. It's a commonly used data type for variables that involve mathematical operations or loop counters.

Long

When there's a requirement to represent very large (or very small) whole numbers, the **long** data type comes into play. Its range starts from -9,223,372,036,854,775,808 and goes up to 9,223,372,036,854,775,807. **long** is especially useful when dealing with massive datasets or calculations involving large numbers.

Short

short is another integer data type but has a more restricted range, spanning from -32,768 to 32,767. Even though it consumes less memory compared to an **int**, its limited range means it isn't as commonly used.

Byte

byte is the smallest of the integer data types, accommodating values from -128 to 127. While it's memory-efficient, its extremely narrow range makes it suitable for only specific scenarios.

Float

For numbers with decimal points, we use the **float** data type. It represents single-precision floating-point numbers, which essentially means they can store values with up to 7 decimal places of precision.

Double

double is another floating-point data type but with double the precision of **float**. It's suitable for values that need up to 15 decimal places of precision, making it the preferred choice for many mathematical computations.

Char

The **char** data type is used to represent individual characters, be it a letter, digit, punctuation, or any other symbol. Characters stored using **char** are enclosed in single quotes.

Boolean

The simplest of all data types, **boolean** can store just two values: **true** or **false**. This binary nature makes it perfect for variables representing conditions, switches, or binary decisions.

By grasping the specificities and memory requirements of each of these primitive data types, developers can make informed decisions, ensuring that their code is both efficient and accurate. Selecting the appropriate data type is a foundational aspect of crafting robust and performant Java programs.

Variables

With data types established, we can now create variables in Java. A variable provides a name to reference a location in memory where a value of a specified data type can be stored and manipulated during program execution. Variables are declared using the following format:

{DataType} {VariableName};

For example, to declare an integer variable called "number" we will type:

int number;

In this example, we have indicated that the variable number will store an int-type value by using the data type int. Some key points about variable declaration:

- Variables must be declared before they are used, specifying the DataType

- The semicolon ";" at the end of every declaration statement is important syntax
- Variable names should be descriptive yet concise, using camelCase formatting
- Variables can be declared at the class level or within blocks like methods

Once declared, variables need to be initialized by assigning them an initial value before they can be used:

```
int number = 0;
```

Now, the number has been initialized to hold the integer value 0. Variable names provide a human-readable identifier to reference a location in memory during runtime. Properly declaring and initializing variables is fundamental to any Java program.

Constants

For values that should never change once declared, such as mathematical constants or configuration settings, Java provides the ability to define constants using the final keyword. Constant variable values are set at compile-time rather than run-time.

To declare a constant, we use:

final {DataType} {VariableName} = {Value};

For example:

```
final double PI = 3.14159;
```

Here, PI is a constant variable that is set to approximate π and cannot be reassigned later in the code. This provides benefits like being able to catch potential bugs from accidentally changing a value that should never change. Constants declared at class-level are visible to all methods, while those declared locally are only visible in a particular scope.

A solid understanding of primitive data types, how to declare variables, and how to define constants is the beginning of your Java journey. Mastering these core concepts will allow you to apply them throughout your programs to effectively manage data. In later chapters, you will continue building upon this foundation to create more complex programs using Java's object-oriented features and other language capabilities.

Control Flow: Decisions and Loops

One of the main responsibilities of any programming language is to allow developers to control the order in which instructions are executed during runtime. This sequencing of operations is known as control flow. Java provides several control flow structures that allow your code to make logical decisions and repeat tasks through looping constructs. This chapter will examine Java's essential control flow statements in detail: if/else conditionals and various types of loops. Understanding how to control program execution through decisions and repetition is central to writing effective Java programs.

if/else Conditional Statements

The most basic control structure is the if/else conditional statement, which allows code to execute different blocks depending on whether a given condition evaluates to true or false. The general syntax is:

if (condition) { // code runs if condition is true }
else { // code runs if condition is false }

For example:
```
public class MyClass {
    public static void main(String args[]) {
        int x = 10;
        if (x < 5) {
            System.out.println("x is less than 5");
        }
        else {
            System.out.println("x is greater than or equal to 5");
        }
    }
}
```

Output:
```
x is greater than or equal to 5
```

Here, we check if x is less than 5 and print one message if true or the alternate message if false. The condition can use comparison operators like >, <, ==, !=, or Boolean logic like && and ||. If the condition checks for equality, it's best practice to use == rather than a single = which is for assignment.

Multiple else if blocks can check multiple conditions in sequence:

if (condition1) { // ... }
else if (condition2) { // ... }
else { // ... }

Conditionals are fundamental for writing logical, well-structured programs that can make decisions based on changing inputs or situations.

for Loop

The for loop iterates over a block of code a specified number of times. It has three sections separated by semicolons:

for (initialization; condition; increment) { // code block to repeat }

Typical usage is counting loops:

```
for (int i = 0; i < 10; i++) {
  System.out.println(i);
}
```

This initializes i to 0, checks if i is less than 10 each iteration, prints i, then increments i by 1 each time before repeating. The initialization, condition, and increment allow precise control over iteration.

while Loop

A while loop repeats as long as a condition remains true:

while (condition) { // code block }

It's useful when the number of iterations is unknown:

```
int i = 0;
while (i < input) {
  i++;
}
```

Here, we don't know the input, so a for loop can't be used, but it allows repeating until the condition is met.

do-while Loop

Similar to while, but the block is guaranteed to run at least once even if the condition is false initially:

do { // code block } while (condition);

For example, displaying a menu until a valid choice is made:

```
do {
  displayMenu();
  choice = get input();
}
while (!isValid(choice));
```

Loop Control Statements

Loop control statements in Java dictate the flow of loops, allowing programmers to have finer control over repetitive operations. They make it possible to break out of loops, skip an iteration, or evaluate conditions before proceeding with loop iterations. Given their versatility, these loop control statements are indispensable when working with iterative structures like arrays, and lists or when simulating real-world systems and algorithms.

Break Statement

The break statement is used to exit a loop prematurely. When a specific condition is met and a break is executed, the loop is immediately terminated, and the program continues with the next line of code after the loop.

Example: Imagine you're searching for the number 5 in an array. Once you find it, there's no need to continue the loop.
```
for(int i=0; i<arr.length; i++) {
  if(arr[i] == 5) {
    System.out.println("Number 5 found!");
    break;
  }
}
```

Continue Statement

The continue statement skips the current iteration and jumps to the next one. This is particularly useful when a specific condition in a loop iteration doesn't need further execution, but the loop shouldn't terminate entirely.

Example: Suppose you want to print all numbers from 1 to 10 except 5.
```
for(int i=1; i<=10; i++) {
  if(i == 5) {
    continue;
  }
  System.out.println(i);
}
```

Loop Conditions

These are the conditional checks in loops like for, while, and do-while. These conditions determine if a loop should continue or terminate. A loop runs as long as its condition remains true.

Example: Using a for loop to print numbers 1 to 5:
```
for(int i=1; i<=5; i++) {
  System.out.println(i);
}
```
Using a while loop to print numbers until a counter reaches a limit:
```
int counter = 1;
while(counter <= 5) {
  System.out.println(counter);
  counter++;
}
```

The strategic use of loop control statements allows for more efficient and readable code. For instance, when traversing complex data structures, the ability to skip unnecessary iterations or exit a loop once the desired outcome is achieved saves computational resources. Similarly, when simulating real-world scenarios, precise control over repetitive actions is crucial. Think of a simulation where you're modeling the behavior of cars on the road; the ability to skip a specific car's movement or stop the simulation when a particular event occurs is crucial for accuracy and efficiency.

Java's Object-Oriented Paradigm: A Gentle Introduction

While the previous chapters established Java's fundamental programming constructs, the language truly differentiates itself through its object-oriented (OO) nature. OO programming uses classes, objects, inheritance, and polymorphism to model real-world entities and problems in software. This paradigm provides many benefits but can seem daunting at first. This chapter will introduce core OO concepts in Java at a gentle, conceptual level to give you a working knowledge without overwhelming technical details. By learning the principles behind OO design, you will lay the foundation to develop quality, maintainable applications down the road.

Classes and Objects

At the core of object orientation is the class. A class defines the attributes and behaviors that characterize some entity. For example, a Student class may have name and age attributes, with methods to enroll (), pay tuition (), etc.

Classes act as a template or blueprint to create multiple objects. An object is an instance of a class - a unique entity with its own set of attribute values. We create objects by instantiating classes:

Student Sarah = new Student();

This declares a Student object called Sarah using the Student class template. Objects encapsulate both data (stored in attributes) and functionality (through methods) into a single programmatic representation. Classes and objects form the basic building blocks of any OO program.

Inheritance

A key benefit of classes is the ability to inherit common traits from a parent class. For example, our Student class could extend a Person class:

class Person {   String name;   //... }

class Student extends Person {   int student;   //... }

The student now gains all attributes and methods of Person automatically. Inheritance creates an "is-a" relationship, as a Student "is-a" Person with additional student-specific details.

Polymorphism

Along with inheritance, polymorphism is another pillar of OO design. It allows subclasses to override or implement methods from a parent class in different ways:

```
class Person {
  public void speak(){
```

```java
      System.out.println("Hello!");
   }
}

class Student extends Person {
  @Override public void speak(){
    System.out.println("Hello, I'm a student!");
  }
}
```

Now, speak() acts polymorphically based on the actual object type, even if it's accessed through the parent Person reference type. This allows behavior to vary in a type-safe, readable way.

Abstraction and Encapsulation

Two other key OO principles are abstraction and encapsulation.

Abstraction models the essential characteristics of an entity independent of implementation details. A class serves as an abstraction of a concept. Encapsulation binds together the data and functions that manipulate the data and prevents external code from accessing or manipulating them directly. In Java, fields are declared private for encapsulation, with public getter/setter methods providing controlled access. Together, abstraction and encapsulation promote loose coupling and high cohesion that results in flexible, reusable class designs. These principles scale with large, complex systems.

Example Program

To summarize OO concepts, let's build a simple grading program. Save the following code in two separate files:

Student.java
```java
class Student{
  private String name;
  private int score;
  public Student(String name) {
    this.name = name;
  }

  public void setScore(int score) {
    this.score = score;
  }
  public String getName() {
    return name;
  }
  public int getScore() {
    return score;
```

}
}

GradingProgram.java

```
class GradingProgram {
  public static void main(String[] args) {
    Student student = new Student("John");
    student.set score(95);
    System.out.println(student.getName() + ": " +
        student.getScore());
  }
}
```

Compile both files from the command line:
```
javac Student.java GradingProgram.java
```

Run the GradingProgram class:
```
java GradingProgram
```

This should produce the output:
```
John: 95
```

This demonstrates core OO principles through encapsulated classes and objects that model real-world entities in code.

While there are certainly more advanced OO concepts to explore later, this introduction provided a high-level overview of key OO paradigms in Java - classes, objects, inheritance, polymorphism, abstraction, and encapsulation. Mastering these principles is the cornerstone for fluently designing robust, maintainable Java applications. In future chapters, we will build upon this foundation to apply OO techniques and best practices to bigger, more complex problems.

Chapter 3: Diving into Object-Oriented Programming

Classes and Objects: The Blueprint of Java

In object-oriented programming, classes and objects are the fundamental building blocks around which entire applications are designed. This section will provide a detailed explanation of these concepts and their relationship to each other.

What is a Class?

A class is a blueprint or template that defines the common properties and behaviors that apply to all objects of a particular kind. It acts as a generalized description for a set of real-world entities.

For example, if we want to model dogs in a programming context, we could define a Dog class. This class would specify that all dog objects have attributes like a name, breed, color, etc. It would also define common behaviors expected of dogs, like barking, fetching, wagging the tail, and so on. These would be represented as data fields and method declarations in the class.

The key aspects of a class are:

- It encapsulates data in the form of fields/attributes that describe the object.
- It encapsulates behaviors through method declarations that the object can exhibit.
- It establishes a common foundation on which similar objects can be based.
- A class is a logical entity rather than a physical one - it does not create actual objects by itself.

Some important points to note about classes:

- A class only provides a template - it is not an instance of the actual object itself.
- Classes are defined using the class keyword in Java.
- They can contain fields, methods, and constructors required to characterize objects.
- Fields defined in a class are called attributes or instance variables.
- Classes act as the building blocks based on which object instances are created.

What is an Object?

In object-oriented programming (OOP), the term "object" carries immense significance. At its core, while a class serves as a blueprint outlining specific characteristics and behaviors, an object is the tangible manifestation of that blueprint—a living, runtime entity constructed based on the class definition. To draw an analogy, if a class is akin to an architectural blueprint, an object would be the actual building constructed from that blueprint.

Let's delve deeper using an illustrative example: If we were to conceptualize a class named 'Dog', this class would delineate the general attributes and behaviors associated with a dog—like its breed, color, and ability to bark. Now, when we instantiate objects from the 'Dog' class, each resulting object represents a distinct dog—be it Max, Bella, Charlie, or Daisy. These individual dog objects have the following features:

Unique Identity: Just as every individual being in the real world is identifiable through unique characteristics, each object boasts a distinct identity based on its attributes and properties.

State: An object's state is a combination of its attributes' values at any given point in runtime. Max might be a 'Golden Retriever' while Bella could be a 'Labrador', for instance.

Lifetime: From the moment of its creation to its eventual deletion or garbage collection, an object has a defined presence in memory.

Behaviors: Every object can exhibit certain behaviors or methods, which are derived from its parent class definition.

Some salient points about objects include:

They come to life at runtime via the use of the **new** keyword followed by the class's name. Each object has a distinct identity, often tied to its memory address or specific properties. While objects can have property values assigned either during their creation (via constructors) or later, they all possess behaviors as declared in their parent class. Objects can also dynamically interact with one another during program execution.

Relationship between Class and Object

The interrelationship between a class and its objects is foundational to OOP. A class is fundamentally a logical construct—a template if you will, that outlines the structure and behaviors of potential objects. Conversely, objects are the physical manifestations created during runtime, crafted meticulously using the class as a mold.

It's crucial to note the following about this relationship:

A single class can be the progenitor for countless objects, each with its distinct state. While each object is unique in its state, it uniformly inherits properties and behaviors from its parent class. Any modifications to the class's definition ripple through, affecting all instantiated objects from that class.

This intricate dynamic between classes and objects underpins the entirety of the Java programming framework and OOP at large. In subsequent sections, we'll explore how objects are initialized and given life during their creation, primarily through constructors.

Constructors: Giving Life to Objects

Now that we understand the concepts of classes and objects, the next logical question is - how are objects instantiated and initialized? This is where constructors play an important role in OOP. Constructors help bring objects to life by setting up their initial state during creation.

What is a Constructor?

A constructor is a special type of method in a class that is executed whenever a new object is instantiated. The job of a constructor is to initialize the new object by assigning values to its attributes and performing any other initialization logic.

Some key properties of constructors:

- Constructors are invoked implicitly by Java at object creation time (using a new keyword).
- They must have the same name as the class in which they are defined.
- Constructors cannot have a return type, not even void.
- If no constructor is defined by the programmer, a default no-arg constructor is provided by Java.

For example, in our Dog class, we may want to initialize the name attribute when new Dog objects are created. We can do this using a constructor:

```
public class Dog {
  String name;
  public Dog(String dogName) {
    name = dogName;
  }
}
```

Now, whenever we do Dog d = new Dog("Max"), the constructor will set the name to "Max" before returning the object.

Types of Constructors

Constructors in Java play a pivotal role in the object-oriented paradigm. Their primary function is to initialize an object when it's created. The power of Java constructors lies in their flexibility—Java allows multiple variations of constructors based on their parameterization. This caters to diverse initialization scenarios for objects. Let's dissect each type in detail:

No-Arg Constructor

The no-argument (no-arg) constructor is a constructor variant that doesn't take any parameters. It's especially handy when you don't need to initialize an object with specific data during its creation. Often, such constructors will initialize an object with default values or perform other setup operations that don't require external input.

Example: Creating a default user:

```
public class User {
  String name;
  int age;

  // No-Arg Constructor
  public User() {
    this.name = "Default User";
    this.age = 0;
  }
}
```

Parameterized Constructor

As the name suggests, a parameterized constructor takes parameters. It's used to initialize an object's attributes using values passed during the object's instantiation. This provides a convenient method to set initial values for an object upon its creation.

Example: Initializing a user with a name and age:

```
public User(String name, int age) {
  this.name = name;
  this.age = age;
}
```

Copy Constructor

A copy constructor is a unique type that is employed to create an object by copying values from another pre-existing object of the same class. It's beneficial when you want to clone an object or create a new object that should start with the state of another object.

Example: Copying a user object:

```
public User(User existingUser) {
  this.name = existingUser.name;
  this.age = existingUser.age;
}
```

Overloaded Constructors

Overloading in Java refers to defining multiple methods or constructors with the same name but different parameters. Overloaded constructors enable the creation of objects under varying scenarios by providing different sets of initialization values. This enhances the flexibility of object creation, ensuring that various use-cases and initialization scenarios are supported.

Example: Overloaded constructors for a user:

public User() { /*... default values ...*/ }

public User(String name) { /*... initialization ...*/ }

public User(String name, int age) { /*... initialization ...*/ }

For example, we could add a no-arg constructor to Dog to handle cases where the name is unknown:

```
public Dog() {
  name = "Unknown";
}
```

What are Constructors Called?

Constructors hold a special place in the Java programming paradigm. They are not mere methods but rather essential mechanisms that breathe life into objects. When an object is created using the **new** keyword, the Java Virtual Machine (JVM) leaps into action, automatically invoking the relevant constructor. This automatic invocation is instrumental as it ensures that the object is suitably initialized and primed for use right from its inception.

The crux of a constructor is its initialization logic. This logic sets the foundation, establishing the initial state of the object. It is this state that forms the backbone of subsequent interactions and operations involving the object. It's worth noting that this initialization, driven by the constructor, is not an iterative or recurring process. In the lifetime of an object, the constructor is called just once, precisely at the moment of its creation.

Furthermore, the sequence of events during object instantiation is meticulously orchestrated. The constructor does its job, setting up the object before any reference variable is assigned to it or before it's returned to the caller. This ensures that by the time any part of the program interacts with or references the object, it's already in a stable and defined state, preventing unforeseen behaviors or errors.

For example:

```
Dog d = new Dog("Max");
// constructor called to initialize d before it's returned
```

Importance of Constructors

In the vast expanse of Object-Oriented Programming (OOP), constructors emerge as foundational elements. They act as gatekeepers, ensuring that every object starts its lifecycle on the right footing. Without them, objects would be like buildings constructed without a solid foundation.

One of the primary tasks of constructors is to assign initial values to an object's attributes. Think of this as the first brush strokes on a canvas, setting the scene for the masterpiece to come. This initialization is crucial because it ensures that the object begins its journey in a well-defined state, minimizing unpredictabilities in its subsequent interactions.

Beyond just assigning values, constructors often wear the hat of a validator. They scrutinize the parameters passed to them, ensuring they align with the expected criteria. This validation mechanism is vital in preserving the integrity of the object and preventing aberrant behaviors that could arise from unchecked or erroneous data.

Objects in OOP are not solitary entities; they often exist within a web of relationships with other objects. Constructors facilitate the establishment of these relationships. They can, for instance, link an object to its siblings, superiors, or subordinates, setting the stage for intricate interactions down the line.

Moreover, while the act of creating an object might seem straightforward, it can sometimes be fraught with challenges. There might be exceptions or unforeseen circumstances during object construction. Constructors step in here, handling such exceptions gracefully and ensuring that the process of bringing an object to life is as smooth as possible.

In their essence, constructors standardize the object creation process. They offer a consistent, reliable mechanism to birth objects, ensuring that every object is created following a well-defined protocol.

Interestingly, the Java language is quite forgiving. If a developer forgets to define a constructor, Java doesn't leave the object high and dry. It automatically provides a default no-argument constructor. Nonetheless, for clarity and precision, it's always advisable for developers to explicitly define constructors, outlining the object creation process in detail.

Methods: Adding Behavior to Objects

So far, we have seen how classes provide a template for objects and constructors initialize them. But objects would be pretty useless without behaviors - the actions they can perform. This is where methods come in. Methods define the functionality or behaviors that objects of a class can exhibit.

What is a Method?

The method is reminiscent of what a function represents in procedural languages. Nestled within a class, a method is a well-defined block of code dedicated to executing a particular task pertinent to that class. Unlike the free-floating nature of functions in some languages, methods are intimately tied to classes and, by extension, to the objects of those classes. They are framed within the class structure, and their accessibility is often governed by specific access modifiers like public or private.

A method's declaration offers a glimpse into its purpose and behavior. It showcases its name, which is often indicative of the action it performs, the parameters it accepts, and the type of value it returns. This signature is a testament to the method's intent and capabilities. At the heart of a method lies its implementation—a sequence of statements that collectively fulfill the method's purpose.

One of the compelling features of methods is their ability to act upon objects. Once a class defines a method, any object instantiated from that class can invoke this method, triggering the actions encapsulated within it. This binding of methods to objects is a cornerstone of the object-oriented paradigm, enabling objects to not just hold data but also to exhibit behaviors.

Furthermore, methods champion the cause of modularity in programming. Instead of a monolithic codebase where every action is intricately woven into a vast tapestry, methods help fragment the code. They carve out distinct, reusable segments, each entrusted with a specific responsibility. This modularity enhances clarity, fosters code reuse, and simplifies maintenance, making methods an indispensable asset in Java programming.

For example, a bark() method in the Dog class would define the behavior of a dog barking:

```
public void bark() {
   System.out.println("Woof woof!");
}
```

Types of Methods

In Java, methods are the conduit through which objects manifest their behaviors. These behaviors are varied and tailored to the myriad needs of a program. Reflecting this diversity, methods themselves come in several variations, each catering to a specific context or requirement.

At a foundational level, the categorization of methods hinges on two pivotal aspects: parameters and return types. Some methods neither accept parameters nor return any value. These are straightforward actions that don't need external inputs or outputs. In contrast, some methods do accept parameters, harnessing them to perform their tasks, but once they've executed their logic, they don't give back any results. Conversely, there are those methods that remain aloof, not requiring any parameters, but upon execution, they graciously return a value. Then there's a synthesis of the two: methods that both accept parameters and, after some internal machinations, return a result.

In addition to these categorizations, there's the realm of static methods. Unlike the typical methods, which require an object for invocation, static methods belong to the class itself and can be called without creating an instance of the class.

Going a step further, methods can also be classified based on their intended functionality. Getter methods, for instance, are guardians of an object's attributes, offering outsiders a glimpse of these values. Their counterparts, setter methods, stand at the gates, allowing or disallowing modifications to these attributes. Then there are business methods, the heartbeats of an object, where the core logic resides. Rounding off this categorization are utility methods, the unsung heroes that facilitate reusable operations, providing consistent functionality across the board.

Invoking these methods is an art in itself. Since most methods are tied to objects, the first step usually involves creating an instance of the class. Once this object is brought to life, invoking a method becomes a simple dance of using the dot operator on the object's reference variable, followed by the method's name, and passing in any required parameters. This sequence brings the method into action, allowing the object to exhibit the behavior encapsulated within the method.

For example:

```
Dog d = new Dog();
d.bark(); //invoke bark method on d object
```

Here, bark() is called on the d object instance, which was created from the Dog class.

Chapter 4: Advancing with Object-Oriented Concepts

Understanding Inheritance: Leveraging Existing Code

Inheritance is one of the core concepts of object-oriented programming that allows programmers to leverage existing code by building upon existing classes. Not only does inheritance facilitate code reuse, but it also makes code more modular and maintainable over time. This chapter will explain in detail how inheritance works in Java and how to properly implement inheritance in your own classes.

What is Inheritance?

Inheritance allows a subclass to inherit attributes and behaviors from a parent or superclass. The subclass extends the parent class and inherits all of its properties and behaviors while also being able to add its own additional properties or overwrite existing behaviors. This principle of extending existing functionality is what enables programmers to reuse code and avoid rewriting similar logic from scratch for every new class.

For example, you may have a superclass called Vehicle that defines common behavior like having wheels, an engine, and the ability to move. Then, subclasses can be inherited from Vehicles like cars, bikes, Boats, etc. Each subclass can focus only on the new unique characteristics it introduces without redefining common vehicle behaviors already defined in the parent Vehicle class.

Inheritance provides an "is-a" relationship. A car IS A vehicle, so it inherits from the Vehicle class. A key benefit is that code written for the parent Vehicle class automatically applies to any subclass like Car without needing modification. New subclasses can extend Vehicles as new vehicle types are introduced without impacting existing vehicle codes, increasing flexibility.

Implementing Inheritance in Java

In Java, the extends keyword is used to establish inheritance between classes. A subclass extends a single-parent class, gaining all its attributes and behaviors.

For example:
```
public class Car extends Vehicle {
  // car-specific fields and methods
}
```
The Car subclass now inherits everything already defined in the Vehicle class, like wheels, engine, move() method, etc., and can add new fields and behaviors related to being a car. The subclass augments but does not replace the parent class. Both could still be used independently as needed.

Access Modifiers and Inheritance

In the object-oriented tapestry of Java, inheritance stands as a pivotal mechanism, enabling classes to inherit attributes and behaviors from their predecessors. However, not all that is part of a class is meant to be freely inherited. The landscape of inheritance is often crisscrossed with boundaries and access points, and it's here that access modifiers come into play, guiding the flow of inheritance.

Access modifiers determine the scope of visibility and accessibility for classes, methods, and fields. They act as gatekeepers, deciding what parts of a class can be reached and from where. In the realm of inheritance, they play a definitive role in delineating how subclasses interact with the inherited code from their parent classes.

Consider the **public** access modifier, which is akin to an open invitation. Classes or members tagged as **public** proclaim their availability far and wide. Whether you're in the same package, a different package, or even in a subclass, **public** members throw open their doors to you.

Contrast this with the **protected** modifier, which is more selective. While it allows members to be accessed within their own package, its unique offering is its openness to subclasses. Subclasses, even if they are in a different package, can freely access the **protected** attributes and methods of their parent, making this modifier particularly significant in the inheritance paradigm.

However, not all members are as forthcoming. Some prefer to stay confined to their local neighborhood—their package. Members adorned with the package-private access level (signified by the absence of an access modifier) are accessible only to classes within the same package. Subclasses outside the package are left at the door.

The most restrictive of all is the **private** access modifier. Guarded and exclusive, **private** members are resolutely introverted. They allow access exclusively within their class, shutting out everyone else, including subclasses. This means that even if a class intends to pass on its legacy through inheritance, its **private** members remain untouched, un-inherited, and unseen by its descendants.

When crafting classes with the intent of inheritance, it's paramount to choose the access modifiers wisely. **Public** and **protected** members are typically preferred, for they can be seamlessly carried forward to subclasses. However, **private** members, given their inaccessibility, should be designed with the understanding that they remain an internal affair of the class, untouched by the currents of inheritance.

Overriding Methods

A key feature of subclasses is overriding or extending existing methods of the parent class. This is done by using the same name and signature for the method. For example:

```
public class Vehicle {
  public void move() {
  // generic movement logic
  }
}
public class Car extends Vehicle {
  @Override
public void move() {
  // car-specific movement logic
  System.out.println("Vroom vroom!");
  }
}
```

Here, the subclass overrides the move() method to provide specialized logic for cars. This is how polymorphism emerges - an instance can be treated as the parent type and call move() while getting the specific subclass implementation at runtime.

Overriding Methods Correctly

Overriding methods is a quintessential aspect of object-oriented programming, particularly in the context of inheritance. However, doing it right requires adhering to certain rules and conventions. When a method is overridden in a subclass, its signature should mirror exactly what's specified in the parent class, ensuring consistency across the hierarchy. While the access level of the method can be adjusted, it should always be tilted towards broader accessibility; narrowing it down further can lead to accessibility issues.

For those abstract methods that the parent class only declares without implementing, it falls upon the shoulders of the subclasses to provide a concrete implementation. To ensure you're genuinely overriding a method and not mistakenly creating a new one, it's advised to use the **@Override** annotation. This small but powerful annotation catches unintended errors stemming from typographical mistakes. If a situation demands invoking the superclass version of a method from within its overridden counterpart, one can use the **super.method()** construct.

Best Practices for Inheritance

While method overriding is pivotal, understanding the broader dynamics of inheritance is equally essential. In the journey of object-oriented design, it's often recommended to lean more towards composition than inheritance. This entails using other classes as components rather than inheriting from them, promoting flexibility. When opting for inheritance, ensure the parent classes are robust representations of clear and appropriately abstract concepts. The cornerstone of inheritance should be a genuine "is-a" relationship between the subclass and the superclass and not merely an avenue for code reuse.

For classes that aren't meant to be part of an inheritance hierarchy, marking them as **final** can shield them from being subclassed. Moreover, it's prudent to avoid deep inheritance hierarchies that sprawl with too many subclasses, as they can become challenging to manage and understand. It's often beneficial to encapsulate interactions between subclasses and parents behind interfaces, laying down a common contract. Adhering to these practices ensures that inheritance serves its purpose effectively, leading to cleaner, more extensible, and organized code structures.

Polymorphism: Flexibility in Action

Polymorphism refers to the ability of objects belonging to different types to be accessed through a common interface. This flexibility in programming allows for code to be reused in a variety of contexts. This chapter will explore how polymorphism gives Java code greater reusability through dynamic binding and inheritance.

Defining Polymorphism

The word polymorphism means "many forms", - which refers to the ability of an entity, like a method, to exhibit multiple forms. In object-oriented programming, this is usually seen as a parent class reference being used to call a subclass-specific implementation of a method.

For example, we could have an Animal parent class with a method makeSound(). Subclasses could override this to define specific sounds:

```
class Dog extends Animal {
  @Override
  public void makeSound() {
    System.out.println("Woof!");
  }
}
```

```
class Cat extends Animal {
  @Override
  public void makeSound() {
    System.out.println("Meow!");
  }
}
```

Even though the code uses an Animal reference variable, the actual object type could be a Dog or Cat. Polymorphism allows calling makeSound() and getting the appropriate subclass implementation at runtime based on the object's actual type.

This provides flexibility where code written for the parent class can still work transparently with any subclass. New animal types can be added without modifying existing code.

Achieving Polymorphism with Inheritance

As seen above, polymorphism is achieved in Java through inheritance and method overriding. For a method to be polymorphic:

- It must be present in the parent class.
- Subclasses must override this method and provide their own implementation.
- Child object reference must be accessed through a parent-type variable.

The latter point ensures the JVM performs dynamic binding at runtime to determine the appropriate implementation based on the actual object type. With a parent reference, makeSound() could call any subclass override transparently.

Other Applications of Polymorphism

Polymorphism allows code to be written more generically and increases reusability across contexts. Beyond method overriding, some other examples include:

- Concrete vs abstract classes - The abstract parent class defines the common interface, and subclasses provide concrete implementations.
- Interfaces - Define only method signatures; polymorphic implementations exist across multiple classes.
- Generics - Type parameters allow defining a common method signature that accepts subclasses of a type.
- Collections - Heterogeneous collection of mixed object types handled via their common interface.
- Factories - Produce subclasses through a common factory interface without coupling code to concrete classes.

So, in summary, polymorphism is a key way to write flexible object-oriented code in Java by abstracting up to a common parent interface for improved cohesion and encapsulation.

Implementing Polymorphic Code

When creating polymorphic code, some best practices include:

- Favor abstraction over concrete classes via interfaces or abstract classes as appropriate.
- Declare variables, parameters, and return types as parent interfaces/classes where possible.
- Prefer composition using parent fields over subclassing unnecessarily.
- Program to abstractions vs concrete classes to maximize flexibility.
- Avoid tight coupling between subclasses by minimizing dependencies.
- Favor small, coherent polymorphic class hierarchies instead of overly large inheritance trees.

Proper usage of polymorphism results in well-structured code that accommodates change gracefully by depending minimally on concrete implementation details. Overall, it greatly increases code reusability and flexibility.

Encapsulation: Shielding Your Data

Encapsulation is a fundamental concept in object-oriented design that involves bundling together code and related data and restricting access to that data. This chapter will explore how encapsulation helps programmers design robust and maintainable code through information hiding.

What is Encapsulation?

At its core, encapsulation is about wrapping up code and state into a single unit called a class. This bundling provides many benefits:

- The data is hidden from the outside world, protecting it from corruption or accidental modification.
- Only the public interface of the class is exposed, allowing developers to change internal implementation without breaking existing code.
- Coupling between classes is reduced since only the class's public interactions need to be considered by the dependent code.

Encapsulation allows designing classes as modular black boxes that control access to their inner workings. Data stored in fields is kept private, so only public methods of the class can directly modify it.

Implementing Encapsulation in Java

In Java, encapsulation is achieved primarily through access modifiers on fields and methods:

- Fields are declared as private by default. They can only be accessed directly within the class.
- If a field must be readable/writable from outside the class, public setter and getter methods provide encapsulated access.
- Sometimes, only getter methods are needed to hide the field while allowing reads.
- Methods not intended for external use can also be declared private.

For example:

```java
public class Person {
  private String name;
  public String getName() {
    return name;
  }
  public void setName(String name) {
    this.name = name;
  }
}
```

Here, the name field is hidden while the getter/setter provides controlled access. This shields the field from unintended modification or access when not desired.

Benefits of Encapsulation

Encapsulation, one of the cornerstones of object-oriented programming, offers a myriad of advantages that elevate the integrity and robustness of software design. At its core, encapsulation serves as a protective shield, preventing objects from inadvertently transitioning into undesirable states by meticulously validating inputs via setter methods. Beyond ensuring valid states, it also conceals intricate details of the implementation, affording developers the freedom to make changes to the underlying code without disrupting the external behavior. This hiding mechanism promotes a gentle interdependence, or loose coupling, between classes; they aren't entangled in the nuances of each other's private members. Furthermore, encapsulation paves the way for higher-level abstraction.

By demarcating common interfaces, developers can establish shared blueprints for objects. Another enticing aspect of encapsulation is that it future-proofs code; classes can be refashioned and refined without jeopardizing the functionality of others who rely on them. Moreover, the testing realm sees the virtue in encapsulation. As classes are insulated, they can be evaluated in isolation, devoid of any unpredictable ripple effects from private members. To ensure this integrity remains uncompromised, Java provides a slew of visibility controls, such as 'final' and 'private', that underpin and enforce encapsulation.

Choosing Encapsulation Levels

Transitioning to the topic of setting encapsulation levels, it's salient to note that Java offers various gradations of visibility, catering to the nuanced requirements of different class members. At the highest echelon of visibility, we have 'public', which exposes the member unabashedly to the outside world. While this fosters seamless accessibility, it also firmly entwines users with the API, prompting caution in its use. 'Protected' strikes a balance, revealing members to the same package and subclasses, thus harmonizing the needs of encapsulation and inheritance.

The 'package private' access level, devoid of a specific modifier, restricts visibility to the confines of the package, making it an ideal choice for internal operations. On the other end of the spectrum lies 'private', the zenith of encapsulation, reserving access exclusively for the class itself. Adopting a philosophy of "tight cohesion and loose coupling", developers are encouraged to judiciously use these modifiers. Exposing only indispensable interfaces to the outside while reserving more restricted access for internal components accentuates the efficacy of encapsulation.

Balancing Encapsulation and Usability

However, encapsulation isn't a monolithic practice; it's paramount to strike an equilibrium between restriction and usability. While the primary thrust of encapsulation is to limit access, developers must also ensure that classes remain user-friendly. For instance, compact utility classes may sometimes forego rigorous encapsulation, deeming it superfluous.

Similarly, design patterns like factories and builders tasked with the construction of objects necessitate access to the private realms of those objects. In the realm of testing, frameworks often have to sidestep traditional encapsulation barriers to effectively verify functionality. Furthermore, frameworks designed with extensibility as their linchpin may often opt for a more relaxed encapsulation regimen to foster customization.

Abstraction: Hiding Complexity

Abstraction is a fundamental concept in object-oriented programming that allows programmers to focus on essential details while hiding irrelevant implementation details. This improves the flexibility, portability, and maintainability of code by raising the level of abstraction compared to concrete classes.

What is Abstraction?

Abstraction refers to representing essential qualities of an entity independently of implementation specifics. For example, when driving a car, we interact with the abstract concepts of steering, acceleration, and braking without concerning ourselves with exactly how the electronics or engine work under the hood. In code, abstraction is achieved through abstract classes and interfaces that define only a contract through method signatures without providing concrete implementations. This allows programmers to work with generalized types versus depending on concrete classes directly. At its core, abstraction is about promoting the separation of interface and implementation so that they can vary independently without impacting one another. This decoupling increases flexibility by removing tight bindings.

Interfaces in Java

In the Java programming language, interfaces represent a powerful method of facilitating abstraction. Essentially, they set out a contract of expected behaviors without stipulating how these behaviors are to be carried out. One of the distinguishing features of interfaces is that they exclusively consist of abstract method signatures, which means they don't have an actual method body. Classes, in their role, take on the responsibility of implementing interfaces and offering tangible versions of these abstract methods. Interestingly, Java allows classes to inherit from multiple interfaces, a feature that sets interfaces apart from abstract classes.

To enhance their utility, Java 8 introduced the ability to have default and static methods within interfaces, granting them the capacity to possess rudimentary implementations. Consider the **List** interface in Java as an illustrative example. This interface might lay down common list operations such as **add()** and **remove()**. And then, different classes like **ArrayList** and **LinkedList** will offer their unique implementations, determining how these operations function internally.

Abstract Classes

While abstract classes and interfaces share common ground, they also have distinct characteristics. Abstract classes can encompass both abstract methods (without a defined body) and already implemented ones. A salient feature is that any subclass deriving from an abstract class must provide concrete implementations of its abstract methods. Moreover, abstract classes can store states via fields.

However, you can't create an object directly from them; they serve primarily as a base for subclasses. Visualize a hypothetical **Shape** class, which, while declaring an abstract **draw()** method, also has a default behavior for **fill()**, which every derived shape inherits. In such a structure, specific shapes like **Circle** or **Rectangle** might only need to define their own **draw()** method.

Benefits of Abstraction

Abstraction, as a programming principle, imparts numerous advantages to Java code. It significantly boosts portability, as developers can utilize interfaces and classes without having to engage with their concrete implementations. The design becomes more adaptable since the actual implementations can be modified without affecting the components that rely on them. By emphasizing interfaces and common abstractions, code becomes more reusable. Another notable benefit is the diminished coupling among different classes and software layers, as dependencies are established based on generalized contracts.

Abstraction also simplifies the testing process, as testers can simulate interfaces without needing to dive into the implementation specifics. By keeping intricate details hidden, abstraction ensures that developers can concentrate on pertinent aspects. Hence, in a well-thought-out system, embracing abstraction becomes pivotal for maintaining the distinction between interface, behavior, and the nitty-gritty of implementation. When deployed appropriately, it equips software to accommodate evolving requirements with relative ease.

Best Practices for Abstraction

To harness the full potential of abstraction, certain best practices are recommended. Developers should lean towards programming with interfaces or abstract classes instead of directly with concrete implementations. When defining concrete subclasses, the emphasis should be on simplicity, ensuring they function as clear-cut implementations of interfaces. It's crucial to keep the intricacies of implementations tucked away, preferably within subclasses or inner classes.

In terms of flexibility, it's advantageous to use abstract types for parameters and return values. Within abstract types, the focus should remain on delineating interfaces, avoiding the temptation to introduce concrete operations. Finally, compact and related abstractions are preferable over vast, unfocused contracts. By steadfastly following these guidelines, developers can leverage abstraction to produce code that's loosely tied, evolves independently, and displays resilience against the inexorable shifts in requirements.

Chapter 5: Generic Programming

The Need for Generics

Before generics were introduced in Java 5, collections like ArrayList, LinkedList, HashMap, etc., were raw types with no type safety. This posed significant issues and limitations which generics aimed to resolve.

Lack of Type Safety

Non-generic collections allowed adding any object without restrictions. This compromised type of safety in several ways:

Unexpected object types:

Consider an ArrayList declared as ArrayList list = new ArrayList();. It could contain Strings, Integers, or any object. Retrieving an element would not guarantee its actual runtime type:

```
list.add("Hello");
list.add(1);
Object obj = list.get(0); // obj could be String or Integer
```

This made the code error-prone as operations on retrieved objects assumed types that may not match.

ClassCastExceptions:

When retrieving elements and casting:

```
list.add("Hello");
String str = (String) list.get(0);
// Throws ClassCastException
```

The cast would fail as the element type differs from what was expected. This resulted in runtime errors that generics help prevent.

Incorrect usage:

Developers could inadvertently add incompatible types since the compiler did not enforce constraints:

```
class Employee {
  public String name;
  public int id;
}
ArrayList list = new ArrayList();
list.add("Hello");
```

```
list.add(new Employee());
// Compiler allows but risks issues
```
Such mistakes reduced reliability and increased debugging efforts.

Maintenance Issues

The absence of type information at the collection object level made the code complex and hard to understand:

- It was not obvious what could be stored in a collection just by looking at its declaration.
- Related methods operating on the collection's elements assumed incompatible types.
- Collection APIs were difficult to document as element types varied per usage instead of being fixed.
- Changes to the type of elements added required thorough testing across all code interacting with that collection.
- Refactoring was challenging as element types behaved dynamically instead of being static.

Compile-time Type Checking

Since the actual element types were only known at runtime, compilers could not validate type safety. Bugs remained hidden and only surfaced after running code:

- Incompatible types could be added or retrieved without compiler warnings.
- Methods declared to receive or return element types did not enforce correctness.
- Contracts specifying element types were effectively suggestions without guarantees.

This delayed errors, reduced code quality, and increased debugging efforts compared to compile-time checks in generics.

Erasure Issues

Due to type erasure, the actual runtime element type was erased. So, operations assumed element types differed from what was specified:

- A method declared for a LinkedList<String> could still return a raw LinkedList.
- Iterate and process elements assuming one type, but elements may be of another.
- Persist collections whose type parameters disappear post-compilation.

This broke assumptions and introduced subtle bugs that generics address by preserving type information.

Understanding and Creating Generic Classes

Generics allow defining classes or interfaces whose element types are arguments that can vary per instance. This makes them type-safe and compatible across client code and libraries.

Defining a Generic Class

A generic class is declared by specifying a type variable between angle brackets (<>) in the class declaration. This variable acts as a placeholder for actual types that will be passed at runtime.

For example, to define a generic List class:

```
public class List<E> {
  private E[] elements;
  public void add(E e) {
    // elements array can now only hold type E
  }
}
```

Here, E is the type parameter that will be replaced by actual types like Integer, String, etc. when List is instantiated.

Specifying Type Arguments

The actual type is specified between angle brackets when creating an instance of the generic class:

```
List<String> stringList = new List<String>();
```

Now, stringList can only contain String elements as the type parameter E is replaced by String.

Bounded Type Parameters

Sometimes, we need to restrict the type parameter to specific types or supertypes. This is done using bounded type parameters.

```
public class Box<T extends Comparable<T>> {
  private T item;
  // T must implement Comparable
  public int compareTo(Box<T> b) {
    return item.compareTo(b.item);
  }
}
```

Here, T is bounded to any type that implements Comparable<T>, ensuring compareTo can be called.

Benefits of Generics

Generics, introduced in Java 5, have revolutionized how developers approach type safety and code reusability. At the heart of generics is the principle of type safety. Through generics, the Java compiler is empowered to validate the correct use of types. This means that many potential issues can be flagged at compile-time rather than waiting for runtime, thereby reducing the likelihood of bugs cropping up later.

Furthermore, generics are designed to be backward compatible, ensuring they operate seamlessly with legacy code and libraries without necessitating major overhauls. A major boost to readability comes from the fact that generics make the element types evident right from the class or method signatures, effectively reducing ambiguity and potential misunderstandings.

One of the standout benefits is reusability. With generics, it becomes possible to craft classes and methods that can operate on multiple, yet compatible, types—essentially slashing code redundancy. This robust system means that most issues are highlighted during the compilation phase, vastly reducing runtime failures. Lastly, when APIs employ generics judiciously, their clarity and understandability are enhanced, making them more developer-friendly.

Generics Support Key Java Features

Generics have been seamlessly woven into numerous Java constructs, augmenting their power and type safety. A clear example is the Collections framework. With generics, developers can create collections like lists or maps that securely store objects of specific types, preventing unintended mix-ups. In the realm of inheritance, generics enable the definition of subtypes that can be specialized based on particular type argument combinations. This provides more granularity and specificity in the type system. Additionally, generics play a role in annotations, allowing annotation types to be parameterized based on element types.

Java 8 introduced lambda expressions and the Streams API, both of which deeply incorporate generics. Lambda expressions can use generics for their parameter and return types, making them more versatile. Similarly, the Streams API, which facilitates functional-style operations on sequences of elements, heavily leverages generics, especially in stream processing pipelines, ensuring type-safe operations throughout. Lastly, the Reflection API, which provides the capability to inspect and manipulate class structures at runtime, has been enhanced to support generic types through Type objects.

Bounded Type Parameters

Sometimes, we want to restrict the allowed types for a type parameter to classes that extend or implement a specific type. This is known as bounding the type parameter. Bounded type parameters ensure type safety by enabling the usage of common methods on the generic class's element types.

Basic Syntax

A type parameter is bounded by specifying the bound after the parameter name, separated by the extends/super keyword in angle brackets <>.

For example, to bind a type T to a Number and its subclasses:

```
public class Box<T extends Number>
private T item;
public void set(T item) {
  this.item = item;
  }
}
```

Here, only Number and its subclasses like Integer, Float, etc. can be passed as arguments to Box.

Ensuring Common Methods

A common use case is to bind a type parameter to an interface so objects of that type are guaranteed to have particular methods available.

For example, to create a generic max method:

```
public class Utils{
  public static <T extends Comparable<T>> T max(List<T>
      list)
Copy
T max = list.get(0);
for(T t : list)
   if(t.compareTo(max) > 0)
      max = t;
   return max;
   }
}
```

Here, bounding T to Comparable<T> ensures any type passed implements compareTo(), allowing its usage. The method is now type-safe for any comparable type like String, Date, etc.

Upper Bounded Wildcards

The <? extends T> syntax presents another way to express an upper bound - it allows any subtype of the bound:

```
public void process(List<? extends Number> list){
```

```
for(Number n : list){
    //...
}
}
```

Here, a list can contain any type that extends a Number like Integer or extends it like BigDecimal. Calling methods on each element is type-safe since it is treated as a Number.

Lower Bounded Wildcards

The <? super T> sets a lower bound, specifying argument types that are supertypes of T:

```
public void copy(List<? super Number> dest, List<Number>
        src){
    dest.addAll(src);
}
```

Here, dest allows container types like List<? Super Number> (ex: List<Object>) since objects assignment compatible with supertypes is allowed.

Bounded wildcards are useful when the specific element types are unknown while ensuring certain guaranteed operations. This increases flexibility compared to rigid-type parameters.

Wildcards in Generics

Wildcards help make generics more powerful and flexible by enabling support for unknown type parameters. They allow writing highly reusable generic code that can work with a variety of type arguments.

Wildcard Types

A wildcard type is denoted using the '?' symbol. It represents an unknown type that is either read-only or write-only.

For example, a List with a wildcard type of '?' could hold elements of any unknown type:

```
List<?> list = new ArrayList<>();
```

This list can be passed around, but we cannot add to it since the element type is unknown. It allows only reading/consuming values generically.

Bounded Wildcards

Wildcards can be bounded to specify the unknown type is a subtype or supertype of a known type:

List<? extends Number> - Unknown type that must extend Number

List<? Super Integer> - Unknown supertype of Integer

Bounding provides context on allowable operations. For the first, only get() works assuming Number. The second allows add() of Integers.

Using Wildcards

Wildcards help design highly reusable methods that accept arguments with unknown type parameters:

```
public void process(List<?> list) {
  for(Object o : list)
    // do something
}
```

This processes any list generically without restrictions on element types.

They are also useful in collection APIs like addAll() that need to abstract over varying element types.

Compatibility

Wildcards enhance flexibility and compatibility in generics. For example, a copy method can accept lists with matching but unknown element types:

```
public static void copy(List<? extends E> from,
List<? super E> to) {
   to.addAll(from);
}
```

Without wildcards, this method would only work for lists with the exact same concrete type arguments.

Type Inference

The Java compiler automatically infers the appropriate wildcard types based on context. For example:

```
List<String> strings = new ArrayList<>();
List<Object> objects = strings;
```

Here, objects is inferred as List<? extends String> as only reading is allowed from it.

While wildcards increase flexibility, they also restrict certain operations since the actual type is unknown. Methods cannot generally return wildcard parameterized types.

Chapter 6: Functional Programming in Java

An Introduction to Lambda Expressions

What are Lambda Expressions?

Lambda expressions were introduced in Java 8 to support functional programming features in Java. Lambda expressions allow treating functionality as a method argument or code as data. They enable the implementation of functional interfaces more concisely without anonymous classes. A lambda expression is a non-named method that can be passed around and used without ever being declared or named. It removes a lot of syntactic noise involved in using interfaces and anonymous inner classes as callback definitions.

Lambda Syntax

Lambda expressions use the -> operator to separate the parameter list from the body of the expression. This is known as the lambda operator or arrow operator.

The general syntax of a lambda expression is:

(parameter types) -> { body }

For example, a lambda that takes an integer as a parameter and returns its square is:

(int x) -> { return x * x; }

If the body contains a single statement, return is optional, and braces {} are not required.

(int x) -> x * x

Type Inference

Lambda expressions don't require the lambda parameter types and return types to be defined explicitly. Java compiler performs type inference to determine types from context.

For example, in the following code, the compiler infers that the parameter is an Integer and the result is an Integer:

x -> x * x

Functional Interfaces

Lambda expressions were introduced mainly to provide small, anonymous inline implementations for functional interfaces. A functional interface is an interface that contains only one abstract method.

Examples of functional interfaces in Java are:

- Predicate<T> - evaluates a condition for objects of T type
- Consumer<T> - performs an action on objects of T type
- Function<T, R> - maps input of type T to output of type R

Prior to Java 8, functional interfaces had to be implemented using anonymous classes like:

```
new Predicate<String>() {
  public boolean test(String s) {
    return s.length() > 0;
  }
}
```

Now, with lambda expressions, they can be implemented much more succinctly as:

```
s -> s.length() > 0
```

Method References

In addition to lambda expressions, Java 8 also supports method references to refer to existing methods without rewriting the method implementation.

A method reference is a constant reference to a method that is being passed around like a lambda expression.

For example, a method reference to an existing isEmpty() method is:

```
String::isEmpty
```

This is semantically equivalent to:

```
(String s) -> s.isEmpty()
```

But reads better in a context like collections operations:

```
list.removeIf(String::isEmpty)
```

Multiple Lambda parameters

Lambdas can have multiple parameters separated by commas:

```
(int x, int y) -> x + y
```

Capturing outer scope variables

Lambdas can capture and use local variables from the enclosing scope:

```
int multiplier = 10;
list.forEach(x -> System.out.println(x * multiplier));
```

Here, the multiplier is effectively final, so it doesn't cause problematic side effects.

Generic type inference

Just like generic methods, lambdas also support generic type inference:

```
listOfStrings.forEach(string -> {
  List<Character> chars = new ArrayList<>();
  for(char c : string.toCharArray())
    chars.add(c);   });
```

Here, the generic type of List in chars is inferred from the type of string in the loop.

Method overloading resolution

When a lambda is passed as a method argument, Java resolves the overload based on the target signature matching the functional interface signature.

For example, in Collections. Sort (), the comparator is a functional interface, so lambda is inferred appropriately.

Applications of Lambda Expressions

Some common uses of lambda expressions are:

- As callback handler in Swing/FX event listeners
- Processing streams sequentially
- Implementing simple Runnable or callable tasks for threading
- Sorting/Searching collections using comparator lambdas
- Database querying using predicate lambdas

Lambda expressions make Java code more functional and concise by treating code as data. They have reduced the verbosity in functional interface usage and enabled new functional capabilities in existing class libraries.

Streams: Processing Collections More Elegantly

What are Streams?

Streams introduced in Java 8 provide a new abstraction for processing data sequentially and aggregate operations on them in a declarative way. A stream is not a data structure; instead, it relies on existing data structures but allows extracting and transforming elements from sources in a declarative manner.

Sources of Stream

Any data structure that supports iteration can serve as a source for a Stream. Some common examples are:

- Collections like List, Set, Map
- Arrays

- I/O resources like Files
- Generator functions

Streams vs Collections in Java

Streams and Collections are both core concepts in Java, but they serve distinct purposes and exhibit different behaviors. Collections, as their name implies, are essentially in-memory data structures, like lists, sets, or maps, that store elements. They allow operations that often modify the state of the collection itself. On the other hand, Streams don't hold data in the traditional sense. Instead, they are more like conduits that offer operations to access and transform elements on the fly, usually sourced from Collections or other data sources.

A salient difference arises in how they handle operations. Collections involve modifying their internal state when operations are performed on them. Streams, in contrast, primarily operate using non-mutating methods. This makes Streams inherently more favorable for concurrent or parallel operations, as they avoid the pitfalls of shared mutable state. Furthermore, Stream operations are designed to be chained, allowing multiple transformations to be executed sequentially in a pipeline. Unlike Collections, where each operation is typically executed independently and immediately, Streams defer execution, processing elements on-demand.

Stream Operations and Their Characteristics

Streams in Java are equipped with a range of both intermediate and terminal operations. Intermediate operations, such as **filter**, **map**, and **sorted**, return a new Stream. These operations are lazy, meaning they don't do any actual computation until a terminal operation demands results. This behavior is foundational to the efficiency of Streams, as it enables operations to be set up in advance, with actual computation deferred until genuinely required.

Terminal operations, like **forEach**, **count**, and **collect**, however, produce a result or a side-effect and mark the end of the Stream processing pipeline. Once a terminal operation is invoked, the stream is consumed, meaning it can't be reused.

One of the defining features of Streams is pipelining. By chaining together multiple intermediate operations, developers can craft intricate data flow pipelines. When a terminal operation is finally called, these operations are executed in sequence, processing the elements through the pipeline.

Lazy Evaluation and Optimization in Streams

The lazy nature of Streams brings about several benefits. Operations set up in a stream pipeline aren't executed immediately. Instead, they wait patiently until a terminal operation kickstarts the computation. This deferred execution model aids in conserving resources, executing computations only when results are genuinely necessary. Additionally, it paves the way for certain optimizations. For instance, Streams can employ short-circuiting, where computation ceases once the desired outcome is achieved, preventing unnecessary processing.

Parallel Streams and Their Advantages

Java Streams also provide support for parallel processing. By employing parallel streams, the source data can be divided into multiple sub-streams. These sub-streams are then processed concurrently, leveraging multiple threads. After processing, the results from the various sub-streams are aggregated. This model abstracts the intricacies of parallelization and thread coordination, presenting developers with a high-level, efficient mechanism for concurrent data processing. The result is a powerful combination of simplicity and performance, allowing for significant speed-ups, especially with large datasets.

Declarative vs Imperative

Streams make aggregation operations more declarative - concentrating on what rather than how. Passing lambda predicates and functions is more declarative than iterative looping.

This declarative nature makes code easier to read, reason about, and optimize, like enabling parallelism in certain cases.

Common Stream Operations: Filtering, Mapping, and Collecting

Filter Operation

The filter operation allows pruning a stream to only include elements matching a given predicate function. This is an intermediate operation that returns a new stream.

For example, to filter a list of names to only include names starting with 'A':

List<String> names = ... names.stream().filter(name -> name.startsWith("A"))

This filter returns a new stream containing only those elements of the original stream where the predicate name is.startsWith("A") returned true.

The filter predicate can reference immutable state and effectively final local variables from enclosing scope. However, it should not perform any side-effects like mutating external objects or variables.

Some key properties of filter operation:

The **filter** operation is an integral part of Java's Stream API, allowing developers to sift through data and retain only those elements that satisfy a given condition or predicate. Here are the key characteristics of the **filter** operation:

1. Laziness: One of the most defining attributes of the filter operation is its lazy nature. When filter is invoked, it doesn't immediately evaluate the predicate against the elements. Instead, it sets up a condition that will be checked later, precisely when a terminal operation is called on the stream. This ensures that computations are deferred and only executed when results are truly necessary.
2. Chainability: The filter operation can be seamlessly chained with other intermediate operations in a Stream pipeline. This means you can have multiple filter calls one after the other or interleave them with other operations like map or sorted. This allows for the construction of complex data processing pipelines that are both efficient and readable.
3. Short-Circuiting: While the filter operation itself doesn't inherently short-circuit, its behavior in combination with certain terminal operations can lead to short-circuiting. For instance, when combined with findFirst in a Stream, the processing will stop as soon as an element that satisfies the predicate is found. However, it's crucial to note that the claim "Short-circuits if predicate ever returns false" is slightly misleading. The filter operation will evaluate the predicate for all elements when required, but the resultant stream will only contain those elements for which the predicate returns true.

Common uses of filters include:

The **filter** operation finds extensive use in various scenarios to refine and process data. Some of its common applications include:

1. Criteria-based Extraction: One of the primary uses of filter is to extract elements from a collection based on specific criteria. For instance, you might want to retrieve all even numbers from a list or select all strings of a certain length.
2. Purging Null or Empty Values: In many data processing tasks, it's crucial to cleanse the data of null or empty values to prevent potential errors further down the line. Using filter, you can easily remove such undesired elements from your data stream.
3. Selective Inclusion Based on Object Properties: When dealing with streams of objects, the filter operation proves invaluable in selecting objects based on their attributes. For instance, in a stream of Person objects, you might want to filter out all persons below a certain age or those who live in a specific city.

Map Operation

The map operation transforms each element in the stream through the mapping function provided and returns a new stream containing the results. It applies the function to every element of the stream.

For example, to extract the first name from Person objects:

List<Person> people = ... people.stream().map(person -> person.getFirstName())

This maps each Person to their first name property value and returns a Stream of Strings containing first names.

The mapping function must be non-interfering - producing results based only on its input argument without side effects.

Understanding the Map Operation in Java Streams

In the world of Java Streams, the map operation plays a pivotal role, enabling developers to transform data seamlessly. At its core, the map operation allows for the application of a function to each element in the stream, producing a new stream that holds the transformed elements.

One of the intriguing characteristics of the map operation is its lazy execution. This means that when the map method is invoked on a stream, the actual computation doesn't happen immediately. Instead, the mapping function waits in a dormant state and is only activated when a terminal operation is called on the stream. This behavior ensures efficient resource usage, only carrying out computations when the results are genuinely needed.

Another key aspect of the map operation is its flexibility concerning the type of output stream. The type of elements in the resulting stream is determined by the return type of the mapping function. This flexibility means that the map operation can not only alter the value of elements but can also change their type. For example, a stream of strings can be transformed into a stream of integers based on some conversion logic.

In practical scenarios, the map operation finds a plethora of applications. One common use case is the extraction of specific properties from objects. Suppose you have a stream of Person objects, and you're interested only in their names. Using the map operation, you can extract just the names, resulting in a stream of strings. Another frequent application is the transformation of one type to another. This could involve converting a stream of numbers into their string representations or vice versa. Furthermore, the map operation is instrumental in formatting or modifying elements. This might involve adjusting the format of date strings, capitalizing words, or any other form of data transformation.

FlatMap Operation

The flatMap operation differs from the map in that it further flattens the elements of the outer stream by mapping them to inner streams and then concatenating all inner streams.

For example, to extract all course titles from a list of Student objects:

List<Student> students = ... students.stream() .flatMap(s -> s.getCourses().stream()) .map(Course::getTitle)

Here, each Student is mapped to a Stream of Courses. These inner streams are then flattened to a single stream of Courses, which is further mapped to titles.

FlatMap is useful when elements need to be transformed into multiple elements or traverse hierarchical/nested structures like trees.

FlatMap Operation in Java Streams

In Java Streams, the flatMap operation stands out as a specialized and versatile tool tailored for handling nested or multi-level data structures. While the map operation is geared towards applying transformations to individual elements, flatMap delves deeper, unraveling and streamlining nested structures into a single unified stream.

A prominent characteristic of flatMap is its ability to flatten nested streams. When faced with a stream whose elements are themselves streams or collections, using flatMap can consolidate these into one continuous stream. This ability to transform a Stream<Stream<T>> or a Stream<List<T>> into a Stream<T> is particularly useful in scenarios where the data is inherently hierarchical or multi-layered.

Another essential property of flatMap is its applicability in situations where a single input element can map to multiple output values. Instead of producing a nested structure, flatMap ensures that the output remains as a single, cohesive stream. This behavior ensures that subsequent operations on the stream can proceed without the need to navigate layers of nesting.

Just like the map operation, the type of elements in the resulting stream after applying flatMap is not arbitrary. It's intrinsically tied to the element type of the inner stream or collection that flatMap processes. This implies that the transformation function supplied to flatMap can, and often does, change the type of elements in the stream.

In terms of practical applications, flatMap has a wide array of uses. For instance, when working with nested collections, such as lists of lists, flatMap can flatten these into a singular list, making further processing more straightforward. Additionally, in the context of Java's Optional class, flatMap serves as a means to unpack and process values, especially when these optional values are themselves containers or can result in other optional values. Another intriguing application is in the traversal of object graphs, where an object might contain references to other collections or streams of objects. By employing flatMap, developers can traverse and process these graphs seamlessly without getting bogged down by the intricacies of the nested structures.

Collect Operation

The collect operation accumulates the output of stream pipeline execution and returns the result. It is a terminal operation that causes the stream to be consumed.

It is the only stream operation that can produce a non-stream result. The result can be collected into Collections, summaries like counting, summarization, etc.

For example, collecting names into a List:

List<String> names list = names.stream().collect(Collectors.toList());

And counting names:

long count = names.stream().collect(Collectors.counting());

Java provides collector implementations for common use cases in the Collectors class like:

- toList(), toSet() - collect to Collection
- joining() - concatenating elements
- averaging(), summing() - numerical aggregation
- groupingBy(), partitioningBy() - grouping streams

Custom collectors can also be created when the built-in collectors don't meet the need.

Collect is typically the last operation in the pipeline as it concludes the aggregation result. But it can also act as an intermediate operation to collect results at intermediate stages.

Some common uses of collect include:

- Accumulating stream results into collections
- Producing summaries like counts, sums, averages
- Grouping elements based on classifiers
- Extracting summations extremes from streams

Chapter 7: Java Features Overview

Exception Handling: Dealing with the Unexpected

What are Exceptions?

In programming, exceptions refer to problems, errors, or other unexpected events that occur when a program is executed. These issues are called "exceptions" because they represent situations that are outside of the normal or expected flow of the program. Some common types of exceptions include:

- NullPointerException - Occurs when trying to use an object reference that is null.
- ArrayIndexOutOfBoundsException - Thrown when trying to access an array element with an illegal index (either negative or greater than or equal to the array size).
- ClassCastException - Occurs when an attempt is made to cast an object to a subclass that it is not compatible with.
- FileNotFoundException - Thrown when attempting to open a file that does not exist or cannot be found.
- SQLException - Indicates a problem or error related to working with SQL databases using JDBC.
- IOException - Signals that an input/output exception of some kind has occurred, such as being unable to open or read from a file.

There are many other kinds of exceptions that represent different types of unexpected errors or events that can occur. Some exceptions are low-level and represent system failures or API issues, while others may indicate logical errors in application code.

Dealing with Exceptions

When exceptions occur, they will often cause the program to crash and exit unexpectedly if nothing is done to catch and handle them properly. However, Java provides an exception-handling mechanism to deal with errors gracefully instead of causing failures.

The basic process in Java for handling exceptions works as follows:

- Code that may throw an exception is wrapped in a try block. This is where the work happens.

- The catch block specifies which exception type it wants to catch. It is where the handling code goes.
- Finally, blocks execute whether or not an exception occurs, allowing cleanup code to run.

For example:

```
try {
  // code that could throw exceptions
} catch (FileNotFoundException e) {
  // handling code
} catch (IOException e) {
  // handling code
} finally {
  // cleanup code
}
```

This allows the program to continue executing even if a FileNotFoundException or IOException occurs. The catch blocks define what to do, like displaying an error message to the user. Finally, blocks run cleanup logic after try/catch executions are complete.

Checked vs Unchecked Exceptions

In Java, exceptions are classified as either checked or unchecked. Checked exceptions are usually those that represent problems external to the application code, such as IOException or SQLException. These are "checked" at compile time - methods must either catch these exceptions or specify that they may be thrown so that the calling code is aware.

Unchecked exceptions typically represent logic errors within code, such as NullPointerException, ArrayIndexOutOfBoundsException, or ClassCastException. These types of exceptions are generally not specified in method signatures since they represent bugs in code that should be fixed. Unchecked exceptions are not "checked" at compile time.

To summarize exception handling:

- Try blocks contain code that may throw exceptions
- Catch blocks handle specific exception types
- Finally, blocks run cleanup code regardless of exceptions
- Checked exceptions must be caught or specified in method signatures
- Unchecked exceptions represent logic errors and are not specified

Proper exception handling makes Java programs more robust by allowing errors and problems to be handled gracefully instead of causing crashes or failures. It is considered a best practice to always catch and handle exceptions appropriately based on the context and requirements.

Java Collections: Lists, Sets, and Maps

What are Collections?

In programming, it is very common to need to work with multiple objects or values at the same time. For example, you may want to store a list of customer names or keep track of invoices for many orders. Organizing and managing groups of related objects is where collections in Java are invaluable. Collections provide built-in ways to store, retrieve, manipulate, and search collections of objects. The Java Collections Framework defines several core collection interfaces like List, Set, and Map. It also provides classes that implement these interfaces to handle the low-level details for you.

Using collections allows code to operate on entire groups of objects together in a very clean and organized way. Things like iterating, searching, adding/removing items, and sorting becomes easy and standardized across collections. This chapter will explore some of the most common collection interfaces and how to apply them effectively in software development with Java.

Lists

The List interface defines a collection that maintains ordering and allows duplicate elements. Some key List implementations are:

- ArrayList - Resizable array-backed implementation. Fast indexed access, but slower adds/removes.
- LinkedList - Doubly-linked list. Slow indexed access but faster adds/removes.
- Vector - Legacy synchronized list. Not recommended in most cases.

Elements can be accessed by numeric index like an array. Some common List methods include:

- add(obj) - Add object to the end of the list
- get(index) - Get the object at the specified index
- remove(index) - Remove and return the object at an index
- size() - Get the number of elements in the list

Lists are very useful for maintaining ordered sequences of objects where duplicates are allowed and indexed access is important.

Sets

The Set interface ensures uniqueness by not allowing duplicates and does not maintain ordering. Specific Set implementations include:

- HashSet - Stores elements in a HashMap for quick lookups. Very fast performance.

- LinkedHashSet - Maintains insertion order when iterating. Slightly slower than HashSet.
- TreeSet - Stores in a sorted binary tree. Slowest but provides ordered elements.

Typical Set features involve adding/removing unique elements like:
- add(obj) - Add an object, returning true/false if added
- contains(obj) - Check if the set contains the object
- remove(obj) - Remove and return object, returning false if not present

Sets are useful for ensuring uniqueness among stored elements efficiently. Common uses include tracking unique words in a document or filtering duplicate entries from a collection.

Maps

The Map interface stores objects in key-value pairs for fast retrieval by key. Common Map classes are:

- HashMap - Default Map implementation using a hash table for key/value storage.
- LinkedHashMap - Preserves insertion order during iteration in addition to key-based access.
- TreeMap - Stores keys in a red-black tree for ordered iteration and lookup based on natural or custom sorting.

Maps allow accessing values by key through methods like:
- put(key, value) - Add key/value pair to map
- get(key) - Return value associated with a key
- containsKey(key) - Check if the map contains the key
- remove(key) - Remove key/value pair if the key exists

Maps provide an elegant way to associate objects together and look up values using deterministic keys. Common uses include caching data, indexing database entries by ID, and storing application configurations.

Java Tips and Best Practices

Some best practices to follow when using collections include:
- Choosing the appropriate collection type based on your specific needs.
- Using generics to specify the concrete type of objects in collections for type safety.
- Iterating with for-each loops or Iterator objects instead of indexed iteration when possible.
- Synchronizing collection access in multi-threaded code.

- Defensively copying collection instances when returning from methods to avoid mutations to the internal state.

Following these tips can help maximize performance and prevent bugs when applying collections effectively in Java code. Understanding common patterns and idioms is vital to solving many real-world programming problems with collections.

Concurrency and Multi-threading: Harnessing the Power of Modern Processors

Modern computer processors are capable of executing multiple tasks concurrently through the use of multiple CPU cores. This allows computers to maximize throughput and efficiently perform many operations at the same time. Concurrency in programming leverages this capability through the simultaneous execution of independent threads. Threads are lightweight processes that can run independently and concurrently within a larger application. Code that is not inherently sequential can often benefit greatly from being broken out into concurrent threads of execution. For example, downloading multiple files at once, encoding video frames in parallel, or performing background database operations asynchronously.

Properly using concurrency allows programs to take advantage of modern hardware and feel more responsive by overlapping I/O with computation. However, special care must be taken to correctly synchronize access to shared data between threads. When not managed properly, concurrency can also introduce difficult bugs from race conditions and deadlocks.

The Java Approach

From early on, Java was designed with concurrency as a core concern. It provides robust thread management and synchronization utilities to simplify concurrent programming compared to lower-level languages.

The basic threading model in Java revolves around the Thread class. By extending Thread or implementing Runnable, a class can define the code executed in a concurrent thread context when started. Common features of Thread include:

- Start () - Begin thread execution.
- Run () - Implemented entry point for thread task.
- Join () - Wait for thread completion before continuing.
- Sleep (millis) - Pause the thread for a time period.
- Yield () - Signal willingness to relinquish current use of CPU.

However, directly managing threads can easily lead to issues, so higher-level concurrency utilities are recommended:

- ExecutorService - Manages ThreadPools and simplifies asynchronous/parallel task submission.
- Callable/Future - Provides checked asynchronous execution with return values.
- BlockingQueue - First-in, first-out producer/consumer design pattern.

Synchronization

With concurrency comes the need to synchronize access to shared mutable states across threads. The synchronized keyword in Java can lock entire method sections or code blocks to exclude other thread entries until unlocked. Also useful are atomic object wrappers like:

- AtomicInteger - Thread-safe counter alternative to int.
- AtomicBoolean - Thread-safe boolean flag.
- AtomicReference - Safe reference updates.

Low-level locks allow finer-grained locking of objects or code regions with try/finally via ReentrantLock. These synchronization primitives prevent critical sections from overlapping and introducing race conditions or inconsistencies.

Best Practices

Some concurrency best practices include designing for:

- Independence - Minimize shared mutable state between threads.
- Isolation - Wrap shared access in synchronization.
- Limited scope - Minimize lock holding durations.
- Non-blocking - Use concurrent queue patterns where possible.
- Progress - Ensure threads cannot deadlock or livelock.
- Recovery - Consider exception-handling strategies in concurrent contexts.
- Performance - Profile and optimize bottlenecks.

When applied judiciously, concurrency can significantly improve the performance and responsiveness of Java programs. With care taken for thread safety and synchronization, the full power of multi-core systems can be unleashed. Understanding the Java primitives for managing threads forms a strong foundation for building highly concurrent systems.

Chapter 8: Advanced Java Concepts

Modules: Organizing and Scaling Your Java Projects

As Java applications grow in size and complexity, proper organization and modularization of the codebase becomes crucial. Left unmanaged, a large monolithic codebase can become difficult to understand, update, and maintain over time. The module system introduced in Java 9 provides an elegant way to tackle these scaling challenges.

What are Modules?

Module Basics

In Java, a module is simply a logical separation of code into independent units. It allows you to compartmentalize your code into cohesive packages that represent certain functionality or domains. Each module is self-contained and only exposes certain APIs to other parts of the codebase via its public interfaces.

Modules are declared using a simple module-info.java file at the root of the source directories. This file defines the module name and exports/opens certain packages. For example:

```
module com.example.app {
    exports com.example.app.controllers;
}
```

Here, we define a module named 'com.example.app' that exports the 'controllers' package, making its public classes and interfaces available to other modules.

Under the hood, modules result in separate class loaders so that classes from different modules don't conflict. This modularity helps avoid problems like naming collisions and greatly simplifies dependency management across codebases and applications.

Key Concepts in Modules

Some key concepts related to Java modules:

- Modules - Logical separation of code into independent building blocks

- Requires - Dependencies between modules defined via 'requires' keyword
- Exports - Control which packages are visible to dependent modules
- Opens - Allow reflective access to classes even in non-exported packages
- Services - Publishing and consuming services via the ServiceLoader interface
- Provides/Uses - Resolving module dependencies via services

By exposing only intended contracts through exports and requirements, modules allow the safe composition of independently developed and maintained components.

Application of Modules

Real World Uses

Let's look at some real-world scenarios where modules really help:

Application Framework as Module:

Core framework code can be extracted as a module that cleanly separates application code from framework code. The framework module exports only the interfaces needed by the application code.

Plugins/Extensions:

Rewritable modules allow others to extend functionality through plug-ins and extensions that require add-to-original modules functionality.

Library/Utility Modules:

Common utilities, database libraries, etc., can be packaged as modular JARs that export only agreed-upon APIs for safe consumption.

Microservices:

Each microservice can be defined as a module boundary with strict requirements/export definitions between autonomous services.

IDE/Build Tools Integration:

Modules define explicit compile-time and run-time dependencies that building/packaging tools can leverage for tasks like building, testing, packaging, and deploying modules.

The key benefits of modularizing Java code include reduced coupling, improved readability, testability, upgradeability, and overall manageability of large and complex codebases over time. Though the use of modules is optional in Java, they offer immense promise for future-proofing applications as systems evolve.

Defining Modules

Let's look at how to construct modules in practice:

1. Define module-info files:

As mentioned earlier, each module is declared using the module-info.java file at the root of the source directory.

2. Structure code into packages:

Group related functionality into cohesive packages under the module.

3. Specify required clauses:

Define other module dependencies via the required keyword.

4. Export/Open packages:

Use exports/opens to selectively publish APIs for external use.

5. Resolve dependencies:

Address any dependency conflicts or issues during compilation.

6. Build and package modules:

Build tooling like Maven can produce modular JARs and modular layouts.

7. Run modular applications:

Use the java command with --module-path and --modules flags to run modular apps.

With a little refactoring effort upfront, modules can pay huge dividends as code evolves from small to very large scales over time.

Java modules provide an effective way to organize large and complex codebases into cohesive bundles. By reducing tight coupling between components and defining explicit dependencies, modules greatly aid code readability, maintainability, and scalability. While optional currently, modules enable future-proofing Java applications as a preferred approach for componentization going forward. When applied correctly, modules can unlock immense gains for projects of all sizes.

Annotations: Adding Metadata to Your Code

Annotations

Annotations in Java are a form of metadata that can be embedded directly in code using the '@' symbol. They allow attaching additional information to various language elements like classes, methods, fields, etc., without modifying their behavior. This metadata can then be consumed and acted upon through reflection at both compile-time and run-time.

Annotations provide a non-intrusive way to enrich code with extra semantic information that can help tools, frameworks, and developers better understand code purpose and intent. Common uses include validation, serialization, injection, and more. Though optional, annotations streamline many development tasks and improve overall productivity.

Builtin Annotations

The Java platform ships with several useful predefined annotations:
- @Override: Ensures a method properly overrides a superclass one by throwing a compilation error if not
- @Deprecated: Marks a symbol as deprecated and instructs users against its usage. Generates warning message during compilation.
- @SuppressWarnings: Suppresses specific compilation warnings like deprecated, unused, etc., by attaching to fields, methods, or classes.
- @FunctionalInterface: identifies a functional interface type - an interface with a single abstract method that can be assigned to lambda expressions.
- @SafeVarargs: Prevents unintended warnings caused by type erasure due to polymorphic array parameters in generics.
- @repeateable: Indicates an annotation can be applied multiple times to the same program element.

Custom Annotations

For custom behavior not covered by default, annotations can also be defined through a simple annotation type.

For example:
```
@Retention(RetentionPolicy.RUNTIME)
@Target(ElementType.METHOD)
public @interface LogCall {
   String calledBy();
}
```
Here, we define a custom @LogCall annotation specifying its target, retention policy, and the calledBy() attribute it contains. This annotation can then be used on methods:
```
@LogCall(calledBy="doSomething()")
public void myMethod() {
   //...
}
```
Reflection is then used at runtime to dynamically access annotated elements and their metadata. This opens up annotations to a whole world of possibilities.

Applying Annotations

Annotations have many real-world applications:

- Dependency Injection: Frameworks like Spring use annotations to declaratively wire beans and service endpoints.
- Validation: JSR-303 validations add constraints via annotations processed by Bean Validation.
- JSON/XML Conversion: Jackson/Gson examines annotations to automate POJO to JSON conversion.
- Caching: Implementations use annotations to mark cache-eligible methods.
- Logging: Frameworks leverage annotations to parameterize logging behavior.
- Testing: JUnit uses annotations for setup/teardown and ignoring test cases.
- Documentation: Javadoc extracts annotations for API documentation.

Through judicious use, annotations significantly reduce code complexity by removing metadata from the implementation itself. They enforce the separation of concerns as an additional layer on top of the code. Overall, this makes applications more robust, lightweight, and extensible.

Defining Custom Annotations

To define a reusable custom annotation, follow these steps:

1. Choose an appropriate retention policy
2. Designate target elements - types, methods, etc.
3. Define the annotation interface with attributes
4. Add default values for attributes if needed
5. Specify runtime retention for reflective access
6. Process annotations within the code
7. Consider repeatable if multiple instances are allowed
8. Document usage through JavaDocs
9. Package the annotation for external use
10. Provide tooling/APIs to leverage annotation

With care and planning, custom annotations create powerful abstractions over code that are self-documenting and aid many automated tasks.

Best Practices

Some best practices when using annotations:

- Use only for metadata, not program logic
- Keep small, focused and avoid multiple nested annotations
- Choose targets wisely based on semantic meaning
- Default/repeatable policies, where applicable
- Document thoroughly with JavaDocs

- Validate annotations during compilation
- Thoroughly test runtime behavior
- Version annotations with care during changes
- Avoid abuse that harms code readability

When applied judiciously, annotations are a highly effective technique to enrich Java code with semantics. They significantly aid the readability, automation, and maintenance of large modern applications.

Java I/O: Interacting with External Data

No Java program is complete without the ability to interact with external data sources like files, network endpoints, databases, etc. The Java platform provides robust and flexible I/O capabilities through its java.io package and associated classes for working with streams of data at varying levels of abstraction.

Core I/O Classes

Some core classes that form the building blocks of Java I/O include:

- File: Represents files and directories on the local filesystem.
- InputStream: Read-only sequence of bytes from a source (Files, network, etc).
- OutputStream: Write-only sequence of bytes to a sink (Files, network, etc).
- Reader: Read-only sequence of characters from a character-based source.
- Writer: Write-only sequence of characters to a character-based sink.
- Buffered*: Wraps an I/O stream/reader to provide buffering capabilities.

Using these classes either directly or via convenience wrappers, Java can interact with local files, network endpoints, database tables/records, and more.

Streams vs. Reader/Writer

The key difference between Streams and Reader/Writer classes is:

- Streams deal with sequences of raw bytes, agnostic of character encoding.
- Readers/Writers work at a higher character abstraction layer using a specified character encoding like UTF-8 to translate bytes to characters and vice versa.

For text-based files using encodings, Readers/Writers are preferred over raw Input/OutputStreams. Streams are useful for binary data or when encoding is unknown.

Working with Files

Common file-handling operations include:

- Create/Open: File and RandomAccessFile classes
- Read: Using FileReader/BufferedReader for text; FileInputStream for binary
- Write: FileWriter/BufferedWriter; FileOutputStream
- Operations: rename(), delete(), length(), canRead/Write() etc.

For example, to read the entire contents of a file:

BufferedReader br = new BufferedReader(new FileReader("file.txt"));
String line;
while((line = br.readLine()) != null) {
  //process line
}

Java 7+ brought many conveniences like try-with-resources and NIO.2 for file system navigation/watching capabilities.

Network I/O

URL-based classes enable fetching resources over HTTP/HTTPS protocols:

- URL: location representation
- URLConnection: obtain streams for a URL
- HttpURLConnection: extended connection for HTTP verbs

For raw socket communication:

- ServerSocket listens for client connections
- Socket for a client connecting/communicating with the server
- Datastreams provide a common interface over network/file streams.

Database Access

For relational databases, the ubiquitous standard is JDBC - the Java Database Connectivity API.

It defines interfaces and classes to connect to RDBMS, execute SQL queries, and retrieve/manipulate results using:

- DriverManager: loads appropriate driver class
- Connection: represents a live connection to DB
- Statement: executes basic SQL statements
- PreparedStatement: for parameterized query execution
- ResultSet: fetches data from queries row-by-row

ORMs like Hibernate abstract over JDBC for object-relational mapping.

NoSQL stores often provide their own Java driver implementations. MongoDB, for instance, uses a robust driver API for operations over data collections.

Overall, I/O provides Java with versatile connectivity across the board - making data availability a core language capability. When combined with streams and appropriate wrappers, it enables clean, efficient information flow in programs.

Best Practices

Some best practices for reliable, efficient, and maintainable Java I/O include:

- Close resources explicitly in final blocks
- Wrap streams in Buffered variants for substantial performance gains
- Leverage try-with-resources where possible for auto-closing
- Use character streams for text, binary for unknown data
- Connection pooling for database access
- Asynchronous I/O for non-blocking network ops
- Validate user inputs before parsing
- Consider serialization for persistent object storage
- Compress/encrypt where applicable before transmitting

Properly implementing these practices eliminates resource leaks while optimizing throughput. The rich I/O facilities in Java combined with diligent coding make for robust data-driven applications.

Chapter 9: Real-World Java Development

Building a CRUD Application: From Start to Finish

Planning the Application

The first step in building any software application is planning. For a CRUD application, we need to determine what data we will manage and how users will interact with it.

For this bookstore application, we identified that books will be the main data entity. Each book will have fields for title, author, price, and quantity available. These translate directly into columns in the database table that will store book records.

Next, we considered the basic functionality users need. At a minimum, they should be able to:

- View a list of all books
- Add a new book
- View/edit an individual book's details
- Delete a book

These operations map to the standard CRUD operations - Read (view list), Create (add new), Update (edit), and Delete. Additional features like searching and sorting could be expanded on later.

Finally, we thought about how this will be delivered. A web application using JSP/Servlets is a common way to build CRUD systems. Users will interact through web pages displayed in a browser. This allows accessing the application from anywhere without installing additional software.

With the planning done, we had the foundation to start development.

Setting Up the Development Environment

For a Java web application, we need a server environment to run the application code and a persistence layer to store data. We chose Apache Tomcat as our server since it is a lightweight and popular open-source Java Servlet container. It was downloaded and configured on our development machines. For the database, H2 was selected as it is an in-memory SQL database ideal for development/testing. Its JDBC driver was also downloaded. To connect Tomcat and H2, we added the required JDBC libraries to Tomcat's classpath. This allows our Java code to communicate with the database. H2 has a built-in browser-based console to view and manipulate data. We used it to create the 'books' table with the four book fields as columns. This completed the basic infrastructure preparation.

Creating the Model Layer

Next, we implemented the model layer that represents our application's data. This included:

1. Book entity class: A simple POJO mapping to the database table with fields and getter/setter methods
2. DAO interfaces: Defined database access methods like findAll(), save(), update(), delete()
3. DAO implementations: Contain JDBC code to execute CRUD SQL and return results

The DAOs abstracted JDBC for cleaner code. Utility methods like connection opening/closing were also created.

To summarize, the model layer focuses on managing the data and interacts with the database infrastructure behind a clean interface. Its role is to retrieve and persist Book objects.

Building the View Layer

JSP allows the creation of attractive and dynamic web pages simply. We designed the view layer to:

1. Books.jsp - Display all books in a table with edit/delete links
2. and add books.jsp - Form to add a new book with submission to a servlet
3. editBook.jsp - Pre-populate form with book details for updating
4. message.jsp - Display status/errors returned from servlets

Simple HTML constructs, JSP expressions to embed Java variables, and SQL tags to iterate over data allowed building these pages quickly.

We followed best practices like separating presentation from logic, using consistent formatting/ styling, and keeping pages focused on a single task. The result is cleanly designed templated content for users to interact with.

Implementing the Controller Layer

Servlets act as controllers that bridge the view and model layers. We implemented:

1. BookServlet - Handle HTTP requests, call DAO methods, forward to views
2. AddBookServlet - Accept form data, save to database, show success/error

3. EditBookServlet - Update existing book details from the form submit
4. DeleteBookServlet - Remove a book record by id

Servlets validate input, interact with the DAO layer as needed, and then dispatch to appropriate JSP views. Parameters are passed between requests using the HTTP session.

Finally, utility classes were written for common tasks like request handling user input validation. They reduce redundant code across servlets.

Integrated Testing

Thorough testing ensures quality and prevents regressions. We covered:

- Model layer tests: Use JUnit to test DAO functionality independently of other layers
- Controller layer tests: Mock model interactions, validate servlet responses
- Integration tests: Mimic real usage with edge cases by making full HTTP requests

Continuous integration using Jenkins automates running the full test suite on code changes. This lets developers focus on features while knowing existing logic is unchanged.

The testing establishes trust in the application to handle real-world usage reliably as features are added over time.

Putting it All Together

To launch the finished application:

1. Create war file packaging classes, JSPs, dependencies
2. Deploy war to the Tomcat server
3. Access the homepage and try all CRUD operations
4. Integrate with continuous delivery using Jenkins
5. Release version 1.0 of the bookstore app

The completed project showcases applying core Java technologies end-to-end. It demonstrates architecture best practices like separation of concerns, unit testing, and extensibility at each layer to create a robust application.

The examples and explanations give readers practical knowledge to develop their own functional and maintainable CRUD systems using Java/JSP for real business needs, and learning objectives are fully covered.

Connecting Java with Databases

Choosing a Database

The first step in connecting a Java application to persistent data storage is selecting an appropriate database. There are several options to choose from:

- Relational Databases: Like MySQL, Oracle, PostgreSQL - Store data in tables with rows and columns. Support structured querying via SQL.
- Non-Relational Databases: Like MongoDB, Cassandra - Flexible document or key-value data models. Distributed computing oriented.
- In-Memory Databases: Like H2, HSQLDB is primarily for development/testing. Data resides only in RAM.

For most Java enterprise applications, a relational database provides the right balance of structure, performance, and functionality. The two most common choices are MySQL for open-source and Oracle for large commercial projects.

Key factors in deciding are data model needs, query requirements, scale expectations, budget, and vendor support availability. Relational databases excel when data can be organized into logical relationships.

Setting Up the Database

Once the database is selected, it needs to be installed and configured for use with Java code.

For MySQL, the server software is downloaded, installed, and started. A default database and user account are also created during setup.

For connectivity, the MySQL JDBC driver JAR file must be placed on the Java classpath. This is typically done by copying it to the Tomcat/lib folder for web apps.

Setting an environment variable for the database URL like:

export DB_URL=jdbc:mysql://localhost:3306/books

Allows programs to connect without hardcoding server details.

To confirm installation and access, tools like MySQL Workbench can be used to interact with the database in the exact same way Java code will - submitting queries and viewing results.

This verifies the database is ready to use as a persistent data store for the Java application.

Connecting with JDBC

The Java Database Connectivity (JDBC) API provides a standard way for Java code to communicate with all major relational databases through SQL. JDBC follows the typical data access steps:

1. Load driver class
```
Class.forName("com.mysql.cj.jdbc.Driver");
```

2. Get a database connection
```
Connection
        conn=DriverManager.getConnection(DB_URL,DB_USERNAME
        ,DB_PASSWORD);
```

3. Create SQL statement
```
String sql = "SELECT * FROM books";
```

4. Execute statement
```
Statement stmt = conn.createStatement();
```

5. Process ResultSet
```
ResultSet rs = stmt.executeQuery(sql);
```

6. Close resources
```
rs.close();
stmt.close();
conn.close();
```

While simple, raw JDBC is verbose and error-prone. Most code delegates data access to specialized classes instead.

Simplifying Data Access

Code to interact with the database is abstracted behind DAOs (Data Access Objects). DAOs provide cleaner interfaces focused on core data operations.

For example, a BookDAO may define methods like:
```
Public interface BookDAO {
  List<Book> findAll();
  Book findById(long id);
  void save(Book book);
  void update(Book book);
  void deleteById(long id);
}
```

Their implementations handle all JDBC calls without cluttering other classes.

Frameworks like Spring JDBC Template provide pre-built DAO functionality with only domain logic code specific to each entity. This drastically simplifies the data access code.

Libraries like Hibernate take it further by automatically mapping objects to database tables and handling SQL under the hood completely transparently.

Overall Benefits

The major benefits of using a standard relational database with JDBC/DAO approach include:

- Formal data structure with integrity constraints enforced by the database itself.
- Persistent storage of objects independent of the application lifecycle.
- Isolation from specific database versions through abstraction layers.
- Leverage decades of database optimization, security hardening, and scalability features.
- Easy migration between database vendors if needed.
- Industry-standard skillset applicable industry-wide.

By understanding the fundamentals of selecting and connecting to a database through JDBC, developers are equipped to design and build robust, scalable Java enterprise applications backed by powerful yet approachable persistence capabilities.

Best Practices: Writing Clean, Maintainable Code

Object-Oriented Design Principles

Object-oriented design promotes code organization, reuse, and extensibility through concepts like encapsulation, loose coupling, and high cohesion. Encapsulation groups related data and behavior within classes. Exposing only necessary public methods hides implementation details. This allows flexibility to change internals without affecting other code. Loose coupling minimizes interdependencies between classes. For example, interfaces can be implemented instead of concrete classes, so classes are only aware of method signatures, not implementations.

High cohesion means classes have a well-defined, narrowly focused responsibility. There should be a clear relationship between a class's methods and attributes. This makes classes easier to understand and reuse. Proper utilization of objects, interfaces, abstraction, and other core OO principles results in code that ages better when requirements change over time.

Separation of Concerns

Large applications involve many distinct areas of functionality. Separation of concerns modularity principles tackle complexity by dividing code into logical sections, each of which has a clear purpose.

Common separations include:

- Model - Represent and interact with application data
- Controller - Handle user input and flow of control
- View - Generate output and display UI

Separating the implementation of distinct activities makes code more readable and maintainable by developers. It also allows teams to work independently on isolated concerns.

Naming Conventions

Meaningful identifier names are crucial for comprehension. Consistent conventions like:

- Classes as nouns (User, Product)
- Methods as verbs (save(), delete())
- Variables like userName rather than u
- Constants as ALL_CAPS
- Packages as lowercase with periods (com.my company.app)

Allow scanning code and immediate understanding purpose with minimal additional context needed. Prefixes/suffixes help differentiate types like DAO vs DTO.

Modularity and Reusability

Extensible design means code can be adapted easily to changing situations. Some techniques include:

- Unix philosophy of small, independent, single-purpose modules
- Component-based architecture with well-defined interfaces
- Avoid duplicated logic with utility/helper classes
- Use templating to support common use cases in a customizable way
- Favor composition over inheritance where possible

This makes code easier to understand at a glance, as well as reuse parts to create new functionality quicker.

Error Handling

Defensive coding anticipates errors to improve reliability. Techniques such as:

- Validate user inputs with format/range checks
- Add parameter checking in public methods
- Handle exceptions gracefully with descriptive messages
- Isolate failure-prone code in try-catch blocks
- Return error codes or enums instead of exceptions for non-critical issues

Help applications withstand unintended usage without crashing. It also eases debugging when problems do occur.

Testing

No code is bug-free initially. Automated testing provides confidence through each change:

- Unit Tests - Check individual classes/functions in isolation
- Integration Tests - Verify components work together correctly
- System Tests - Validate end-to-end scenarios
- Contract Tests - Ensure public interfaces function as expected
- Regression Tests - Catch when prior code breaks unexpectedly

Well-tested code releases anxieties about unintended consequences of changes and allows refactoring fearlessly. There are frameworks like JUnit, Mockito, and Selenium to support different testing levels.

Documentation

Self-documenting code minimizes the need for comments by following conventions. But documentation also includes:

- Module/class summaries explaining purpose and usage
- Javadocs explaining public APIs
- Design documents for complex algorithms
- Configuration files for deployment/runtime
- Changelogs with release notes

Documenting assumptions, caveats, improvements, or why certain decisions were made benefits future understanding. Standards like Markdown optimize readability. Overall, well-documented code acts as a knowledge base for others.

By applying these practices comprehensively, development teams can collaboratively produce Java code that withstands testing, extension, and maintenance over long product lifecycles in a consistent, organized manner. Clean code is a prerequisite for successful long-term software.

Chapter 10: Addressing Frustrations and Overcoming Challenges

Common Mistakes and How to Avoid Them

As a beginner Java programmer, you will inevitably make mistakes as you learn. Mistakes are a natural part of the learning process, as they help reinforce concepts and highlight areas you need more practice with. However, repeated mistakes can grow frustrating and hinder your progress. This section will explore some of the most common mistakes made by beginners and provide tips on how to avoid them.

Typos

One of the easiest mistakes to make is a simple typo. When first learning the syntax of a new language, it is easy to accidentally mistype a variable name, method name, operator, or other code element. Typos can be difficult to spot, as the code may still compile and run with errors. Some common typo mistakes include:

- Missing or extra characters like semicolons, parentheses, braces
- Incorrect spelling of variable/method names
- Accidentally typing equals ("=") instead of double equals ("==") in conditional statements

To avoid typos, take your time when coding and double-check your work. Having clean, formatted code with proper indentation makes typos more obvious as well. Consider using an IDE with code completion features, which can catch typos as you type. You should also thoroughly test any code you write before moving on, which will catch runtime errors from typos.

Syntax Errors

Closely related to typos are syntax errors, which occur when the structure or formatting of your code does not follow Java's rules. Some common syntax mistakes include:

- Forgetting to close opened curly braces or parentheses
- Incorrect placement or missing semicolons
- Incorrect usage of operators like += instead of =
- Incorrect declaration or initialization of variables

- Incorrect method signatures

Like typos, syntax errors can prevent code from compiling or cause unexpected runtime behavior. The best way to avoid syntax mistakes is to learn Java's rules inside and out. Refer to language references when unsure of proper syntax constructs. Use an IDE with intelligent code assists, and always compile and test your work. Taking time to format code neatly also makes syntax issues stand out and easier to spot.

Logical Errors

Even if code successfully compiles, it may still contain logical errors that cause unexpected or incorrect program flow. Some common logical mistakes include:

- Infinite loops from incorrect termination conditions
- Off-by-one errors in loops or arrays
- Faulty conditionals resulting in wrong program paths
- Invalid assumptions about how code should behave
- Incorrect calculations due to the order of operations mistakes

Catching logical errors can be tricky since the code itself may be syntactically valid. Walk through your code step-by-step using print statements or a debugger to verify that the program flow matches expectations. Test edge cases, invalid inputs, and expected successful and failure scenarios. Consider adding validation checks for assumptions. With experience, your intuition for catching logical flaws will improve over time.

Null Pointer Exceptions

A very common runtime error encountered by beginners is a NullPointerException. This occurs when you attempt to access or call a method on a reference variable that has been assigned the value null, meaning it references no object. Some typical causes of NullPointerExceptions include:

- Forgetting to initialize reference variables before use
- Returning null from methods without checking for it
- Passing null as a parameter when non-null is expected

To avoid NullPointerExceptions:

- Initialize reference variables when declaring them
- Check for null values before calling methods or accessing fields
- Consider defensive coding methods to return non-null or throw exceptions
- Handle null checks gracefully rather than letting exceptions occur

This is an error that becomes less frequent with experience validating reference variables are non-null before use.

Unused Variables

Declaring variables that are never read or assigned can introduce bugs, waste memory, and obscure mistakes. Some unnecessary variable pitfalls are:

- Declaring variable never referenced in the code scope
- Declaring variable only assigned but value never used
- Declaring multiple variables with similar names causes confusion

IDEs like Eclipse and IntelliJ help catch unused variables with code inspections. It's also good practice to purposefully initialize all variables as you declare them to avoid inadvertent bugs later. Consistent naming styles avoid similar variable names masking issues as well.

Input/Output Errors

Dealing with user input and output streams, like reading from the console or writing to files, introduces new categories of bugs for beginners. Some common I/O issues include:

- Forgetting to close streams after use, causing resource leaks
- Not handling exceptions from I/O operations
- Invalid assumptions about the format of input data
- Incorrect format specifiers when reading/writing different data types

Proper error handling around I/O is important. Use try-with-resources blocks to ensure streams close automatically. Validate input matches expectations before use. Consider defensive coding practices like parsing input as generic objects and handling specific data types later to avoid assumptions.

Static and Dynamic Errors

Two other categories of errors result from improper usage of static and dynamic program elements:

Static Errors:

- Calling non-static methods/variables from a static context without object
- Defining static members that should be instance members

Dynamic Errors:

- Forgetting to instantiate objects before using them
- Attempting to access object fields/methods before construction
- Not accounting for state changes over time in mutable objects

Following best practices like favoring instances over static members guides the correct use of static and dynamic elements in Java. Always construct objects properly before interacting with them as well.

As demonstrated, beginners face many common pitfalls when first learning Java. However, with practice and experience, mistakes become much less frequent as good coding habits and intuition develop over time. Understanding where errors typically occur empowers you to proactively avoid issues through things like thorough testing, early validation, proper naming/formatting, and defensive coding techniques. While you will likely still encounter bugs, learning from mistakes leads to continuous improvement. Stay determined, and before long, handling frustrations will feel routine as mastery grows.

Overcoming Impostor Syndrome in the Tech World

As beginners embark on learning to code, it's common to experience feelings of self-doubt and insecurity, known as impostor syndrome. With so much information to absorb and constant exposure to more experienced developers online, feeling like a fraud or that superficial abilities will be exposed is understandable. However, it's important to recognize impostor syndrome for what it is—a collection of irrational thoughts, not reality. With awareness and coping strategies, feelings of not belonging or being capable can be overcome.

What is Impostor Syndrome?

First, it's useful to understand specifically what impostor syndrome entails. At its core, it involves internalizing feelings of intellectual phoniness despite objective evidence of success or skills. Symptoms typically include:

- Chronic self-doubt about abilities and expertise
- Fear of incompetence and being exposed as a "fraud."
- Difficulty internalizing accomplishments
- Attribution of success to external factors like luck
- Perfectionism that prevents risk-taking

Though impostor syndrome was traditionally thought to only affect high-achievers, it actually impacts individuals across all experience levels, genders, and backgrounds. The tech industry tends to exacerbate these feelings due to the constant exposure to others' accomplishments online. But it's important to remember impostor syndrome reflects irrational thoughts, not reality or ability.

Challenging Irrational Beliefs

A key part of overcoming impostor syndrome is recognizing when unhelpful thought patterns are occurring and challenging them rationally. Some common cognitive distortions include:

- Catastrophizing mistakes — believing a single error means overall failure
- Polarized thinking - believing you're either perfect or useless
- Mind reading - assuming others see you as incompetent without evidence
- Fortune telling - predicting future disaster without facts
- Labeling - calling yourself a "fraud" rather than acknowledging room to grow

When these thoughts come up, take a step back to evaluate them objectively. Consider alternative, more balanced perspectives. Remind yourself you're still learning, and mistakes don't define you or your potential long-term.

Focus on Progress over Perfection

Perceiving yourself as a perfectionist plays into impostor feelings. Shifting to focus on progress rather than flawless performance is healthier. Set small, attainable goals that acknowledge your stage of learning. Enjoy small wins and view setbacks as normal rather than failures. Reward progress-driven effort rather than results alone. Compare yourself to who you were yesterday rather than unrealistic standards.

Build Confidence through Action

Rather than avoiding risks that might expose imperfections, take the initiative to build competence. Consider side projects that apply new skills without pressure. Try teaching others - explaining concepts strengthens your own understanding. Ask questions to fill gaps versus fearing looking silly. The more you code, the more natural it will feel over time. Faking it til you make it can help you gain real confidence, too.

Promote Well-Being

Negative self-talk thrives when we're stressed or tired. Make self-care a priority. Get enough sleep, stay hydrated, and fuel your body/mind. Spend time offline, too - it's easy to compare yourself non-stop online. Find balance through hobbies unrelated to your career to reduce perfectionist tendencies. Surrounding yourself with supportive people helps relieve pressure as well.

Know You're Not Alone

Sharing impostor feelings or thoughts with others can alleviate their power. Chances are others, especially in tech, can relate on some level. When doubts arise, remind yourself virtually all programmers question themselves sometimes - it's part of being human. Leaders you admire likely wrestled with insecurity, too, at some point. Reframe negative self-talk by acknowledging it's normal and common.

Change Negative Labels

Resist calling yourself things like "fraud" or "impostor." This creates psychological barriers. Replace destructive labels with empowering ones like "student," "amateur," "in training." Shifting language shifts mindset more positively over time. View yourself on your journey versus what you are not yet. Identity comes with competence, not the inverse.

Look for Validation Internally

Place less weight on outside validation as the arbiter of your inherent worth or competence. You must believe in yourself even without positive reinforcement. Learn to feel satisfied from intrinsically motivating accomplishments rather than trophies/badges. Define success in your own terms focused on growth versus image. Inner confidence is a must to overcome self-doubt in the long term.

The Path to Confidence

Gaining confidence takes time and intentional practice, flexing more positive thought patterns and self-talk. Mistakes won't abruptly stop, nor will all doubt vanish overnight. But recognizing impostor syndrome and making an effort leads further down a less self-critical path over the long run, freeing you to focus outward on coding passion versus insecurity. With patience and persistence, you can overcome feeling like a fraud to become the programmer you aim to be through experience alone.

Resources and Communities to Support Your Learning Journey

As a beginner programming student, it's important to utilize available resources and join coding communities. No one learns effectively alone - connecting with others provides numerous benefits to motivate continued progress. This chapter section explores beneficial resources as well as local and online communities for supporting your Java learning experience.

Online References & Documentation

Official documentation sites maintained by Oracle provide thorough Java specifications, tutorials, API documentation, and more to augment classroom or self-study materials. Key references include:

- Java Tutorials (docs.oracle.com/javase/tutorial/) - Modules, language concepts
- Java API Documentation (docs.oracle.com/en/java/) - Class and interface details
- Java Language Specification - Formal language design & syntax rules

YouTube is also full of tutorial channels like Thenewboston, Dereck Banas, and Corey Schafer that explain Java concepts through video lessons. As a supplement to textbooks/courses, documentation sites ensure you learn straight from the source and find answers quickly. Save frequently used pages for easy future access.

Online Forums & Q&A Sites

When specific code questions or errors arise, online forums allow peeking into discussions from a vast community. Java forums like Stack Overflow and Reddit's r/javahelp are especially active, with Java experts ready to assist newcomers. Before posting, search existing threads - chances are your issue has already been discussed. However, forums are a great place to get personalized guidance and validate conceptual understanding by explaining problems to others. Just be sure to search thoroughly before adding new threads where possible.

Code Practice & Learning Platforms

For hands-on practice, interactive learning platforms like codingame.com, codingbat.com, and hackerrank.com offer Java problems to sharpen skills. Udemy, Coursera, and edX also host MOOCs (massive open online courses) from top universities for in-depth Java learning paths.

Many platforms include tutorials, reference materials, and gamified challenges to keep the study engaging. Code practice is essential to move beyond theoretical knowledge - these resources provide structured exercises and projects for applied learning in a low-pressure environment.

Open Source Projects

Contributing to open-source Java projects provides real-world experience beyond simplified exercises. Browse repositories on GitHub, exploring areas like algorithms, frameworks, or tools you find interesting. Look for beginner-friendly issues labeled "good first issue" for simple fixes, documentation changes, or new features. Ask project maintainers for guidance on suitable first tasks. Shadowing code from open-source projects also grows understanding of code structure and best practices. Just be sure to thoroughly review contributing guidelines.

Coding Tutorial Books

Programming books from publishers like O'Reilly, Manning, Packt, and No Starch Press offer in-depth tutorials on Java concepts, frameworks, APIs, and more. E-books are convenient for mobile or tablet access on the go. Visit your local library to check out coding books for free or purchase low-cost titles online. Books provide digested knowledge on specialized topics in a structured format.

Local User Groups & Meetups

Connecting with local programming communities in person through user groups and meetups boosts learning through networking, knowledge sharing, and mentorship. Events cover everything from Java basics tutorials to tech talks on libraries/tools.

Many large cities host Java-focused groups to build relationships within your geographic coding network. Meetup is a major platform for finding tech events worldwide. Say hello, ask questions, and share your own journey and skills - you never know who you'll meet!

Coding Bootcamps

If you're considering a career change, full or part-time coding bootcamps deliver intensive skill-building over weeks or months. With project-based curricula and one-on-one support, boot camps rapidly take students from novice to job-ready rates. Despite costs, graduates often see increased earnings and new career prospects afterward. Research programs thoroughly based on outcomes, curriculum, and support services.

Online Peer Learning

Websites coupling mentorship with project collaboration foster learning through helping others. At Anthropic, experienced developers review AI safety work by newcomers. Rust Together matches beginners with mentors for open-ended Rust projects. Sites like this build skills through guided teaching and social motivation. Some offer credentials and job opportunities, too.

Educational YouTube

While passive video consumption alone doesn't replace practice, channels like Coding Garden and Java Brains present concepts through visual, clear lessons. ProgrammingPlaylist curates comprehensive Java learning paths from fundamentals to frameworks. With so much free content, YouTube supplements formal coursework nicely. Discover channels matching your interests and goals.

Combining online references, communities, and practical projects leverages different strengths to accelerate your Java journey. Stay motivated through utilizing diverse available resources for well-rounded, engaging skill growth. With determination and community support, your programming abilities will advance rapidly. Maintain a growth mindset - each new resource further fuels your potential as a developer.

Chapter 11: Future of Java and Beyond

Keeping Up with Java's Evolution

Since its initial release in 1995, Java has evolved tremendously to stay relevant in an ever-changing technological landscape. As one of the most popular and widely used programming languages, Java continues to receive regular updates that add new features and capabilities. For Java developers seeking to remain employable and on the cutting edge of their field, it is critical to make keeping up with Java's ongoing evolution a priority. This chapter will explore Java's history of changes and innovations, examine some of the major upcoming new additions to the language, and provide tips for effectively tracking and learning new Java developments.

A Brief History of Java's Evolution

Java was created by Sun Microsystems in the early 1990s under the guidance of James Gosling and was first launched in 1995. The original goals for Java included being simple, object-oriented, distributed, robust, secure, architecture-neutral, portable, high-performance, and interpreted. From the beginning, Java was designed with the vision of being platform-independent so that applications could be easily deployed across different operating systems and hardware without modification.

Some key milestones and versions in Java's evolution include:

- JDK 1.0 (January 1996) - The first official public release that established the core Java standard libraries and APIs.
- J2SE 1.2 (December 1998) - Introduced important new features like collection classes, reflection, regular expressions, and Java IDL.
- J2SE 1.3 (May 2000) - Enhanced performance, security, internationalization, new APIs, and minimum VM requirements.
- J2SE 1.4 (February 2002) - Major new additions such as generics, regular expressions in the core API, improved compilation speed, and Just-In-Time compilation.
- Java SE 5.0 (September 2004) - Dubbed "Tiger", it introduced annotations, autoboxing/unboxing, enumerated types, varargs, and enhanced for loops.

- Java SE 6 (December 2006) - Codenamed "Mustang", it focused on improved productivity, manageability, and larger throughput. New features included Scripting API, Java EE 5 support, and convenience methods in core API classes.
- Java SE 7 (July 2011) - Known as "Dolphin", it brought switch expressions, try-with-resources, string switches, and improved type inference for generic instance creation.
- Java SE 8 (March 2014) - A hugely influential update called "Lambdas" added lambda expressions, default methods in interfaces, date and time API, streams API, type annotations, and more.
- Java SE 9 (September 2017) - Modularity was the headline, allowing Java code and dependencies to be packaged into custom units called "modules". Other updates included reactive streams and private interface methods.
- Java SE 11 (September 2018) - Minor LTS release with changes to ThreadLocal to reduce memory usage, further modularity aids, and launch single-file source-code programs.
- Java SE 17 (September 2022) - The latest major version introduces pattern matching for switches, records, switch expressions, and text blocks.

As this brief history shows, Java's core development team, now at Oracle, has consistently delivered major upgrades to the language every few years that expand its capabilities to keep pace with technological and industry changes. This steady progression has allowed Java to remain a very relevant and widely adopted programming platform.

Upcoming New Features in Java

Let's examine in more detail some of the most prominent new features that have recently been added or are planned for upcoming releases. Understanding additions to the core Java language will help keep skills sharp and resumes and portfolios marketable as a Java developer.

Records (Java 16+)

Records provide a convenient way to define simple classes whose main purpose is to transport data from one place to another. Records are like classes but behave differently in that their fields are public, implement hashCode()/equals() in terms of their fields, and have a nicely formatted toString() method. Records eliminate much boilerplate code and help developers focus on the intent rather than implementation details for plain data objects.

Switch Expressions (Java 14+)

This enhancement to the switch statement allows expressions instead of statements in the case blocks, enabling a more flexible code flow. Now, switch expressions return a value instead of always falling through case blocks sequentially. This makes switch blocks more readable and reusable for common tasks like value mapping without overwhelming else-if blocks.

Text Blocks (Java 16+)

Text blocks provide an easy way to handle multiline strings through the use of a specially formatted string literal and without the need to concatenate each line. This avoids messy string concatenations and improves readability when dealing with large blocks of text content. Text blocks use triple quotes before and after the content to indicate multi-line strings.

Pattern Matching for Switch (Java 15+)

Switch statements gained a major boost with the addition of pattern-matching capabilities. Now, case labels can utilize patterns to match multiple options rather than just a single constant value. This allows matching against enums, subtypes, and more complex predicates, simplifying switch logic that previously required the use of instance checks.

Dynamic CDS Archives (Java 17+)

With class data sharing (CDS), metadata can be extracted from a set of classes and archives during compilation. Subsequent Java processes reuse this data, improving ahead-of-time compilation speed when applications are started up again. CDS archives go further with dynamic updates, allowing archive contents to change based on class loading without forcing JVM restarts.

These are some of the most important new features added to Java in recent versions, with more improvements on the horizon over time. Keeping familiar with language innovations helps modern Java programmers stay on top of their skills.

Tips for Tracking Java's Evolution

With regular releases that may introduce breaking changes or deprecate established APIs, it is a job in itself to track the evolution of the Java platform. Here are some suggestions for developers seeking to keep abreast of ongoing Java developments:

1. Read Release Notes - Carefully review documentation describing what is new for each major Java version and any behavioral changes. Oracle provides detailed notes on the contents of each upgrade.
2. Monitor Blogs/News Sites - Subscribe to various Java-centric blogs and news sites to get notified of the latest news, previews of

upcoming features, and articles on newly introduced APIs/functionality.
3. Follow Core Developers - Follow key members of the Java development team on social media to see updates directly from the source on changes being planned and worked on.
4. Check GitHub Repos - Browse the GitHub repos for OpenJDK to see proposed new features and current development activity before releases.
5. Watch Conferences - Events like JavaOne and Devoxx provide early sneak peeks at future Java roadmaps and evolutionary paths straight from Oracle.
6. Try Early Access Previews - Sign up for early access programs from Oracle/OpenJDK to test unreleased Java versions yourself before general availability.
7. Read Books/Documentation - Purchase books on major versions after release to learn about all new additions through in-depth tutorials and explanations.

With active effort spent tracking changes, Java developers can ensure their skills smoothly evolve as the language advances rather than fall behind as it modernizes. Staying aware of new developments helps professionals position themselves and their portfolios for the latest industry trends and job opportunities.

Since its initial launch in 1995, Java has continued to greatly expand and refine its capabilities through regular releases that introduce important new functionality. To stay competitive in the industry, Java programmers must invest time into learning about ongoing updates and innovations to the language. Understanding recent additions and roadmaps for future changes allows developers to both write better code leveraging new Java features and market themselves as experts employing cutting-edge techniques. By actively tracking Java's steady evolution, programmers can keep their skills and careers continually progressing along with an ever-evolving technology.

Exploring the Java Ecosystem: Frameworks and Tools

Beyond just learning the core Java language syntax and programming concepts, developing real-world applications requires leveraging the rich ecosystem of frameworks, libraries, and tools that surround Java. The wide array of options available helps developers rapidly build robust applications, simplify common tasks, and focus efforts on business logic rather than infrastructural programming. This chapter will explore some of the most popular technologies within the Java ecosystem and provide guidance on efficiently navigating and learning these frameworks.

Major Java Application Frameworks

As an object-oriented language, Java lends itself well to framework-based programming. Let's examine several of the most widely adopted frameworks across various domains that millions of applications rely on:

Spring Framework

Known as the de facto application development framework for Java, Spring is used in everything from simple web applications to large enterprise systems. It handles aspects like dependency injection, transaction management, and web integration. Popular modules include Spring MVC for building web UIs, Spring Boot for creating microservices, and Spring Security for authentication and authorization.

Hibernate ORM

An object-relational mapping tool that handles data persistence by converting database tables into Java objects and vice versa. Hibernate automates common data access tasks and improves developer productivity significantly compared to handwritten SQL. Its query language, HQL, makes building sophisticated database queries intuitive.

Java Server Faces (JSF)

A server-side MVC framework for building web UI components and pages using XML configuration and built-in tag libraries. JSF applications leverage the MVC pattern to cleanly separate user interface views from business logic components. Managed beans power the backing code. JSF applications are easily portable to any Java application server.

Struts

Another popular MVC framework that predates JSF, Struts, inspired many later web development frameworks through its clear model-view-controller structure. The framework leverages Apache Velocity and XWork libraries for view rendering and action handling. Struts is a mature solution suitable for large legacy Java web applications.

Java EE

An umbrella technology is making Java the best platform for server-side development. The Java EE platform powers everything from servlets and JSPs to Enterprise JavaBeans and web services. Major Java application servers like WildFly and GlassFish implement industry-standard Java EE specifications.

Exploring Other Framework Categories

Beyond application-specific frameworks, many reusable libraries assist Java development in other categories:

Testing Frameworks

JUnit - The de facto standard for unit testing in Java since its introduction in 2002. Easy to use and extend.

TestNG - A more robust alternative to JUnit that supports advanced testing concepts.

Mockito - Popular mocking framework used alongside tests for stubbing dependencies.

Web Service Frameworks

JAX-WS - Standards-based API for building web services using annotations or WSDL documents.

Jersey - Lightweight RESTful framework based on JAX-RS that facilitates building REST APIs.

ORM/Database Libraries

Apache Commons DBCP - Established connection pool framework for efficiently managing database connections.

H2 Database Engine - Lightweight, embedded SQL database used for testing and rapid prototyping.

Dependency Injection

Guice - Dependency injection framework from Google that provides a clean alternative to Spring.

Dagger - Compile-time dependency injection for Android/JVM based on Guice and annotation processing.

JavaScript Integration

GWT - Google Web Toolkit for building full-featured Web UIs with Java that compile into optimized JS/HTML.

ReactJS on the JVM - Expose Java classes through interop utils for integration into React-based front-ends.

This list highlights just some of the key frameworks, tools, and libraries for Java that expand its functionality and simplify development at each layer of an application stack. Let's now explore guidance for learning these ecosystems.

Navigating the Java Framework Ecosystem

With such an expansive selection of frameworks across different domains, new Java developers can feel overwhelmed in deciding where to start. Here are some tips:

- Focus on core application platforms like Spring Boot first for building microservices or web apps. These offer the widest industry reuse potential.
- Look for frameworks used by companies you admire - examine the tech stack of open-sourced projects at firms like Netflix and Adore to guide selections.
- Pick frameworks related to your specific interests, like web, data access, and testing, to get hands-on faster. Learn the database tier next.
- Don't try to learn everything at once. Instead, incrementally expand breadth over time as you learn new application layers in-depth.
- Consider frameworks recommended as part of training, like Java EE for Appendix Z certification studies.
- Look for frameworks that match your problem domain for real-world projects rather than just learning for learning's sake.
- Evaluate framework popularity and maintenance activity levels on GitHub for stability and longevity potential.
- Experiment with multiple options before committing fully - test common code patterns on frameworks.
- Java tools tend to converge on a handful of leaders, so focus energy where the community appreciates contributions.
- Reference tech articles, tutorials, and books covering standard Java setups using leading frameworks

Properly navigating the ecosystem will lead to an efficient learning process and marketable skills. A solid foundation of industry-leading frameworks paired with focused app development provides developers with the expertise recruiters desire.

Major Development Tools

Beyond frameworks, many tools are indispensable for productive Java coding:

- Integrated Development Environment (IDE)
- Eclipse - Open-source heavyweight with powerful refactoring and debugging capabilities. Very customizable.
- IntelliJ IDEA - Cross-platform IDE from JetBrains admired for code intelligence and inspections.

- NetBeans - Full-featured but lighter IDE good for web and Java EE projects.

Build Tools

- Maven - De facto standard build tool that handles dependencies, compilation, testing, and deployment.
- Gradle - Flexible alternative to Maven that embraces code as the primary configuration.

Version Control

Git - Ubiquitous distributed VCS behind major platforms like GitHub and Bitbucket.

Code Quality Tools

- Checkstyle - Customizable static analysis tool for enforcing code conventions.
- PMD - Finds common programming flaws and unintended code patterns.
- FindBugs - Advanced static analysis tool for detecting bugs related to correctness.
- JaCoCo - Jacamo Java Code Coverage Library for integration into builds.

Debugging & Profiling

- YourKit Java Profiler - Feature-rich profiler for troubleshooting performance problems.
- JProfiler - Another top-tier profiler and memory analyzer.
- Java Platform Debugger Architecture (JPDA) - Standardized API for debugging tools.

Automation

- Maven Release Plugin - Manages automated version updates and deployments in Maven.
- Gradle Build Automation Tool - Scriptable build language for sophisticated continuous integration.
- Jenkins - Open-source automation server for building, testing, and deploying software.

Overall, mastering at least one IDE, build tool, debugger, and other productivity enhancers helps developers leverage the full power of Java frameworks and results in more code delivered daily.

Exploring Emerging Technologies

While established frameworks cater to standard Java use cases, it is also worthwhile evaluating emerging technologies that promise to transform how Java applications are built in the future:

Microservices with Spring Boot/Cloud

- Spring Boot's ease of setup makes it ideal for microservices that comprise self-contained business logic units.

Containerization with Docker

- Docker allows packaging Java apps into lightweight Linux containers for simplified deployment to any infrastructure.

Serverless Computing on AWS Lambda

- Serverless computing provides scalable, on-demand computing for event-driven Java functions without managing servers.

Cloud-Native Development on Kubernetes

- Kubernetes facilitates portable deployments of containerized Java microservices to cloud platforms.

Reactive Programming with RxJava

- Asynchronous and event-driven architectures are enabled through reactive streams and immutability.

JavaScript Interoperability

- Exposing Java classes to JavaScript and integrating with modern frontends like React expands usage scenarios.

Machine Learning Frameworks

- Apache Spark, Deeplearning4j, TensorFlow, and other ML libraries make Java a competent language for data science, too.

While not suitable for all use cases today, staying aware of evolving technologies helps Java developers anticipate future industry shifts. Selectively exploring emerging areas enhances professional portfolios for coming developments.

The Java ecosystem extends far beyond just the core programming language syntax and features. An immense number of frameworks, libraries, and development tools power real-world applications across industries. Mastering some of the leading frameworks alongside IDE proficiency, version control, and other productivity tools positions Java professionals optimally for success. Careful navigation of the extensive ecosystem options through focused learning and hands-on projects provides meaningful skills applicable to both present and future opportunities.

The Road Ahead: Furthering Your Java Career

As technologies and industries continuously evolve, it is crucial for Java professionals to actively manage their career development and skills portfolio. While foundational Java knowledge establishes a solid base, simply maintaining the status quo is insufficient for long-term success in this dynamic field. This discussion will delve deeper into strategies outlined in the previous chapter for Java developers seeking enduring, rewarding careers. With proactive efforts to update competencies, expand perspectives, and specialize capabilities, endless opportunity remains ahead.

Advancing Technical Skills

Technical excellence remains the cornerstone for Java careers. Continuous learning keeps skills on the cutting edge:

Online Courses

Websites like Coursera offer numerous specialized Java courses taught by industry experts. For example, Object Oriented Design Patterns taught by the University of Alberta help solve real problems efficiently using common patterns like Factory Method and Singleton. While online, the interactive nature cements learning better than passive reading. Challenging courses broaden capabilities beyond everyday work scenarios.

Technical Books

In-depth books from publishers like O'Reilly provide opportunities to gain mastery of complex topics not covered sufficiently elsewhere. For instance, Effective Java by Joshua Bloch discusses item 75, "Prefer lambdas to anonymous classes", and explains performance benefits. Books impart a deeper understanding compared to cursory tutorials and retain relevance for reference years later.

Open Source Contributions

Actively participating in open-source projects expands skills through hands-on problem-solving. As an example, contributing to the Spring Framework on GitHub allows for improving widely used libraries and getting feedback from the community. It also strengthens resumes and builds networks vital for referrals. Combined, these methods augment skills at the developer's own pace daily in bite-sized or more intensive modules. Technical excellence compounds over the long run to attain senior abilities dominating emerging trends. Continuing education resources ensure competitiveness during career transitions, too, by closing expertise gaps.

Developing Business Skills

While technology enables innovation, business objectives drive priorities. Strong "soft skills" open non-coding opportunities:

Formal Education

An MBA increases understanding of business fundamentals like finance, management, and marketing, often lacking in technical-only roles. It cultivates a strategic, enterprise-level perspective complementing technical depth. MBA graduates find more diverse, remunerative, non-technical roles as architects and program managers.

Workplace Exposure

Accepting rotational assignments exposing strengths beyond just coding expands business acumen. For example, working closely with product managers on requirements elicitation and demos sharpens communication and analytical thinking attributes that similarly skilled careers require.

Communications Practice

Conferences offer networking opportunities like informal discussions and scheduled developer meets. Practicing clear explanations to non-technical audiences here and in documentation builds persuasive communication talents valued industry-wide. Well-rounded business understanding combined with technical mastery sets leaders apart when overseeing complex initiatives later on. It also enables fluid industry changes by developing transferable "soft" career skills instead of job-specific technical skills alone.

Specializing Knowledge

By directing learning towards important emerging domains, opportunities arise:

Cloud Architecture

Obtaining AWS Certified Solutions Architect - Associate certification proves cloud design expertise is increasingly required as infrastructure shifts off-premises. Hands-on projects applying Docker/Kubernetes to microservices demonstrate savviness. These open doors to challenging cloud roles transforming businesses digitally.

Data Science

Coursera's Machine Learning course from Stanford, combined with side projects applying skills to problems, establishes data analysis credentials. Proficiency in analyzing datasets using frameworks like Spark broadens career prospects to high-growth analytics specializations.

Overall, specializing in strategically selected areas maximizes desirability given their prominence and the openings they afford. Profiles convey deeper thought leadership and solutions-focused mindsets attractive to forward-thinking companies.

Participating in Communities

Active software engineering communities accelerate learning while elevating professional profiles:

Meetups

Attending local Java User Groups introduces diverse perspectives beyond workplace silos. Discussing innovative architectures with architects sparks new ideas. It establishes a valuable network supporting career pivots.

Conferences

Presenting in "lightning talks" helps share knowledge developed through painful learning experiences benefitting others. Distinguished papers published commemorate contributions while impressing prospective employers.

Open Source

Projects providing a platform to showcase skills garner recognition. For example, Pull Requests addressing serious issues in popular repos gain commit access and peer endorsements, elevating status within that community.

Social Media

A perfectly optimized personal brand acts as a virtual resume. Posts on LinkedIn demonstrating an adept grasp of relevant topics via thought-leadership comments make you discoverable to exciting ventures.

Participation keeps skills at the forefront through interactive learning and puts the best attributes center stage to influencers who fuel career advancement through connections and referrals over conventional alumni networks.

Cultivating a Learning Mindset

Passive consumption risks obsolescence versus an entrepreneurial spirit embracing inevitable change:

Experiment Fearlessly

Try new technologies before fully adopting them, and reduce risk from rushed decisions. Sandboxes to test concepts prevent blocking progress.

Take Calculated Career Risks

Temporary roles outside the comfort zone expand perspectives for groundbreaking career pivots unrestrained by precedents. Consider strategically valued opportunities scaling skills.

Stay Teachable

Humility to accept superior perspectives maintains agility in adapting to market swings. Outdated views rigidly clung to hinder reinvention.

Continually Reinvent

Discover new passions fueling lifelong curiosity through personal projects regardless of imminent necessities. Sustained exploration unlocks opportunities invisible to complacent peers.

Glossary of Common Java Terms

Abstract Class - A class that is declared as abstract using the abstract keyword. It cannot be instantiated but serves as a base for subclasses to extend from.

Abstract Method - A method declared as abstract using the abstract keyword that must be implemented by a concrete subclass.

Access Modifier - Keywords like public, private, and protected that determine access/visibility of classes, methods, fields, etc.

Anonymous Class - An unnamed class defined and instantiated within code without a class declaration statement.

API - Application Programming Interface provided by classes, packages, and frameworks that define how others can interact with them.

Argument - Values passed into a method or constructor to execute its logic. Alternative to parameter.

Array - A data structure that stores multiple elements of the same type in contiguous memory locations.

ArrayList - The most commonly used implementation of the List interface. Stores elements dynamically with access by index.

Bounded Type Parameter - A generic type restricted to classes within a specified class hierarchy via a wildcard.

Bytecode - The intermediate format instructions that are generated from Java source code and executed by the JVM.

Class - A blueprint used to create objects. Classes define what properties the object has and what actions it can perform.

Collection - A generic framework in Java used to work with groups of objects. Interfaces like List, Set, Queue.

Compilation - The process of converting Java source code files to bytecode that can be understood by JVMs.

Constructor - A special type of method used to initialize objects. It has the same name as the class.

Encapsulation - The grouping of related attributes and methods within a class and restricting access to them. Safeguards the data.

Enum - A special reference type that represents a group of constants like days of the week.

Exception - An error condition that occurs during program execution that can be caught and handled.

Field - Attributes defined within a class to store data for objects of that class. Also called variables or properties.

Final - Marks a class, variable, or method that can't be overridden or reassigned once assigned.

Generics - A language feature that allows classes, interfaces, and methods to operate on objects of various types while providing compile-time type safety.

IDE - Integrated Development Environment used for developing, debugging, and testing Java programs.

Immutable - Describes objects that cannot be modified after construction. Prevents unwanted side effects.

Inheritance - A mechanism where one class acquires the properties and behaviors of another class. The child class extends the parent class.

Interface - A blueprint of methods that can be implemented by classes. Defines behavior without implementation.

JDK - Java Development Kit used for developing Java applications and includes development tools, compilers, debuggers, etc.

JVM - Java Virtual Machine that executes Java bytecode at runtime on various platforms.

Lambda Expression - Anonymous functions that can be used to simplify the creation of anonymous implementation classes.

Method - A function defined within a class that contains a series of statements to perform an action related to that class.

Override - Ability to redefine inherited methods to modify behavior using the @Override annotation.

Package - A namespace that organizes related classes and interfaces. The equivalent of a directory.

Parameter - Variables defined within parentheses in methods or constructors that accept/pass data.

Polymorphism - The ability of different classes to share the same method name while having different implementations.

Primitive Type - Predefined types in Java like int, boolean, and char that have no methods. Value types rather than reference types.

Static - References a static member/method that is not associated with any object instance but the class itself.

String - A sequence of characters represented by the String class as objects. Commonly used as a primitive.

Wrapper Class - A class that wraps around primitive data types like int to provide more functionality.

Conclusion

We have come to the end of our journey learning the fundamentals of Java programming. In this book, we aimed to give you a solid foundation to get started with Java - from installing the development environment to exploring core concepts like classes, objects, inheritance, and more. I hope you have gained an appreciation for object-oriented programming and how Java makes programming easier and more intuitive through its various features.

This is by no means an exhaustive resource covering everything there is to know about Java. Java is a vast ecosystem with endless possibilities. However, my goal was to provide you with enough material to get comfortable with the basics and set you on the right path to becoming a Java programmer. You should now have a working knowledge of Java syntax, logic, and problem-solving approach. I encourage you to take what you have learned and start building your own simple programs to reinforce these concepts.

As with any programming language, continued practice is key to mastering Java. Don't be afraid to experiment, get your hands dirty with code, and most importantly - have fun with it! Learning to program does require patience, but the rewards of seeing your ideas come to life are extremely gratifying. Don't fret over small mistakes; we all go through that as part of the learning curve. Focus on continuously improving and expanding your skills. While this book focused primarily on the core Java language, it's important to note that Java is just one part of a massive overall ecosystem.

Staying motivated and continuously self-educating are important habits for any programmer. Remember, Java is evolving rapidly, so you must evolve with it. Consider specializing in an area that aligns with your interests, like mobile apps, big data, machine learning, etc. There will always be opportunities for talented Java developers, so keep learning! It's also important to stress continual self-improvement through practices like code katas, reading technical articles, taking online courses, participating in programming challenges, and giving conference talks. There are always new things to learn, so make learning part of your daily routine. And remember, no one is expected to know everything - having a growth mindset and a willingness to learn from others are true strengths for any developer. I hope exploring related technologies and engaging in ongoing learning helps expand your skills and career opportunities. Never stop developing as a programmer, and the world of possibilities with Java will truly be limitless.

I want to sincerely thank you for choosing this book as a starting point in your Java journey. I hope this book has provided you with a solid foundation to begin your career as a Java developer. There may be ups and downs, but never lose your passion and curiosity for code. I wish you the very best as you progress forward and sharpen your skills. You now have the power to build virtually anything with Java - the possibilities are endless! I'm excited to see what great things you will create. Keep programming, and keep enjoying the journey.

SQL for Beginners

Introduction

Welcome to "SQL for Beginners"! We will explore the powerful world of SQL (Structured Query Language) and relational databases, providing a comprehensive overview of the fundamentals, advanced techniques, and real-world applications of this essential data management tool.

The first section of this book will explain the fundamentals of SQL and relational databases. We'll start by discussing relational databases and how to use SQL to interact with them. We will then go over the fundamental syntax and operations of SQL, such as building and modifying tables, inserting, updating, and removing data, and querying data with basic and sophisticated approaches. Throughout this part, we will give practical examples to assist the reader establish a solid foundation in SQL.

In the second section of this book, we will explore more complex SQL techniques and optimization. We will cover topics such as joining tables, subqueries, grouping and aggregating data, and advanced filtering and sorting techniques. We will also delve into the use of stored procedures, functions, and indexing for performance optimization. This section will provide the reader with real-world applications and best practices to optimize their data management processes and improve the performance of their SQL queries.

In the final section of this book, we will focus on the integration of SQL with other technologies and applications. We will explore importing and exporting data to and from other formats, working with data in a distributed environment, building data pipelines, and automating data processes. We will also discuss the use of SQL in data analysis and business intelligence, and the security and privacy considerations that come with SQL data management. Throughout this section, we will provide practical applications and real-world examples, helping the reader to build the confidence and competence to effectively implement SQL in a wide range of data management contexts.

Whether you are a beginner to SQL or looking to expand your existing knowledge, this book will provide you with the essential skills and knowledge to effectively manage and analyze data using SQL. I encourage you to work through the practical examples provided in each section to reinforce your understanding of the concepts and techniques covered. I hope you enjoy reading "SQL for Beginners" and find it to be a valuable resource in your journey to becoming a proficient SQL user.

Chapter 1: Relational Databases and SQL

A relational database (RDB) is a structure that stores files in an organized way using rows, tables, and columns. In a relational database, information is often organized in one or more tables, and each table has a unique name.

The types of data that can be stored in a table are determined by the columns that make up its structure. A row is a set of data items that correspond to a specific instance of an object in the table. Rows are also referred to as records. Keys are unique values that identify a particular row in a database and are used to link that row to relevant data in another table.

The relationship between the tables is established through the use of keywords, which are the values that distinguish one row from another. The ability of relational databases to store and manage large amounts of structured data, their adaptability in dealing with different data types, and their assistance in maintaining data integrity have led to their widespread adoption. Relational database management systems (RDBMS) that are widely employed include MySQL, Microsoft SQL Server, Oracle, and PostgreSQL. Because of their exceptional suitability, relational databases are designed specifically for use with applications that require complex data links and transactions that involve multiple tables.

A relational database may, for example, contain multiple tables for customers, orders, and products in order to manage product inventory and track customer orders. Relationships between these tables may also be established to facilitate the management of product inventory and the tracking of customer orders.

Advantages of Relational Databases

The use of the relational database model for both data management and storage comes with a variety of benefits, including the following:

- Flexibility: It is simple to add new data, modify existing data, or remove data anytime it is required.
- Durability ensures that any changes made to the database will be retained indefinitely, even if the operating system becomes corrupted.
- For consistency, only information that satisfies the criteria set forth by the data validation rules may be added to the database.

What is SQL?

The acronym SQL stands for Structured Query Language, which is used for maintaining and manipulating database systems. It may be used to conduct activities like building tables and indexes, adding, updating, and removing data, obtaining information from a database, and many other similar tasks. SQL is used in a wide variety of database systems, such as relational databases (such as MySQL, PostgreSQL, and Microsoft SQL Server) and NoSQL databases (such as MongoDB). SQL is a sequence of instructions, which means that you explain what it is that you want the database to do, and the DBMS is responsible for determining the most effective way to carry out your instructions. Because of this, you are free to concentrate on the logical aspects of the operations you perform on your database rather than the specifics of how to carry them out. SQL has existed for more than four decades, and despite its complexity, it continues to enjoy widespread adoption because of its adaptability, sturdiness, and ease of use. Learning SQL is a crucial ability that will help you deal with data more successfully, regardless of whether you are a software engineer, system admin, or data analyst. SQL is a structured query language.

Advantages of SQL

SQL provides many benefits that make it a good choice. A few of the most important benefits include the following:

- Flexibility: SQL is a versatile phrase that can be utilized for a broad range of data-related activities, from basic data retrieval to complicated data processing and analysis. This range of jobs is made possible by SQL's ability to be used for various data-related tasks.
- Accessibility: SQL is a portable dialect used by many relational management systems due to its status as a standard. Because of this, SQL code may be moved from one relational database to the other, making it simple to transition between systems if this is required.
- Accessing data quickly and effectively SQL was developed to be a language that is both efficient and quick when it comes to retrieving data from relational databases. It contains many built-in functions and features that make obtaining, organizing, and analyzing data straightforward.
- SQL is a sophisticated and quite well language with a storied record of dependable performance. Its reliability stems from its lengthy history. Because of this, it is an excellent option for applications that are crucial to the operation of a company.

- Scalability: SQL can handle enormous databases that include millions of entries, so it is an excellent option for businesses that are required to store and retrieve massive volumes of data.
- SQL includes various security tools and features for preserving the integrity and secrecy of sensitive information, managing access to data and preventing unauthorized disclosure.
- When it comes to accessing and maintaining relational databases, utilizing SQL offers several benefits, some of which are listed below. SQL is a strong and adaptable language that may assist you in working with data more efficiently and successfully, regardless of whether you are a system administrator, a data analyst, or a software developer.

Chapter 2: Basic SQL Syntax and Commands

SQL allows users to communicate with databases using a set of fundamental instructions. The following are a few of the frequently used commands:

Create

The *CREATE* command is used to create different objects. One of the most important objects to store information is a database.

Syntax:
CREATE DATABASE database_name;

Code:
```
CREATE DATABASE office;
```

Output:
It results in creating a database named office in the system database folder.

CREATE is also used to create tables within a database. The *CREATE TABLE* command creates the table and also specifies its columns and data types as follows:

Syntax:
CREATE TABLE table_name(column_name DATATYPE);

Code:
```
CREATE TABLE Employee_Tab(Name varchar(20), Age int, Salary
     int, Email varchar(30));
CREATE TABLE Customer_Tab(Name varchar(20), Age int, Email
     varchar(30));
CREATE TABLE Manager_Tab(Name varchar(20), Code int, Email
     varchar(30));
```

Output:

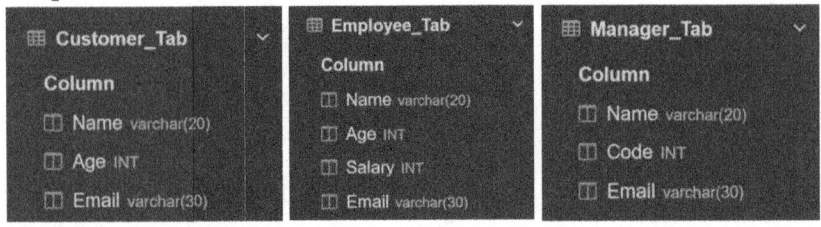

Customer_Tab	Employee_Tab	Manager_Tab
Column	Column	Column
Name varchar(20)	Name varchar(20)	Name varchar(20)
Age INT	Age INT	Code INT
Email varchar(30)	Salary INT	Email varchar(30)
	Email varchar(30)	

It creates 3 tables named Employee_Tab, Customer_Tab and Manager_Tab in the Tables folder of the office database.

INSERT INTO

In SQL, the INSERT INTO statement is used to feed a database with data. In this case, **'table_name'** refers to the tag of the table where you want to insert data. **'column1', 'column2', 'column3'**, etc., are the names of the columns of the table. The values **'value1', 'value2', 'value3'**, correspond to the values you wish to enter into the corresponding columns, denoting them.

It is important to remember that you may insert many records into a table all at once if you use the same INSERT INTO command and add extra sets of information.

Syntax:
INSERT INTO table_name (column1, column2, column3, ...)
VALUES (value1, value2, value3, ...);

Code:
```
INSERT INTO Employee_Tab (Name, Age, Salary, Email)
VALUES ('John Doe', 30, 4000, 'johndoe@gmail.com'),
       ('Jane Doe', 28, 5000, 'janedow@gmail.com'),
       ('Jim Smith', 35, 5000, 'jimsith@gmail.com');

INSERT INTO Customer_Tab (Name, Age, Email)
VALUES ('Janet Yew', 20, 'janetyew@gmail.com'),
       ('Peter Son', 48, 'peterson@gmail.com'),
       ('Andrew Smith', 32, 'smith@gmail.com');
```

Output:
As a result, 3 rows are affected because we have entered three records in the Employee and Customer tables.

SELECT

SELECT will be the starting point for many queries because it tells the database which variables we want to see. We can either give the names of the columns, separated by commas, or use the * symbol, which will return all the columns in the table.

Syntax:
SELECT * FROM table_name;

Code:
```
SELECT * FROM Employee_Tab;
SELECT * FROM Customer_Tab;
```

Output:
```
John Doe|30|4000|johndoe@gmail.com
Jane Doe|28|5000|janedow@gmail.com
Jim Smith|35|5000|jimsith@gmail.com

Janet Yew|20|janetyew@gmail.com
Peter Son|48|peterson@gmail.com
Andrew Smith|32|smith@gmail.com
```

If you want to extract data from specific columns you have to replace * with the names of the columns.

Syntax:

SELECT column1, column2

FROM table_name;

Code:
```
SELECT Name, Age FROM Employee_Tab;
SELECT Age, Email FROM Customer_Tab;
```

Output:
```
John Doe|30
Jane Doe|28
Jim Smith|35

20|janetyew@gmail.com
48|peterson@gmail.com
32|smith@gmail.com
```

UPDATE

The UPDATE command in SQL changes the data already in a table.

The table name refers to the table title that this command will update. The SET clause allows you to specify the columns and values you wish to modify. The WHERE article governs which rows should be changed depending on the given conditions.

Because changing the wrong rows might result in inaccurate data, it is essential to utilize the WHERE clause with extreme caution. Before altering the data, it is recommended to validate your UPDATE statement using a SELECT query to validate the row that the change would impact.

Syntax:

UPDATE table_name

SET column1 = value1, column2 = value2

WHERE condition

Code:
```
UPDATE Employee_Tab
SET Name = 'Houston'
WHERE Salary = '4000';

SELECT * FROM Employee_Tab;
```

Output:
```
Houston|30|4000|johndoe@gmail.com
Jane Doe|28|5000|janedow@gmail.com
Jim Smith|35|5000|jimsith@gmail.com
```

The name John Doe is updated to Houston as his Salary was 4000 according to the condition mentioned.

DELETE

When you want to remove records already in a table, you may use the DELETE command in SQL.

Because accidentally removing the incorrect rows might result in lost data, it is essential to utilize the WHERE clause with extreme caution. Before removing the data, it is a good idea to validate your DELETE statement using a SELECT query to validate the rows the deletion could impact. This is a recommended best practice.

Be aware that the data you delete using DELETE statements is irretrievably destroyed and cannot be recovered under any circumstances. This information is gone forever. It is important to keep regular backups of your data to prevent it from being lost in the event it is inadvertently deleted.

Syntax:
DELETE FROM table_name
WHERE condition

Code:
```
DELETE FROM Customer_Tab
WHERE Name = 'Peter Son';
SELECT * FROM Customer_Tab;
```

Output:
```
Janet Yew|20|janetyew@gmail.com
Andrew Smith|32|smith@gmail.com
```

Code:
```
DELETE FROM Employee_Tab
WHERE Name = 'Jim Smith';
SELECT * FROM Employee_Tab;
```

Output:
```
Houston|30|4000|johndoe@gmail.com
Jane Doe|28|5000|janedow@gmail.com
```

Code:
```
DELETE FROM Customer_Tab
WHERE Age = '32';
SELECT * FROM Customer_Tab;
```

Output:
```
Janet Yew|20|janetyew@gmail.com
```

DROP

It is used to remove the table's structure and any entries. You must use the DROP statement with extreme care since it will irreversibly erase the object you provide together with all its contents. The data that has been destroyed cannot be retrieved once the DROP instruction has been carried out.

The DROP command may be used to destroy additional database objects and tables. Some examples of these other database objects are indexes, views, and databases. There may be particular subtle modifications in the syntax of these objects, but the fundamental idea remains the same.

Syntax:
DROP TABLE table_name;

Code:
```
DROP TABLE Manager_Tab;
```

Output:
It results in dropping the table named Manager_Tab from the table's folder.

Chapter 3: SQL Data Types

Basic SQL Syntax

There are several fundamental principles and rules to keep in mind when using SQL Let's have a look to the most important rules:
- Although SQL keywords do not care about capitalization, it is best practice to write them with all capital letters.
- The semicolon is required after SQL statements (;).
- In SQL, the keywords are almost always typed with an uppercase letter.
- String values are required to be encapsulated in single quotation characters (').
- Executing SQL instructions is impossible until the semicolon has been reached.
- SQL statements rely on the lines of text they are written on. We can utilize a single SQL query on more than one text line if necessary.
- SQL queries are processed starting at the left and working to the right.
- It is not necessary to put numerical numbers in quotation marks.
- SQL comments are denoted by a pair of hyphens (--) at the opening of the line and continue to the decision.
- You can carry out most of the tasks in a database using SQL statements.
- Structured Query Language relies on Tuple Relationship Calculus and Relational Algebra.

Data Types

A data type in SQL Server specifies the information that may be found in a database column or variable. In the process of creating a table, this phase is required and very necessary. Inappropriate data types in a table may contribute to various problems, including ineffective query optimization, poor performance, and truncated data.
- Data types that deal with numbers are called Numeric, such as INT, TINYINT, BIGINT, FLOAT, and REAL, amongst others.
- Date and time-related data types include dates, TIME, and DATETIME, among others.

- Data types for characters and strings include the likes CHAR, VARCHAR, and TEXT.
- Data types that correspond to Unicode character strings, such as NCHAR, NVARCHAR, and NTEXT, among others.
- Binary data types include things like BINARY and VARBINARY, amongst others.
- Miscellaneous data types include CLOB, BLOB, XML, CURSOR, and TABLE.

SQL is equipped with several fundamental data types that may be used to save various kinds of information in a database. These are the details of the data type as mentioned above

INT

INT stands for "integer" and is the data type used to hold entire numbers and integers. The size of an INT may vary depending on the particular SQL implementation, although it generally falls between the range of -2147483648 and 21473647.

Syntax:

variable_name INT

Code:
```
CREATE TABLE Employee_Tab(
    Age INT
);
```

BIGINT

BIGINT is a whole integer data type that may be used to store bigger integer values. BIGINT values normally fall in the range of -9223372036854775808 to 9223372036854775807; however, the size of a BIGINT might vary depending on the particular SQL implementation.

Syntax:

variable_name BIGINT

Code:
```
CREATE TABLE Employee_Tab(
    Salary BIGINT
);
```

DECIMAL

The DECIMAL data type for decimal numbers is used to hold numbers with a decimal point that is always the same. Depending on the SQL implementation, the length of a DECIMAL may vary anywhere from -1038+1 to 1038-1, although, in general, it falls somewhere in that region.

Syntax:

variable_name DECIMAL

Code:

```
CREATE TABLE Manager_Tab(
    Income DECIMAL,
);
```

FLOAT

FLOAT is a floating-point number data type that is used for the storage of values that have a fractional component. A FLOAT's size may vary according to the particular SQL implementation, although it is more often than not in the range of -1.79E+308 to 1.79E+308.

Syntax:

variable_name FLOAT

Code:

```
CREATE TABLE Manager_Tab(
    Average_Salary FLOAT
);
```

DOUBLE

DOUBLE is a floating-point number data type that stores bigger values that include a fractional component. The type is called DOUBLE. A DOUBLE's length varies according to the particular SQL implementation; however, the range for this value is normally between -2.23E+308 and 2.23E+308.

Syntax:

variable_name DOUBLE

Code:

```
CREATE TABLE Manager_Tab(
    Yearly_Allounce DOUBLE
);
```

CHAR

CHAR is a string data type with a predetermined length used to store character strings. The size of a CHAR is measured in characters and has a variable limit that may fall between 0 and 255.

Syntax:

variable_name CHAR(char_length)

Code:

```
CREATE TABLE Customer_Tab(
    Email CHAR(30)
```

);

VARCHAR

It is a variable-length string data type used to hold character strings. VARCHAR stands for "variable character." The length of a VARCHAR is measured in characters and has a width that may be anything from 0 to 65535 characters long.

Syntax:

variable_name VARCHAR(varchar_length)

Code:
```
CREATE TABLE Customer_Tab(
    Name VARCHAR(20)
);
```

TEXT

TEXT is a data type that can hold a variable number of bytes of text and has a string length that may vary. A TEXT's size may vary according to the particular SQL implementation, although the range of possible values is normally between 0 and 231 -1 character.

Syntax:

variable_name TEXT

Code:
```
CREATE TABLE Order_Tab(
  Order_Details TEXT
);
```

DATE

DATE is a data type for dates that can store dates in the format of YYYY-MM-DD. You may save dates using this type.

Syntax:

variable_name DATE

Code:
```
CREATE TABLE Order_Tab(
  Order_date DATE
);
```

TIME

TIME is a data type for times that are stored in HH:MM: SS.

Syntax:

variable_name TIME

Code:
```
CREATE TABLE Order_Tab(
  Order_time TIME
);
```

Chapter 4: SQL Data Structures

Databases are organized to provide straightforward access, administration, and modification of the data sets they contain.

They are used by businesses to track all operations, get insight into what will help them function more effectively, and, consequently, assist ownership, managers, and analysts in making better choices.

The term "data structure" refers to the many methods of preserving data on a machine and is a vital component of the style of any central database. The operations that may be performed on these data structures and the instructions given to them to execute them are called algorithms. It is common for the fundamental functions of algorithms to be adapted specifically to the structure of the data structure.

How to Use Data Structures

In addition to enabling Core OS functions and resources and storing newly produced data for data permanence, data structures also store newly created data. Linked lists, trees, and queues are three different data structures that may handle memory allocation, file directories' administration, and processes' scheduling. Packets may be shared by developers using the TCP/IP protocols that are arranged using data structures. For binary search trees, for instance, there are various techniques for efficient ordering and sorting, and priority queues make it possible for programmers to handle objects while adhering to a predetermined order of priority.

Various straightforward methods are available for indexing and searching your data inside the various data structures. In large data applications, data structures also play an important role in ensuring high performance and scalability, which is why these applications are so important.

How to Select Data Structures

A variety of factors may aid the categorization of data structures. For instance, they may have a linear structure, similar to an array, in which the data items occur in a specific sequence. They may have a nonlinear structure like a graph, where the components are not arranged in any particular order.

Homogeneous data structures demand that all components have the same data type, but heterogeneous data structures can store data of various sorts. In contrast, data structures may either be static, in which the sizes and ram locations are predetermined, or dynamic, in which the sizes and storage locations are adjustable according to the requirements of the task at hand.

There is no simple solution to the question of which data structure you can implement. Each data format might have advantages and disadvantages, depending on the use-case situation. As a result, it is essential to consider the operations that you would execute on the data before making a choice about which to utilize.

For example, although retrieving any member of an array using the array's index is simple, linked lists are preferable when you want to resize the items in the array. On the other side, if you use a data structure that is neither appropriate, the duration of your program's execution will be increased, and the program will not respond properly.

When selecting a data structure, developers often take into consideration the following five factors:

- The kind of information you want to save is called the Data Type.
- Use Case refers to how you intend to put the knowledge to use.
- Location refers to the place where data are kept.
- The most effective method for you to arrange things so that it is simple to reach is efficiency.
- How to use your storage reserve and maximize its potential

Stack Data Structure

Stacks are an important data structure in computer science that follows the Last In, First Out (LIFO) principle. This means that the final piece added to the stack will be the first one removed. However, SQL, being a language for managing and querying relational databases, does not inherently support stack operations like a traditional programming language or data structure library.

Nonetheless, you can simulate stack behavior in SQL by using a table and carefully crafting your insert and select statements. Here's a practical example using a SQL table to mimic a stack:

Example: Creating the Stack Table

```
CREATE TABLE Stack(
    id INT PRIMARY KEY AUTO_INCREMENT,
    value VARCHAR(255)
);
```

This table has an 'id' column that auto-increments with each new entry, which helps to keep track of the order in which elements are inserted.

Push Operation (Inserting an Element):

```
INSERT INTO Stack (value) VALUES ('First Element');
```

Every time you insert a new element, it goes to the 'top' of the stack.

Pop Operation (Removing the Last Element):
To simulate the pop operation, you need two steps:
1. First, select the last inserted element:
```
SELECT value FROM Stack ORDER BY id DESC LIMIT 1;
```
2. Then, delete the last inserted element:
```
DELETE FROM Stack ORDER BY id DESC LIMIT 1;
```
This combination of SELECT and DELETE commands simulates the pop operation.

Checking if the Stack is Empty:
```
SELECT CASE WHEN COUNT(*) = 0 THEN 'Stack is empty'
            ELSE 'Stack is not empty' END
FROM Stack;
```

This approach uses a SQL table to mimic a stack's behavior, but it's important to note that this is not a typical use of SQL. SQL databases are designed for efficiently managing large datasets and complex queries rather than acting as a data structure like a stack. In practical scenarios, stack operations are usually handled in the application layer using programming languages.

Tree Data Structure

Tree data structures are not directly supported in SQL as they are in programming languages, but hierarchical data can be represented and managed in SQL databases. A tree structure is typically represented in SQL using a table with a self-referencing foreign key. This is often done in the context of representing hierarchies or parent-child relationships.

Example
Consider an organization where each employee has a manager, creating a tree-like hierarchy. Here's how you can represent this in SQL:
```
CREATE TABLE Employee(
    EmployeeID INT PRIMARY KEY,
    Name VARCHAR(100),
    ManagerID INT,
    FOREIGN KEY (ManagerID) REFERENCES Employee(EmployeeID)
);
```
In this table, EmployeeID is the primary key for each employee, Name is the employee's name, and ManagerID is a foreign key that refers to the EmployeeID of the employee's manager. For the top-level employee (like a CEO), ManagerID can be null.

Inserting Data:
```
INSERT INTO Employee (EmployeeID, Name, ManagerID) VALUES
    (1, 'CEO', NULL);
INSERT INTO Employee (EmployeeID, Name, ManagerID) VALUES
    (2, 'Manager A', 1);
INSERT INTO Employee (EmployeeID, Name, ManagerID) VALUES
    (3, 'Manager B', 1);
INSERT INTO Employee (EmployeeID, Name, ManagerID) VALUES
    (4, 'Employee 1', 2);
INSERT INTO Employee (EmployeeID, Name, ManagerID) VALUES
    (5, 'Employee 2', 2);
```
This creates a hierarchy where 'Manager A' and 'Manager B' report to 'CEO', and 'Employee 1' and 'Employee 2' report to 'Manager A'.

Querying the Tree:

To retrieve the hierarchy, recursive queries are used, especially in systems that support Common Table Expressions (CTEs) like SQL Server, PostgreSQL, and MySQL 8.0+.

Example of a Recursive Query:
```
WITH RECURSIVE EmployeeCTE AS(
    SELECT EmployeeID, Name, ManagerID
    FROM Employee
    WHERE ManagerID IS NULL
    UNION ALL
    SELECT e.EmployeeID, e.Name, e.ManagerID
    FROM Employee e
    INNER JOIN EmployeeCTE ecte ON e.ManagerID =
        ecte.EmployeeID
)
SELECT * FROM EmployeeCTE;
```

Output:
```
1|CEO|
2|Manager A|1
3|Manager B|1
4|Employee 1|2
5|Employee 2|2
```

This query will recursively traverse the tree, starting from the top-level employee (CEO) and going down through all levels of managers and employees.

Linked List Data Structure

A linked list is an elementary data structure in computer science used in many programming languages. It is made up of a series of nodes. Each node has data and a reference to the next node in the chain.

In SQL, which is designed primarily for managing and querying data in relational databases, there isn't a direct, native implementation of linked lists as there is in programming languages like Python, Java, or C++. However, you can simulate a linked list in SQL by using a table structure where each row references another row in the same table, creating a chain of links.

Let's see an example.

Creating the Linked List Table:

```
CREATE TABLE LinkedList(
    NodeID INT PRIMARY KEY,
    Data VARCHAR(255),
    NextNodeID INT,
    FOREIGN KEY (NextNodeID) REFERENCES LinkedList(NodeID)
);
```

In this table, NodeID is a unique identifier for each node, Data is the value stored in the node, and NextNodeID is a reference to the next node in the list. The foreign key constraint ensures integrity by linking NextNodeID to another NodeID in the same table.

Inserting Data:

```
INSERT INTO LinkedList (NodeID, Data, NextNodeID) VALUES
        (1, 'Node 1 Data', 2);
INSERT INTO LinkedList (NodeID, Data, NextNodeID) VALUES
        (2, 'Node 2 Data', 3);
INSERT INTO LinkedList (NodeID, Data, NextNodeID) VALUES
        (3, 'Node 3 Data', NULL);

SELECT * FROM LinkedList;
```

We insert nodes into the list, specifying the NextNodeID to create the links. The last node's NextNodeID is set to NULL, indicating the end of the list. The output will be the following:

```
1|Node 1 Data|2
2|Node 2 Data|3
3|Node 3 Data|
```

Traversing the Linked List:

Traversing a linked list in SQL can be complex, especially if the list is long. You may need to use recursive queries or stored procedures, depending on your SQL database's capabilities.

```
WITH RECURSIVE LinkedListCTE AS (
    SELECT NodeID, Data, NextNodeID
    FROM LinkedList
    WHERE NodeID = 2 -- Assuming we start from the 2nd node
    UNION ALL
    SELECT ll.NodeID, ll.Data, ll.NextNodeID
    FROM LinkedList ll
    INNER JOIN LinkedListCTE cte ON ll.NodeID =
        cte.NextNodeID
)
SELECT * FROM LinkedListCTE;
```

This recursive query will traverse the linked list starting from NodeID = 2. The output will be:

```
2|Node 2 Data|3
3|Node 3 Data|
```

Chapter 5: Working with Tables

In the previous chapters we have created tables with the command CREATE TABLE.

In this chapter we will explore more in detail the different options SQL offers for handling tables. This includes altering table structures, manipulating data, and employing advanced techniques to maximize the potential of our databases.

Creating Tables

Creating tables in SQL is a fundamental task for structuring and storing data in a database. The process involves defining the table and its columns, specifying data types for each column, and setting any necessary constraints like primary keys. Here's a step-by-step guide on how to create a table using SQL:

1. Choose a table name: select a meaningful name for your table that reflects the data it will store.
2. Define columns and data types: for each column in the table, you need to specify a name and a data type. The data type specifies what kind of data the column can store (e.g., integer, text, date, etc.).
3. Set constraints (optional): constraints are rules that table columns must follow to ensure data integrity. Common constraints include:
    a. PRIMARY KEY: Uniquely identifies each record in the table.
    b. FOREIGN KEY: Links data between two tables.
    c. NOT NULL: Prevents a column from containing a NULL value.
    d. UNIQUE: Prevents a column from having two identical values.
    e. CHECK: Verifies that the value in a particular column meets a certain criterion.
    f. DEFAULT: Assigns a default value to a column when no value is given.
4. Create the table using use the CREATE TABLE statement.

Example

Let's say you want to create a simple table named Customers, which stores customers' information with columns for customer ID, name, and email:

```
CREATE TABLE Customers (
    CustomerID INT PRIMARY KEY,
    Name VARCHAR(100),
    Email VARCHAR(100) NOT NULL
);
```

In this example:

- Customers is the name of the table.
- CustomerID, Name, and Email are column names.
- INT and VARCHAR(100) are data types. INT is for integers, and VARCHAR(100) is for variable-length strings up to 100 characters.
- PRIMARY KEY is a constraint on CustomerID to ensure each customer has a unique ID.
- NOT NULL on the Email column ensures that every customer must have an email address.

Output

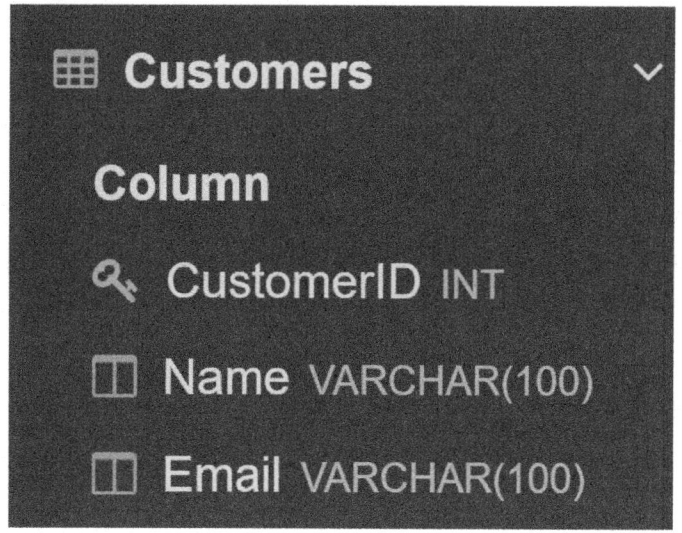

```
⊞ Customers                        ∨

Column

  ⚷  CustomerID INT

  ⊞  Name VARCHAR(100)

  ⊞  Email VARCHAR(100)
```

It's crucial to plan your table structure carefully, considering how the data will be used and the relationships between different tables.

Altering Tables

Altering tables in SQL is a common task that involves making changes to the structure of an existing table. This could include adding new columns, modifying existing columns, deleting columns, or changing constraints.

Let's use the Customers table from the previous example to illustrate various ALTER TABLE operations.

Adding a New Column:

To add a new column, for example, a column for storing the customer's phone number:

```
ALTER TABLE Customers
ADD PhoneNumber VARCHAR(15);
```

This command adds a new column named PhoneNumber with a data type of VARCHAR(15).

Modifying an Existing Column:

If you need to change a column's data type or size, use the MODIFY or ALTER COLUMN command (syntax can vary between SQL databases). For instance, extending the Email column to allow 150 characters:

```
ALTER TABLE Customers
MODIFY Email VARCHAR(150) NOT NULL;
```

Deleting a Column:

To remove a column, use the DROP COLUMN command. For example, removing the PhoneNumber column:

```
ALTER TABLE Customers
DROP COLUMN PhoneNumber;
```

Adding a Constraint:

You can also add constraints. For example, adding a unique constraint to the Email column to ensure all email addresses are unique:

```
ALTER TABLE Customers
ADD UNIQUE (Email);
```

Altering a table can have significant implications on data integrity, especially when modifying or deleting columns. Be cautious with tables that have relationships with other tables. Changes can affect foreign keys and related data.

Altering tables is a powerful feature in SQL that allows you to evolve your database schema as requirements change. However, it should be used judiciously to maintain data integrity and system stability.

Inserting Data

In SQL you can enter data into a database with the help of the INSERT INTO command. The table name in this context refers to the table title into which you want to put data. The names of the different columns included in the table are given in the form of their column numbers, such as column 1, column 2, column 3, etc. The values value1, value2, and value3 relate to the values you want to put into the respective columns, indicating them. Those values may be found in the respective columns.

Syntax:

INSERT INTO table_name (column1, column2, column3, ...)

VALUES (value1, value2, value3, ...);

Let's see an example.

Inserting a Complete Row

To insert a new row into the Customers table, you need to provide values for all the columns since all are mandatory (assuming we didn't change the original structure):

```
INSERT INTO Customers (CustomerID, Name, Email)
VALUES (1, 'John Doe', 'john.doe@example.com');
SELECT * FROM Customers;
```

In this example, you are adding a new customer with a CustomerID of 1, name 'John Doe', and email 'john.doe@example.com'.

Output

```
1|John Doe|john.doe@example.com
```

Inserting Multiple Rows

You can also insert multiple rows in a single statement by providing multiple sets of values:

```
INSERT INTO Customers (CustomerID, Name, Email)
VALUES (2, 'Jane Smith', 'jane.smith@example.com'),
       (3, 'Emily Johnson', 'emily.johnson@example.com');
SELECT * FROM Customers;
```

Output

```
1|John Doe|john.doe@example.com
2|Jane Smith|jane.smith@example.com
3|Emily Johnson|emily.johnson@example.com
```

This statement adds two more customers, each with their own ID, name, and email address.

Updating Table

In SQL, the UPDATE command is executed whenever you need to modify the data already stored in a database.

Syntax:

UPDATE table_name

SET column1 = value1, column2 = value2

WHERE condition

Example
```
UPDATE Customers
SET Email = 'new.email@example.com'
WHERE CustomerID = 1;

SELECT * FROM Customers;
```

Output
```
1|John Doe|new.email@example.com
2|Jane Smith|jane.smith@example.com
3|Emily Johnson|emily.johnson@example.com
```

It's often a good practice to run a SELECT statement first to ensure you're updating the correct records, especially in tables with many rows.

Consider backing up your data before performing mass updates, as an incorrect UPDATE can alter all rows in a table.

Deleting Data

You can use the DELETE command in SQL to delete records from a table if you already have entries in the table and wish to remove them.

Syntax:

DELETE FROM table_name

WHERE condition

Example
```
DELETE FROM Customers
WHERE CustomerID = 1;
SELECT * FROM Customers;
```

Output
```
2|Jane Smith|jane.smith@example.com
3|Emily Johnson|emily.johnson@example.com
```

In this example, WHERE CustomerID = 1 is the condition that specifies which record(s) to delete. In this case, it's the record where CustomerID equals 1.

Chapter 6: Basic and Advanced Query Techniques

SQL facilitates communication with relational databases. The following is a list of some fundamental and sophisticated methods for choosing data:

JOIN

The JOIN operation combines the data from two or more tables, given that there is at least one common column between them.

Syntax:

SELECT * FROM table1
JOIN table2
ON table1.column1 = table2.column2

Code:
```
SELECT *
FROM Store_Tab
JOIN Staff_Tab
ON Store_Tab.Store_id = Staff_Tab.Staff_id;
```
Output:

Store_Name	Store_id	Staff_Name	Staff_id	Staff_salary	Staff_email

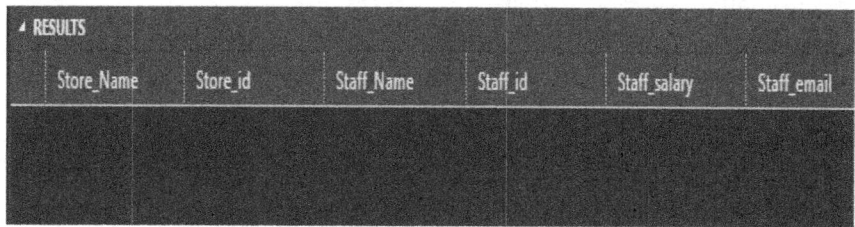

GROUP BY

This function groups data according to your column and produces aggregate statistics such as SUM, AVG, MIN, MAX, etc.

Syntax:

Select column_name , SUM(column_name)
From table_name GROUP BY column_name

Code:
```
SELECT Store_id, SUM(Store_id)
FROM Store_Tab
GROUP BY Store_id;
```

Output:

	Store_id	(No column na...
1	22	22
2	30	30

HAVING

The HAVING clause is a filter that sorts groups according to a certain condition.

Syntax:

Select column_name , SUM(column_name)

From table_name Group By column_name

Having SUM(column_name) [Condition]

Code:
```
SELECT Store_id, SUM(Store_id)
FROM Store_Tab
GROUP BY Store_id
HAVING SUM(Store_id) > 10;
```

Output:

	Store_id	(No column na...
1	22	22
2	30	30

UNION

The UNION operator combines the findings of many SELECT queries into a single overall set of findings.

Syntax:

SELECT column_name FROM table_name UNION SELECT column_name FROM table_name

Code:
```
SELECT Store_Name
FROM Store_Tab
UNION
SELECT Staff_Name
FROM Staff_Tab;
```

Output:

▲ RESULTS	
	Store_Name
1	Andrew Smith
2	Grocery Store
3	Janet Yew
4	Printer Store

ORDER BY

We can sort the output of a query in SQL by using the "ORDER BY" clause, which allows you to sort the results in either descending or ascending order. When sorting the results of the SELECT mainly depending on one or even more columns, the "ORDER BY" phrase is utilized in the statement.

Syntax:

Select column 1, column 2

From table_name

Order column_name

Code:
```
SELECT Store_Name,Store_id
FROM Store_Tab
ORDER BY Store_id
```

Output:

⊿ RESULTS		
	Store_Name	Store_id
1	Grocery Store	22
2	Printer Store	30

ORDER BY DESC

It is possible to categorize the outcome set in ascending or descending directives using the ORDER BY command.

The ORDER BY command will default sort the result set using an ascending sorting order. Use the DESC keyword to sort the entries in descending order from highest to lowest.

Syntax:

Select column 1, column 2

From table_name

Order column_name DESC

Code:
```
SELECT Staff_Name, Staff_salary, Staff_id
FROM Staff_Tab
ORDER BY Staff_id DESC;
```

Output:

⊿ RESULTS			
	Staff_Name	Staff_salary	Staff_id
1	Andrew Smith	2500	35
2	Janet Yew	5000	20

ORDER BY Ascending example:

Syntax:

Select column 1, column 2

From table_name

Order column_name ASC

Code:
```
SELECT Staff_Name,Staff_salary,Staff_id
```

```
FROM Staff_Tab
ORDER BY Staff_id ASC;
```

Output:

	Staff_Name	Staff_salary	Staff_id
1	Janet Yew	5000	20
2	Andrew Smith	2500	35

INTERSECT

The UNION command and the INTERSECT operator work on a single set of SQL statements, whereas the INTERSECT operator acts on two statements. The INTERSECT and UNION operators function as OR operators. However, the INTERSECT operator also functions as an AND operator. This is the chief difference between the two.

Syntax:

SELECT column_name FROM table_name

Intersect

SELECT column_name FROM table_name

Code:

```
SELECT Store_id FROM Store_Tab
INTERSECT
SELECT Staff_id FROM Staff_Tab;
```

Output:

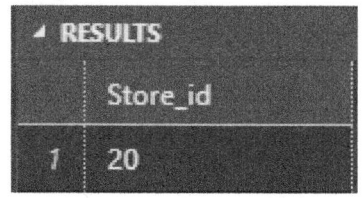

	Store_id
1	20

MINUS

The MINUS command also works on two different SQL queries simultaneously. The MINUS command begins by retaining the result from the first statement. It then takes the result received from the second statement and subtracts it from the result acquired from the first statement to arrive at the final result. If the second statement produces outcomes that were not obtained from the first statement, then the first result will be disregarded, and the second result will be considered valid. It is important to notice that the MINUS command may only choose values unique from one another.

Syntax:

SELECT column_name FROM table_name

MINUS

SELECT column_name FROM table_name

Code:

```
SELECT Store_id FROM Store_Tab
MINUS
SELECT Staff_id FROM Staff_Tab;
```

Output:

	Store_id
1	30
2	22
3	20
4	48

	Staff_id
1	20
2	35

Chapter 7: Advanced SQL Techniques and Optimization

Joining Tables and Working with Multiple Data Sources

In many scenarios, it can be challenging to work with data that is spread across multiple tables or data sources. This is where the concept of joining tables comes into play. Joining tables is the process of combining data from numerous tables into a single result set. This is achieved by identifying a common column between the tables that can be used to match the rows. By doing so, we can create a more comprehensive and useful dataset that can provide valuable insights and aid in decision-making.

Joining tables in SQL is a fundamental technique that is widely used in data management and analysis. It allows us to retrieve data from different tables and combine it into a single result set. Joining tables are performed using the JOIN operator, which can be used with different types of joins, such as inner joins, left outer joins, and right outer joins. The type of join used depends on the desired result.

Inner joins are the most common sort of join in SQL. They only fetch rows with matching values from both tables. Therefore, rows with no matching values will be excluded from the result set. On the other hand, left and right outer joins retrieve every row from one table and any matching rows from the other. In case there are no matching rows, the non-matching rows will have NULL values. This is useful when we want to retrieve all data from one table but only the matching data from the other.

Joining tables in SQL can be a difficult task, especially if dealing with huge datasets. It's important to understand well the data structure and how the tables are connected. However, once mastered, it is an extremely effective tool for data analysis and management. By merging data from multiple sources, we can gain a more comprehensive understanding of our data and make more enlightened decisions based on the insights gained.

In conclusion, joining tables is an essential technique in SQL for working with data that is spread across multiple tables or data sources. It allows us to combine data from different tables into a single result set, providing us with more comprehensive and useful data for analysis and decision-making. By using different types of joins, we can retrieve the desired data and gain valuable insights into our data. While it can be complex, mastering this technique can greatly improve our ability to manage and analyze large and complex datasets.

Joining tables is an essential skill for anyone who works with relational databases, and it is used extensively in data analysis, reporting, and other data management tasks.

INNER JOIN

The INNER JOIN keyword returns only the rows where there is a match in both tables based on the specified join condition.

Syntax:
SELECT *
FROM table1
INNER JOIN table2
ON table1.column = table2.column;

LEFT OUTER JOIN

LEFT OUTER JOIN returns all left table rows and matching right table rows. The right table's columns will be NULL if there is no match.

Syntax:
SELECT *
FROM table1
LEFT OUTER JOIN table2
ON table1.column = table2.column;

RIGHT OUTER JOIN

The RIGHT OUTER JOIN keyword returns all right table rows and matching left table rows. The left table's columns will be NULL if there is no match.

Syntax:
SELECT *
FROM table1
RIGHT OUTER JOIN table2
ON table1.column = table2.column;

FULL OUTER JOIN

The FULL OUTER JOIN keyword returns all the rows from both tables and includes NULL values for the columns that do not match.

Syntax:
SELECT *
FROM table1
FULL OUTER JOIN table2
ON table1.column = table2.column;

CROSS JOIN

The CROSS JOIN keyword returns the Cartesian product of both tables, meaning every row from table1 is combined with every row from table2.

Keep in mind that not all databases allows you to perform every join type. Also, when using the JOIN keyword without specifying an explicit type of join, an INNER JOIN is assumed.

For example, suppose a business has two tables: one with customer information and another with purchase information. By joining these tables on a common column, such as customer ID, it is possible to get a complete picture of each customer's purchase history.

Syntax:
SELECT *
FROM table1
CROSS JOIN table2;

Let's see an example. Assume we have two tables: **'employees'** (with columns **'employee'**, **'employee_name'**) and **'departments'** (with columns **'department_id'**, **'department_name'**). Each employee is assigned to a department, represented by **'department_id'** in both tables.

The INNER JOIN keyword selects records that have matching values in both tables.

```
SELECT employees.employee_name, departments.department_name
FROM employees
INNER JOIN departments ON employees.department_id =
     departments.department_id;
```

This query retrieves a list of employees along with the names of their respective departments, but only for employees who have a corresponding **'department_id'** in both the **'employees'** and **'departments'** tables.

The LEFT OUTER JOIN keyword returns all records from the left table (**'employees'**), and the matched records from the right table (**'departments'**). The result is NULL from the right side if there is no match.

```
SELECT employees.employee_name, departments.department_name
```

```
FROM employees
LEFT OUTER JOIN departments ON employees.department_id =
        departments.department_id;
```
This query includes all employees, even those without a department assigned. If an employee does not belong to a department, the **'department_name'** will be NULL.

The FULL OUTER JOIN keyword returns all records when there is a match in either left (**'employees'**) or right (**'departments'**) table records. Records without a match in the other table are also included, with NULL in the place of missing values.
```
SELECT employees.employee_name, departments.department_name
FROM employees
FULL OUTER JOIN departments ON employees.department_id =
        departments.department_id;
```
This query shows all employees and all departments, with NULLs appearing for employees without departments and for departments without employees. (Note: Not all SQL databases support FULL OUTER JOIN natively, such as MySQL.)

The CROSS JOIN keyword produces a Cartesian product of the two tables, combining each row of the first table with each row of the second table.
```
SELECT employees.employee_name, departments.department_name
FROM employees
CROSS JOIN departments;
```
This query returns a combination of every employee with every department, regardless of whether the employee is associated with the department or not. It's important to note that CROSS JOIN can produce a very large number of rows if both tables have many entries.

Subqueries and temporary tables

Subqueries are queries within queries that are used to perform more complex data manipulations. They are a powerful tool for data analysts and can be used to extract data from multiple tables, filter data based on complex conditions, and perform aggregations.

For example, a subquery could be used to find all the customers who have made purchases over a certain amount and use that data to perform further analysis.

Temporary tables are another way to work with complex data sets. They are tables that are created on the fly and are used to store the intermediate results of a query. This can be helpful in situations where the data is too large to fit into memory or when a query needs to be broken down into smaller, more manageable steps.

Subqueries and temporary tables are advanced SQL techniques that can significantly improve the efficiency and flexibility of SQL data management.

Assume you have two tables: **orders** and **customers**. The columns of the **orders** table are **'order_id'**, **'customer_id'**, and **'order_amount'**. The **customer** table has **'customer_id'**, **'customer_name'**, and **'customer_email'**.

We want to find the total amount of orders made by customers who have a Gmail email address. We can use a subquery to filter out the customers with non-Gmail email addresses and then use a temporary table to store the intermediate result:

Code:
```
CREATE TEMPORARY TABLE temp_customers AS
SELECT customer_id
FROM customers
WHERE customer_email LIKE '%@gmail.com';
SELECT SUM(order_amount) AS total_order_amount
FROM orders
WHERE customer_id IN (SELECT customer_id FROM
        temp_customers);
```

Output:
```
total_order_amount
------------------
$12,345.67
```

The first query creates a temporary table called temp_customers that contains only the customer IDs of customers with a Gmail email address. The LIKE operator is used to match any email address that contains "@gmail.com". The second query uses the temporary table to filter the orders table and retrieve the total order amount made by those customers.

The output of this query would be a single row with the total amount of orders made by customers with Gmail email addresses.

Note that the use of temporary tables and subqueries can greatly improve the efficiency and flexibility of SQL data management, especially when dealing with complex data manipulations. However, it's important to use them judiciously and optimize queries for performance, as they can also lead to slower query execution times if not used correctly.

Grouping and Aggregating Data

Grouping and aggregating data are important methods for summarizing large data sets and extracting insights from them. Grouping involves combining rows based on shared values in one or more columns, while aggregation involves computing summary statistics like counts, sums, averages, and max/min values for each group. For instance, grouping customer purchase data by date can reveal sales trends over time, while aggregating by product category can show which products are most popular. These techniques are widely used in data analysis and reporting and are indispensable for anyone working with large data sets.

Let's consider a table named "sales" that has columns for product, date, and amount. We want to determine the total sales amount for each product.

Code:
```
SELECT product, SUM(amount) AS total_sales
FROM sales
GROUP BY product;
```

Output:
```
product | total_sales
--------+------------
A       | $10,000
B       | $15,000
C       | $5,000
```

Now, let's say we want to calculate the total amount of sales for each product, grouped by year and quarter.

Code:
```
SELECT product, DATE_TRUNC('quarter', date) AS quarter,
       DATE_TRUNC('year', date) AS year, SUM(amount) AS
       total_sales
FROM sales
GROUP BY product, quarter, year;
```

Output:
```
product | quarter | year | total_sales
--------+---------+------+------------
A       | Q1      | 2022 | $3,000
A       | Q2      | 2022 | $5,000
B       | Q1      | 2022 | $6,000
B       | Q2      | 2022 | $9,000
C       | Q1      | 2022 | $2,000
C       | Q2      | 2022 | $3,000
```

Finally, let's say we want to calculate the average sales per day for each product.

Code:
```
SELECT product, AVG(amount) AS avg_sales_per_day
FROM sales
GROUP BY product, DATE_TRUNC('day', date);
```

Output:
```
product | avg_sales_per_day
--------+------------------
A       | $1,111.11
B       | $2,000.00
C       | $714.29
```
In summary, grouping and aggregating data are essential techniques for summarizing and gaining insights from large data sets, and SQL provides powerful tools for performing these operations efficiently and effectively.

Advanced Data Filtering and Sorting Techniques

Filtering and sorting data are fundamental SQL techniques, but advanced techniques can enhance these tasks. SQL offers various operators like LIKE, IN, and BETWEEN to filter data based on complex criteria. Additionally, SQL enables sorting data by multiple columns with different sort orders for each column. These advanced filtering and sorting techniques help identify patterns and trends in large and complex data sets, making them essential for anyone working with such datasets.

Using the LIKE operator to filter data based on pattern matching:

Code:
```
SELECT * FROM employees WHERE last_name LIKE 'S%';
```
Output:

emp_id	first_name	last_name
1	John	Smith
4	Sarah	Sanders

Using the IN operator to filter data based on a list of values:

Code:
```
SELECT * FROM products WHERE category IN ('Electronics',
        'Home Appliances');
```
Output:

prod_id	product_name	category
1	TV	Electronics
3	Refrigerator	Home Appliances
4	Microwave	Home Appliances

Using the BETWEEN operator to filter data based on a range of values:

Code:
SELECT * FROM sales WHERE amount BETWEEN 1000 AND 5000;

Output:

sale_id	date	amount
1	2021-01-01	2000
3	2021-02-01	3000
5	2021-03-01	4000

Stored procedures and functions

Stored procedures and functions are pre-written blocks of code that can be executed within SQL. They are a way to encapsulate complex SQL logic into reusable modules, which can be called from other parts of the code. Stored procedures and functions can improve the efficiency and maintainability of SQL code, as

well as provide a way to modularize complex data manipulation tasks.

For instance, a stored procedure could be used to calculate the average order value for a customer, which could then be used in other parts of the code to make decisions about how to market to that customer.

Stored procedures and functions are critical tools for database administrators and developers as they can help to simplify the management of large, complex databases.

Example 1: Creating a stored procedure

Suppose we have a table called Orders with columns OrderId, CustomerId, and OrderAmount. We want to create a stored procedure that calculates the average order amount for a given customer. Here's how we can create the stored procedure:

Code:
```
CREATE PROCEDURE CalculateAvgOrderAmount
    @customerId INT
AS
BEGIN
    SELECT AVG(OrderAmount) AS AvgAmount
    FROM Orders
    WHERE CustomerId = @customerId
END
```

The CREATE PROCEDURE statement creates a new stored procedure called CalculateAvgOrderAmount. This stored procedure takes one input parameter @customerId, which is used in the WHERE clause to filter the orders for the given customer. The SELECT statement calculates the average order amount for the given customer and returns the result in a column called AvgAmount.

To execute the stored procedure and see the output, we can use the EXEC statement.

Code:
```
EXEC CalculateAvgOrderAmount @customerId = 123
```

This will calculate the average order amount for a customer with CustomerId = 123 and return the result in a column called AvgAmount.

Output:
```
Query OK, 0 rows affected
```

Example 2: Creating a function

Suppose we want to create a function that calculates the discount amount for a given order amount. The discount amount is calculated as follows:

If the order amount is less than 100, the discount amount is 0%

If the order amount is between 100 and 500, the discount amount is 5%

If the order amount is greater than 500, the discount amount is 10%

Here's how we can create the function:

Code:
```
CREATE FUNCTION CalculateDiscountAmount
    (@orderAmount DECIMAL(10, 2))
RETURNS DECIMAL(10, 2)
AS
BEGIN
    DECLARE @discountAmount DECIMAL(10, 2)
    IF @orderAmount < 100
        SET @discountAmount = 0
    ELSE IF @orderAmount <= 500
        SET @discountAmount = @orderAmount * 0.05
    ELSE
        SET @discountAmount = @orderAmount * 0.1
    RETURN @discountAmount
END
```

The CREATE FUNCTION statement creates a new function called CalculateDiscountAmount. This function gets one input argument, @orderAmount, that is used to determine the discount amount. The RETURNS clause indicates that the function will return a decimal value with a 10 digits accuracy and a 2 digits scale.

We use an IF statement within the function to compute the discount amount depending on the order amount. The result is stored in the variable @discountAmount and returned with the RETURN command.

To execute the function and see the output, we can use the SELECT statement:

```
SELECT OrderId, OrderAmount,
       dbo.CalculateDiscountAmount(OrderAmount) AS
       DiscountAmount
FROM Orders
```

This will calculate the discount amount for each order in the Orders table using the CalculateDiscountAmount function and return the result in a column called DiscountAmount.

Output:

```
+------------------+
| avg_order_value  |
+------------------+
| 49.333333333333  |
+------------------+
1 row in set (0.00 sec)
```

Indexing and performance optimization

Indexing is a crucial aspect of performance optimization in SQL. When a database table contains a large number of records, the database engine may take longer to search for specific data within the table. This is where indexing comes into play. An index is a type of data structure with information about the information stored in one or more columns of a table, allowing the database engine to rapidly find the desired rows. It works similarly to a book's table of contents, allowing readers to locate relevant sections quickly and easily.

To construct an index in SQL, use the CREATE INDEX statement, which provides the index's name, the table and column(s) to be indexed, as well as other parameters like index type and sort order.

Remember that indexing isn't always the answer to slow query performance. In some cases, indexing too many columns or creating indexes on columns that are rarely used can actually slow down query performance. Therefore, it's essential to analyze the query execution plan and determine which columns would benefit from indexing.

In addition to indexing, there are other techniques that can be used to optimize SQL queries for better performance. One of these techniques is query optimization, which involves rewriting queries to minimize the use of subqueries, selecting appropriate data types and normalization, and using efficient join techniques.

Another technique for optimizing SQL queries is to use appropriate data types and normalization. For example, if a column in a table contains only numeric data, it's best to use a numeric data type (such as INT or FLOAT) rather than a text data type (such as VARCHAR). This can help to optimize memory while improving query performance.

Normalization is the process of structuring data in a database to decrease redundancy and increase consistency. By breaking up large tables into smaller tables and establishing relationships between them, normalization can help to eliminate duplicate data and improve query performance.

If indexing and query optimization do not improve query performance, the database administrator may consider partitioning data across multiple servers or using advanced techniques such as sharding or replication. Partitioning is the process of splitting a large table into smaller, easier to manage sections depending on specified criteria like date range or geographic area. Sharding distributes data over several servers using a predetermined sharding key, whereas replication creates multiple copies of the same data on multiple servers.

In conclusion, indexing and performance optimization are critical techniques for managing large and complex databases. By creating indexes on commonly used columns and optimizing SQL queries through

Example 1: Indexing

Suppose we have a table named "users" with columns "id", "username", "email", and "created_at". To improve query performance, we can create an index on the "username" column, which is commonly used in queries:

Code:
```
CREATE INDEX idx_username ON users (username);
SELECT * FROM users WHERE username = 'jdoe';
```
Output:
```
| id | username  | email             | created_at          |
|----|-----------|-------------------|---------------------|
| 1  | jdoe      | jdoe@example.com  | 2022-01-01 12:00:00 |
```

Example 2: Performance optimization

Suppose we have a table named "orders" with columns "id", "customer_id", "product_id", and "quantity". To optimize the performance of a query that calculates the total order value for each customer, we can use the SUM() function to aggregate the order values and GROUP BY the "customer_id" column:

Code:
```
SELECT customer_id, SUM(quantity * price) AS
       total_order_value
```

```
FROM orders
JOIN products ON orders.product_id = products.id
GROUP BY customer_id;
```

This query joins the "orders" and "products" tables on the "product_id" column and calculates the total order value for each customer by multiplying the "quantity" and "price" columns and aggregating the results with SUM(). The GROUP BY clause groups the results by the "customer_id" column.

Output:

```
| customer_id | total_order_value |
|-------------|-------------------|
| 1           | 150.00            |
| 2           | 75.00             |
```

These examples demonstrate how indexing and performance optimization can be used to improve the performance of SQL queries and make them more efficient for managing large, complex databases.

Example 3: Normalization

Suppose we have the following table called "Orders":

Order ID	Customer Name	Item Name	Quantity	Price
1	John Smith	T-Shirt	2	20
2	Jane Doe	Jacket	1	50
3	John Smith	Jeans	1	30
4	Bob Johnson	T-Shirt	3	20
5	Jane Doe	Hat	2	10

This table violates the first normal form (1NF) because some columns contain multiple values. Specifically, the "Item Name" column contains multiple values, which makes it difficult to query the data. We can fix this by creating two new tables: one for the customers and another for the items.

The "Customers" table would look like this:

Customer ID	Customer Name
1	John Smith
2	Jane Doe
3	Bob Johnson

The "Items" table would look like this:

Item ID	Item Name	Price
1	T-Shirt	20
2	Jacket	50
3	Jeans	30
4	Hat	10

We can then create a new "Orders" table that references the "Customers" and "Items" tables:

Order ID	Customer ID	Item ID	Quantity
1	1	1	2
2	2	2	1
3	1	3	1
4	3	1	3
5	2	4	2

This new "Orders" table is now in second normal form (2NF) because it does not have any partial dependencies. Specifically, the "Quantity" column is dependent only on the "Order ID" and "Item ID" columns, and the "Price" column is dependent only on the "Item ID" column.

It is also in the third normal form (3NF) because it does not have any transitive dependencies. Specifically, the "Price" column is not dependent on the "Customer ID" column, only on the "Item ID" column.

Code:
```
SELECT o.OrderID, c.CustomerName, i.ItemName, o.Quantity,
       (o.Quantity * i.Price) AS TotalPrice
FROM Orders o
INNER JOIN Customers c ON o.CustomerID = c.CustomerID
INNER JOIN Items i ON o.ItemID = i.ItemID
```

Chapter 8: Integrations with other Data Management Tools

What is Data Management?

According to the definition provided, data management is "an extensive set of techniques, ideas, procedures, and processes along with a wide variety of associated systems that enable an organization to take ownership of its data resources." "Data Management as a usually headed participates with the full lifespan of a given set of data assets from its classic creation point to its final savings, how it proceeds and changes throughout its entire life through to the internal (and external) data feeds of an enterprise." "Data Management as a reached the spot is engaged with the full lifespan of a provided data asset out of its original conception point to its final superannuation, how it advances and changes throughout its

Products for managing data are quite well recognized in the business sector. Many of the most successful firms in the world, like IBM, Oracle, Amazon, Microsoft, Google, and Dell, have developed collections of data management solutions to fulfil their customers' needs. Because of the adaptability of these

goods for every organization, they can construct a chain of processing of information based on the firm's data.

Data Management Functions

- Creating, accessing, and updating data across multiple data levels.
- Maintain copies of data locally as well as on the cloud.
- Use the data across your applications, analytics, and algorithmic processes.
- Offer both high availability and a recovery plan in the event of a calamity.
- Secure data and give privacy.
- Using the retention standards and compliance requirements as guides, archive the data and then delete it.

Approach to Data Management

- Access to the data means capturing and gathering information regardless of where it is kept.

- Data quality ensures that data is correct and useable for the purpose it was collected from beginning to finish. Regardless of the amount or kind of data, it assists in producing better and cleaner results.
- Preparing data for analytics and reporting is called "data preparation."
- Integration of data refers to the processes carried out to merge several sorts of data.
- Data federation is the process of virtually integrating data in such a way as to make it possible to see combined data drawn from several different sources, all without having to relocate and store the integrated view in a new place.
- Data governance may be defined as the rules and choices that assist in managing data to ensure harmony between the digital strategy and the business plan. It makes it possible to effectively manage all vital data assets, irrespective of their size, nature, or location.
- Identifying, organizing, and maintaining all necessary and common data in a single hub is called master data management, or MDM for short.
- Examining data as it is generated is known as "data streaming." It allows users to filter, purify, and rectify rapidly changing data before it's saved, enabling them to receive immediate, concrete benefits in real-time and via a single interface.

SQL Data Management Tools

There is a wide selection of SQL data management solutions on the market today, and the particular requirements of the company or the individual user often determine the tool selection. The succeeding is a list of samples of tools for managing SQL data:

- MySQL is a well-known, fully accessible SQL management system for databases often used for developing web applications.
- Microsoft SQL Server is a powerful database management system that is widely used. It is available in multiple versions to satisfy the needs of a wide range of businesses.
- Oracle Database is a strong SQL management system for databases that is both comprehensive and scalable. It also has many built-in security measures.
- SQLite is a compact and identity SQL database system that is frequently utilized in integrated devices, portable devices, and web browsers.

- IBM DB2 is a robust and scalable SQL management system for databases that many major enterprises utilize. It is marketed under the brand name "DB2."
- MariaDB is a community-driven MySQL derivative with many new capabilities and significant speed enhancements.
- MySQL, Oracle, SQL Server, and PostgreSQL are just some of the prominent database engines that Amazon RDS, a cloud-based databases management service support.
- MySQL and PostgreSQL are two of the database management systems that are supported by Google Cloud SQL, which is a cloud-based SQL database management service.

The following piece of SQL code is an example of operating a data management tool, especially the MySQL Workbench. The program generates a brand-new database and a table inside it.

The MySQL Workbench tool, which offers a graphical user experience for controlling databases, tables, and data, may be used to execute the SQL code provided here. The program first establishes a new database with the name my database, then generates a table with the name my table with the columns id, name, age, and email, adds some info into the table, and then retrieves all of the data from the table.

Code:
```
-- Creating a new database xyz
CREATE DATABASE xyz;
-- Use the new database xyz
USE xyz;
-- Create a new table
CREATE TABLE Emp_Tab
(
    emp_id INT PRIMARY KEY,
    emp_name VARCHAR(50) NOT NULL,
    emp_age INT,
    emp_email VARCHAR(100)
);
-- Insert some data into the table
INSERT INTO Emp_Tab(emp_id,emp_name, emp_age, emp_email)
VALUES
    (1,'Sara', 25, 'sara@example.com'),
    (2,'Janet', 30, 'janet@example.com'),
    (3,'Bobby', 35, 'bobby@example.com');
-- Select data from the table
SELECT * FROM Emp_Tab;
```
Output:

	emp_id	emp_name	emp_age	emp_email
1	1	Sara	25	sara@example....
2	2	Janet	30	janet@example...
3	3	Bobby	35	bobby@examp...

Importing and exporting data to and from other formats

- SQL databases may support a wide range of information import and export protocols. The following is a list of common formats and procedures that may be used to import and export information to and from SQL databases:
- CSV: Comma-separated values (CSV) files are a common format for transferring and importing data from SQL databases. CSV files include values that are separated by commas. Most SQL database management programs include data importation and exportation support using the CSV file format. We can use CSV format by connecting to your host and setting up a new database. Upload the CSV file by utilizing the wizard provided by SQL Server. Put text qualifying matches and column widths into every column using the manual input method.

Code:
```
LOAD DATA INFILE 'data_file.csv'
INTO TABLE data_table
FIELDS TERMINATED BY ','
ENCLOSED BY '"'
LINES TERMINATED BY '\n'
IGNORE 1 ROWS;
```

This code inserts the data loaded from a CSV file referred to as data_file.csv into a table referred to as data table. It is specified in the FIELDS TERMINATED BY clause that commas separate the values in the CSV file, and it is specified in the Wrapped BY clause that the fields are fenced in double-quotes. The LINES TERMINATED BY clause ensures that each row in the CSV file is finished with a newline character. This is the default behavior. The Overlook 1 ROWS clause causes the first row of the CSV file, which is almost often the header row, to be ignored.

Code:
```
SELECT *
```

```
INTO OUTFILE 'data_file.csv'
FIELDS TERMINATED BY ','
ENCLOSED BY '"'
LINES TERMINATED BY '\n'
FROM data_table;
```

A CSV file with the name data_file.csv is created from the data taken from a table with the name data_table. The input file's name and location are specified by the INTO OUTFILE clause. In this scenario, the FIELDS TERMINATED BY, ENCLOSED BY, and LINES TERMINATED BY clauses are used to determine the output file format. Their values are the same of the values used in the previous example.

JavaScript Object Notation, or JSON, is a compact data transmission format that is widely used in web applications. JSON data can be imported and exported to and from some SQL databases. JSON is now the data communication format most often utilized despite its widespread popularity. All online database services, web browsers (such as Firefox and Internet Explorer), and web services that return results either deliver results structured as JSON text or accept input formatted as JSON. The majority of current web-based and mobile-based services return information in this format. Because the information is formatted as JSON text when received from other systems, JSON is also saved in SQL Server 2016 as text.

Code:
```
LOAD DATA INFILE 'data_file.json'
INTO TABLE data_table
FIELDS TERMINATED BY ''
LINES TERMINATED BY '\n'
(@json)
SET my_id = JSON_EXTRACT(@json, '$.my_id'),
    my_name = JSON_EXTRACT(@json, '$.my_name'),
    my_age = JSON_EXTRACT(@json, '$.my_age'),
    my_email = JSON_EXTRACT(@json, '$.my_email');
```

Spreadsheet application Excel: Microsoft Excel is one of the most popular spreadsheet applications available, and the majority of SQL databases include support for exporting and importing data in Excel format. Sharing data with individuals who are not technically savvy or integrating information from different sources are also potential use for this feature.

Code:
```
SELECT id, name, age, email
INTO OUTFILE 'data_file.xls'
FROM data_table;
```

- A common standard for transferring data between programs is XML, which is an "extensible markup language." Some SQL

databases provide functionality for exporting and importing data in XML format.
- Additional formats: In addition to being able to import and export data in fixed-width, tab-separated, and pipe-separated values, SQL databases May also export and import data in other formats.

The succeeding is a list of practices that may be used to import and export content to and from SQL databases:

- Utility programs for the command line Many SQL databases come along with utility programs for the command line that make it possible to import and export data. The MySQL command-line tool, for instance, comes with the mysqlimport command for entering information from CSV files and the mysqldump tool for sending the data to SQL files. Both of these commands may be found in the MySQL documentation.
- Graphical user interfaces. The vast majority of SQL database management systems are equipped with a graphical user interface (GUI) that allows for the importation and exportation of data. These graphical user interfaces normally allow you to choose the type and file to import or export. Some may also give you a choice to choose certain tables, columns, or rows.
- Personalized scripts: Programming languages such as Python and Java may be used to write individualized scripts that can be used for import and export processes that are more complicated. Using the application programming interfaces (APIs) or libraries made available by the database management system, these scripts can communicate with the SQL database.

Chapter 9: Working with Data in a Distributed Environment

What is a Distributed Environment?

Relational databases fall into the category known as distributed SQL, which incorporates the most important aspects of both standard SQL and NoSQL systems. It offers a distributed implementation of a single relational, logical database that may be used across several network hosts. Distributed SQL databases instantly duplicate and distribute data across all servers, often called nodes. Each node in the database can process read and write queries.

Around the middle of the 2010s, distributed SQL databases were available with transactional applications. They provide the fundamental functionality that may be encountered in both relational databases (SQL) and non-relational databases (NoSQL). The database is capable of horizontal scaling and robust consistency and natively supports ACID transactions across unavailability and regional zones in on-premises data centers or the cloud.

Key Features and Concepts of the Distributed Database

- An SQL application programming interface (API) for data modelling and querying, including support for conventional RDBMS, features such as database objects, partial indexing, database objects, and triggers.
- Smart distributed processing execution means that the processing of queries may get closer to the facts rather than the data being sent across the network, which can slow down the response times of queries.
- Intelligent and transparent distributed information storage, comprising data and index that should be continuously shared among various cluster's nodes so that no one node creates a bottleneck in processing requests. Data dissemination and intelligent rebalancing may ensure good performance and high reliability.
- When you spread your data over different servers, you must select how to divide your data. This decision must be made before you distribute your data. To do this, your data will need to be segmented into subsets that will be kept on separate nodes. Several values, such

as a timeframe or geographical location, may be used to divide data. This may assist in increasing the performance as well as the scalability of the system.
- Joining tables in a cloud system hosted on various nodes might be difficult from a performance standpoint due to the distributed nature of the environment. If you want to maximize the efficiency of your queries, you may need to use specific methods such as multicast joins or partitioned joins.
- Maintaining data consistency may be difficult when dispersed over numerous nodes, making errors more likely to occur. To guarantee that any changes made to the data are accurately transmitted across all nodes, you may be required to use distributed protocols or other methods.
- If you have a great number of nodes, it is necessary to ensure that the burden is spread evenly among all the nodes in the system. This process is called "load balancing." You may need to implement a network interface or another strategy to guarantee that the system operates at peak performance.
- Maintaining privacy and integrity becomes an even more pressing concern when data is stored across numerous nodes. You are responsible for ensuring that the data is adequately secured and that use is strictly regulated.

Primary Requirements of the Distributed Database

It is significant to keep in observance that distributed SQL is still a database, and as such, it is needed to meet the baseline requirements necessary for it to be considered a database. Even though the seven requirements listed above are specific to dividing up SQL (well, all of them except for the SQL thing), it is still important to remember that distributed SQL has these requirements. There is a predetermined level of performance expected for the following:

Administration: You should have no trouble installing and configuring the database with the help of a collection of tools based on command lines and graphical interfaces. This comprises the capabilities of controlling the environment and the information lifecycle for backup and restoration, configuring indexes and partitions, constructing new DDL, building new tables, defining the new schema, and applying new schema.

Optimization: The database ought to make it possible for a database administrator (DBA) to obtain information about the effectiveness of queries and their role in improving how they are executed. This includes more complex features like a cost-based estimator and a cloud system that may be challenging to implement and introduces novel ideas.

Authentication, authorization, and accountability are three of the most important aspects of data safety that a database needs to be able to provide. Data safety is an essential component of every corporate software product. It should not be able to function alone and should instead integrate with a single truth source for identity management and governance.

Integration: A database cannot work independently and has to be integrated with the apps you already have using tried and proven drivers. It should be able to interact smoothly with any current ORMs and give the capability to either import or export data in bulk. It should also give essential features that enable it to interact with ETL tools and update data capture features to interface with more modern services such as carried out and the results or cloud storage. In addition, it should have controls that help it to work with ETL tools.

How is data processed in distributed database?

A vast quantity of data enters a distributed data processing system via various distinct entry points. This causes the system to process the data. The act of taking in new information is referred to as data ingestion.

Once the input begins to flood in, the system architecture consists of many layers, each of which divides the processing into several distinct components at various points.

Layer for the Collection and Preparation of Data

This layer is in charge of gathering data from various outside sources and processing it to be analyzed by the system. It also handles any necessary formatting. When there is no consistent format for the data being ingested, in its natural state, it is either raw and unstructured or semi-structured. It could also be tax returns, policy forms, medical bills, etc. The data processing layer is responsible for transforming the data into a consistent and standard format and classifying the data according to the business logic the system will handle. The layer has an intelligence high enough to do all of this without any assistance from a person of any kind.

Layer for Data Security

Moving data exposes it to potential security vulnerabilities. The information security protocol has to guarantee that the data transfer is carried out securely by keeping a close eye on it at all times, using various security protocols, and so on.

Layer for the Data Storage

After the data has been received, it must be stored somewhere permanent. There are many various ways to do this task. When analytics are performed in real-time on streaming data, data storage and management are handled via distributed caches that are kept in memory. On the other hand, if the data is just being handled in a conventional manner, such as batch processing, distributed databases specifically developed to manage large amounts of data are utilized to store the information.

Layer for Processing of Data

This tier processes the data and includes the logic that is the real thing. It is accountable for the layer above it. This layer applies business logic to the data to get information that is useful from the data. The most common approaches for this purpose are machine learning, predictive modelling, descriptive modelling, and decision modelling.

Data Visualization Layer

The data visualization layer is a critical component of the data analysis process. It serves as a bridge between the raw data and the user, presenting complex information in an easily understandable format. Once data has been collected and processed, it is transmitted to the data visualization layer.

Web-accessible dashboards make up the data visualization layer. These dashboards display data in graphs, charts, and infographics. Users can quickly understand data trends and insights.

One of the key benefits of the data visualization layer is that it allows users to interact with the data in real time. This means that users can modify the parameters of the visualization, such as changing the timeframe or selecting specific data sets, to gain a more detailed understanding of the information being presented.

Another benefit of the data visualization layer is that it can be customized to suit the needs of different users. For example, a sales team might use a different dashboard than a marketing team, as their needs and objectives are likely to be different. This flexibility means that the data visualization layer can be tailored to meet the specific needs of different departments within an organization.

Overall, the data visualization layer is an important part of the data analysis workflow. It allows users to acquire insights quickly and easily from complicated data sets and may be tailored to the specific needs of individuals within an organization. Organizations that use data visualization tools effectively can make more informed decisions and acquire a competitive advantage in their marketplaces.

Advantages of the distributed database

- Data warehouses are skilled in modular development, which means that processes can be expanded by introducing new desktops and

local data to a new site and integrating them in a distributed manner without any interruptions. This can be done without disrupting the overall operation of the distributed database.
- When there is an issue with one of the system's centralized databases, the whole thing grinds to a halt. However, with distributed database systems, if a component fails, the system will continue to operate, although with a decreased level of performance, until the issue is resolved.
- Suppose the data is stored close to the areas in which it is used the most. In that case, administrators of distributed database systems may reduce the amount of money spent on communication. In centralized systems, this is not something that can be done.

Chapter 10: Building Data Pipelines and Automating Data Processes

What are data pipelines and their uses?

A data pipeline is a series of components that work together to automate the gathering, organization, mobility, modification, and processing of information as it travels from a source to its destination. This ensures that the data arrives in a form that businesses can use to facilitate the development of a data-driven culture.

Pipelines for data movement are an essential component of every organization's data architecture. Implementing a data pipeline that is well-designed, resilient, and scalable in your organization will assist your company in successfully managing, analyzing, and organizing massive amounts of data to generate business value.

There is a use case for data pipelines in almost every business and sector today. It may be anything as simple as moving data from one location to another, or it could be something as involved as processing data for use in supervised ml recommendation engines that enhance product offers. Some popular data pipeline use applications include:

- Consolidating data from many sources (SaaS tools, databases) into a big data repository (data warehouses, data lakes) to create a single authoritative source for the organization's data is known as data consolidation.
- They are improving the overall performance of the backend system by moving data to huge data stores and minimizing the amount of strain placed on operational databases.
- Ensuring the data's quality, dependability, and consistency across all business units to provide quicker data access

Components of a data pipeline

1. Data sources

The point of origin of the data is the primary focus of the first stage of a contemporary data pipeline. Any system that your company makes use of to create data has the potential to serve as a data source, including the following systems:

- Analytics data (user behavior data)
- Transactional data (data from sales and product records)
- Data obtained from third parties, or data that your organization does not directly acquire but does utilize.

2. The gathering and processing of data:

The ingestion layer is the next element in the data pipeline, and it is responsible for delivering information into the pipeline. This layer connects to a variety of internal and external data sources via various protocols, using tools like Striim. This layer can transport both batch and streaming data to big data storage.

3. Data processing

Through data validation, cleaning, normalization, transformation, and enrichment, the processing layer is responsible for bringing the data to a condition where the system can consume it. This processing component of the data pipeline may be done either before or after the data is saved in the data store. This decision is made based on the firm's unique architecture, either ETL (Extract Transform Load) or ELT (Extract Load Transform). The data is extracted, converted, and fed into the data stores in an Attach processing architecture. This architecture is often used when the data storage is a data warehouse. In systems based on ELT, the data is first imported into data lakes and then converted into a state consumable for various business use cases.

4. Data storage

This component is in charge of supplying the data pipeline with storage that is reliable, scalable, and protected from unauthorized access. Large data repositories, such as database systems (for structured data) and data lakes, are often included in their composition.

5. Data consumption

The consumption layer delivers and integrates scalable, high-performance tools for drawing data from storage locations. In addition, the process of considering layer offers analytics to all users across the company employing function insights tools that allow for analysis strategies such as SQL, shipment insights, documenting scorecards, and machine learning. The data consumption layer can access these analytics.

6. Data governance

The security and oversight layer protects the data in the data layer and the processing resources of all other levels from unauthorized access.

Mechanisms for password protection, encryption, network security, use monitoring, and auditing are included in this tier of the security stack. In addition, the security layer records the activities of all the other levels and generates an exhaustive audit trail. Additionally, the other data pipeline components have native integration with the security and oversight layer.

7. Designing data pipeline in SQL

There are a few stages involved in creating a data pipeline using SQL, including the following:

- Finding where the data came from: Identify the source or sources that will feed into your pipeline. Databases, flat files, application programming interfaces (APIs), and other data sources might be included here.
- Planning the flow of data involves determining how the data will move through the pipeline, determining what kinds of transformations will be made to the data, and determining where the information will be kept.
- The first step in defining a schema is determining the database or file structure that will eventually be used to store the data. Creating the columns, tables, types of data, and any restrictions imposed is a part of this step.
- Writing SQL scripts You will need to write SQL scripts to extract, manipulate, and load the data (ETL). To extract the data, SQL statements such as SELECT, JOIN, and UNION may need to be used. Additionally, this may require the application of filters, the aggregation of data, the cleaning of data, and the joining of databases.
- Testing and validating: Perform testing and validation on the pipeline to check that the information is being processed appropriately and that it satisfies the quality requirements that have been established.
- Monitoring and maintenance: Establish procedures for monitoring and maintaining the pipeline so any problems may be identified and remedied as soon as possible. This will guarantee that the pipeline operates efficiently.

Code:
```
SELECT
p.Name,
p.Age,
p.Email,
p.Name AS s.Name
FROM office.Customer_Tab p
```

```
JOIN office.Customer_Tab p ON s.product_name =
     p.product_name
GROUP BY
s.transaction_date,
s.customer_name,
s.product_name,
s.price,
s.quantity_sold,
p.price
```

Automating data processes in SQL

To automate data operations using SQL, you must schedule SQL scripts to run automatically at predetermined intervals rather than manually perform them. The following is a rundown of the fundamental actions to take:

- To extract, convert, and reload (ETL) data from various sources and to do any required transformations, you will need to write the SQL scripts.
- Determine the scheduling application: Determine the scheduling application you will use to arrange the SQL scripts to execute automatically. Tools for scheduling include Vista Scheduling, cron for Linux/Unix, and SQL Server Agent for Microsoft SQL Server. Some examples of scheduling tools are shown below.
- Put the scripts on your schedule: Make a timetable for the execution of the SQL scripts by using the tool for scheduling tasks. Set the start time and the number of times the scripts execute per day.
- Perform tests on the automation: Perform tests on the automation to confirm that the SQL routines are operating properly and delivering the desired results. This may be done by manually running the scripts to confirm that they function properly and then checking to see whether the results of the regular runs are the same as those of the manual runs.
- Maintain a close eye on the automation: Maintain a close eye on the automation process to ensure that it is operating properly and that any problems are recognized and fixed as soon as possible. This step may require you to set up notifications informing you of any problems or faults.
- It is essential to keep in mind data security, security, and speed while automating data operations in SQL. It would be best if you also described the processes and SQL scripts you use to make it simpler to resolve problems and implement improvements in the future. Lastly, ensure that you follow the best practices for arranging, such as limiting scheduling tasks during high-use hours or overlaps with

other jobs, which might create difficulties with the system's performance.

Using SQL in data analysis and business intelligence

SQL is a useful tool for business intelligence and data analysis because it enables users to extract, process, and analyze massive amounts of data rapidly and effectively. In the areas of data and business intelligence, some of the techniques that SQL may be put to use include as follows:

- Data querying and filtering: SQL lets consumers question and filter massive databases, enabling them to get the information pertinent to their research.
- SQL may join many tables jointly using a single key, enabling users to mix data from various sources and generate deeper insights.
- Data aggregation: SQL can produce aggregate statistics like tallies, sums, means, and medians, which makes it easier to examine huge datasets and detect patterns and trends. SQL can also do data grouping, which groups similar values into a single value.
- SQL may generate views and reports that offer a description of the information, making it simpler to comprehend and express insights. This can be accomplished by creating sorts and reporting that describe the information.
- Data preparation and cleaning: You may use SQL to wash and organize data for analysis by eliminating duplicates, formatting the data, and dealing with missing value situations.
- SQL may be used to develop data models that offer a conceptual representation of the data. This makes it much simpler to comprehend the linkages and dependencies between the various data items.
- To execute data modelling, such as developing predictive models and projecting future trends, SQL may be used in concert with other statistical tools to achieve these tasks.

SQL is also often used in data analysis products like Excel, Power BI, and QlikView. These tools offer user-friendly interfaces to view and analyze data, and they make use of SQL. Users of these tools can generate displays, clickable reports, and data visualizations, all of which assist business users in gaining insights and making choices driven by data. SQL is an important device for data research and business intelligence because it enables users to get useful insights from enormous amounts of data.

Security and privacy considerations in SQL

When dealing with SQL databases, security and privacy are important factors to keep in mind.

Control of access: It is essential to limit direct connections to the SQL server database to just those users who have been specifically permitted to do so. Integrating user authentication and authorization mechanisms such as participation network access and least privilege are two methods that may be used to accomplish this goal.

For example, let's say we want to create a user account named "user1" with password"password1" and grant them permission to select from a table called "employees".

Code:
```
CREATE USER user1 IDENTIFIED BY 'password1';
GRANT SELECT ON employees TO user1;
```

Output:
User "user1" is now created and has permission to select from the "employees" table.

Encryption: Sensitive data stored in SQL databases must be encrypted to safeguard against unwanted access. Encrypting data while it is stored and in transit is one way to accomplish this goal. Examples of such methods include SSL/TLS encrypting the message encryption algorithms.

For example, let's say we want to encrypt a column called "social_security_number" in a table called "customers".

Code:
```
ALTER TABLE customers ADD COLUMN
      social_security_number_encrypted VARCHAR(100);
UPDATE customers SET social_security_number_encrypted =
      AES_ENCRYPT(social_security_number,
      'encryption_key');
```

Output:
A new column called "social_security_number_encrypted" is added to the "customers" table, and the values from the original "social_security_number" column are encrypted using the AES encryption algorithm.

Data mask and anonymization: Data masking and privacy-preserving methods may be used to secure sensitive data. These approaches include replacing actual data with fictional data that maintains the same statistical features as the original data.

For example, let's say we want to mask the "email" column in a table called "users" by replacing the first 3 characters with "xxx".

Code:
```
UPDATE users SET email = CONCAT('xxx', SUBSTR(email, 4));
```
Output:

The first 3 characters of each value in the "email" column are replaced with "xxx".

Audit logging: You may use audit logging to observe and track user engagement in the SQL database. It provides a full record of who accessed the data and what modifications were done. Audit verification can be used to track user activity in the SQL database.

For example, let's say we want to enable audit logging for the "employees" table to track all insert, update, and delete operations.

Code:
```
ALTER TABLE employees ENABLE AUDIT;
```
Output:

Audit logging is enabled for the "employees" table.

Updates and patches regularly: To guard against known vulnerabilities, it is essential to regularly maintain the SQL database and any other software connected with it up to the most current security patches and updates.

For example, let's say we want to update the SQL server software to the latest version.

Code:
```
UPDATE sql_server SET version = '5.0' WHERE id = 1;
```
Output:

The SQL server software is updated to version 5.0

Disaster and backup recovery: It is recommended that backup copies of the SQL server database be taken to guarantee that data is recoverable if lost due to a catastrophe or other catastrophic event.

For example, let's say we want to create a backup of the "employees" table.

Code:
```
BACKUP TABLE employees TO 'backup/employees_backup.sql';
```
Output:

A backup file named "employees_backup.sql" is created in the "backup" directory.

In today's digital age, securing sensitive data is of utmost importance, particularly when it comes to SQL databases. Companies that use SQL databases must adhere to strict privacy and security policies to safeguard against potential security breaches, unauthorized access, and data loss. By doing so, they can ensure the security of sensitive information while complying with applicable legislation and standards.

One crucial aspect of securing sensitive data in SQL databases is controlling access. Direct connections to the SQL server database must be restricted to only those users who have been authorized to do so. Integrating user authentication and authorization mechanisms like participation network access and least privilege can limit access to the database to only authorized users.

Another key aspect of data security in SQL databases is encryption. Sensitive data stored in SQL databases must be encrypted to safeguard against unwanted access. Encrypting data while it is stored and in transit is one way to accomplish this goal. Examples of such methods include SSL/TLS encrypting the message encryption algorithms. Data masking and anonymization are also effective ways of securing sensitive data.

Audit logging is yet another important factor in securing data in SQL databases. It allows companies to monitor and track user activity within the database, providing a full record of who accessed the data and what modifications were made. Audit verification can be used to track user activity in the SQL database.

It is also crucial to regularly update and maintain the SQL database and all associated software up to the latest security patches and updates to protect against known vulnerabilities. Disaster and backup recovery plans should also be in place to ensure that data is recoverable in the event of data loss due to a catastrophe or other catastrophic event.

By adhering to these privacy and security issues, companies can ensure that sensitive data housed in SQL databases are secured and protected against potential security breaches, unauthorized access, and data loss. However, it is essential to do frequent reviews and updates on these safeguards to stay up to date with the constantly shifting vulnerabilities and dangers in the digital world. By taking these measures, companies can ensure the security and integrity of their sensitive data.

JavaScript Programming

Introduction

Welcome to the fascinating world of JavaScript! In today's digital age, where interactivity and dynamic web experiences reign supreme, JavaScript has emerged as a powerful programming language that fuels the modern web. Its versatility and widespread adoption have made it an essential skill for aspiring developers, offering immense potential in the job market.

JavaScript was initially created to enhance web pages by adding interactivity and enabling client-side scripting. However, it has evolved far beyond its humble beginnings and now finds application in a myriad of domains. JavaScript has evolved into a vital tool for creating many different kinds of applications, from front-end development to server-side programming, mobile app development to game development. It has even extended its reach into emerging fields like IoT, where JavaScript is used to control and manage connected devices.

The demand for JavaScript developers is soaring, as numerous tech companies and startups embrace its power. By mastering JavaScript, you open doors to exciting career opportunities, as many organizations are actively seeking professionals with expertise in this language. Whether you aspire to work for renowned tech giants, contribute to cutting-edge startups, or embark on your entrepreneurial journey, JavaScript proficiency can set you on the path to success.

This book aims to equip beginners with the knowledge and skills necessary to dive into JavaScript development confidently.

In chapters 1 to 6, we will cover the fundamental aspects of JavaScript. We will begin with an introduction to JavaScript, providing you with an overview of its history, features, and role in web development. From there, we will dive into the syntax and data types of JavaScript, including strings, numbers, Booleans, null, symbols, and objects. You will learn how to work with variables, understand operators, and explore conditional statements to make your programs more dynamic. We will also cover loops, which allow you to repeat tasks efficiently, and introduce you to functions and objects, two foundational concepts in JavaScript programming.

Chapters 7 to 11 will explore more advanced JavaScript concepts. We will delve into closures, a powerful mechanism that enables encapsulation and control of variable scope. You will gain an understanding of prototypes, an essential part of JavaScript's object-oriented nature, and explore how they contribute to inheritance and code reusability. Additionally, we will explore the Document Object Model (DOM), which provides a structured representation of web pages and enables JavaScript to interact with HTML elements. You will learn about event handling and how to respond to user actions effectively. Finally, we will delve into asynchronous programming, a critical skill in today's web development landscape, where you will discover techniques such as callbacks, promises, and asynchronous functions.

In the final chapter, we will introduce you to JavaScript frameworks and libraries that have revolutionized web development. You will be introduced to React, a powerful library for building user interfaces, and Angular, a comprehensive framework for building robust applications. We will explore Node.js, a runtime environment that allows JavaScript to be executed on the server-side, enabling server-side JavaScript development. Furthermore, you will discover essential tools like npm, Webpack, and Babel, which enhance your JavaScript development workflow and streamline the deployment process.

By the end of this book, you will have a solid foundation in JavaScript and the necessary skills to embark on your journey as a JavaScript developer. Whether you're aiming to create engaging user interfaces, build scalable web applications, or dive into the exciting world of server-side JavaScript, this book will equip you with the knowledge and confidence to bring your ideas to life.

Now, let's begin our exploration of JavaScript and unlock its full potential together!

Why JavaScript

Many people refer to JavaScript as a scripting language for websites since it is a computer language that can be used on several platforms, is lightweight, can be interpreted and can be compiled. It is used in various contexts beyond browsers, including producing web pages, one of its most common applications. Client-side and server-side programming are both possible uses for the computer language JavaScript. JavaScript is a hybrid programming language that combines imperative and declarative statements. JavaScript has a core set of language components, such as control structures, operators, and statements. Moreover, there is a standard library for objects in JavaScript, which includes things like Date, Array, and Math.

Client-Side

It provides control objects for a browser and its Document Object Model (DOM). Client-side extensions let a program insert components on an HTML form and react to user actions such as mouse clicks, page navigation, and form input. Among the useful client-side libraries are ReactJS, AngularJS, VueJS, and many more.

Server-Side

It provides objects required for executing JavaScript on the server. Such as if server-side extensions enable a program to interface with a database, offer information continuity between invocations of an application, or manipulate files on a server. Node.js is currently the most popular and helpful framework available.

Imperative Language

In this form of language, we are mostly concerned with the procedure. It only regulates the flow of computation. The procedural programming technique, object-oriented approach, and async-await fall under this category. We are considering what should be done after an async call.

Declarative Programming

In this form of language, we are concerned with how something will be done; logical computation is required. Here, the objective is to explain the intended outcome without dictating how to get it, as the arrow function does.

You may add JavaScript to your HTML code in two ways:

1. Internal JS

By placing the code within the <script> tag, we may add JavaScript straight to our HTML file. The <script> tag may be put either within the <head> or <body> tags, depending on the situation.

2. External JS

We may create JavaScript code in a separate file with the extension.js and afterwards link this file within the <head> tag of an HTML page in which we want to include it.

Syntax

```
<script>
    // JavaScript Code
</script>
```

Example

```
<!DOCTYPE html>
<html lang="en">

<head>
    <title>
        Basic Example of JavaScript
    </title>
</head>

<body>
```

```
<!-- JavaScript code can be inserted within
    the head or body section -->
<script>
    console.log("Welcome to JavaScript Introduction");
</script>
</body>
</html>
```

Output
Welcome to JavaScript Introduction

History of JavaScript

JavaScript, created by Brendan Eich in 1995, has a rich and fascinating history in the world of programming languages. Originally developed as a scripting language for web pages in Netscape Navigator, it was initially named "Mocha" and later "LiveScript" before settling on its current name, JavaScript. It gained popularity rapidly due to its ability to bring interactivity and dynamic content to the static web. In 1997, the language was standardized as ECMAScript, with subsequent versions being released periodically to introduce new features and improvements. JavaScript is now a strong and adaptable language that can be used for front-end and back-end programming, having changed over time from being largely employed for client-side web development. JavaScript has become a dominant force in the web development industry thanks to the advent of contemporary web apps and the creation of frameworks like React, Angular, and Node.js. These tools allow developers to construct highly dynamic and responsive applications that function across several platforms. Today, JavaScript continues to evolve, with ongoing efforts to enhance its capabilities and address the ever-changing needs of the web development community.

Features of JavaScript

According to a recent poll from Stack Overflow, JavaScript may be the planet's most widely used programming language.

With the advancement of browser technology and the migration of JavaScript to the server with Node.js and other frameworks, JavaScript is now capable of much more. Here are some of the capabilities of JavaScript:

- JavaScript was first developed for DOM manipulation. Before the invention of JS, most websites were static; following its invention, dynamic websites were established.
- In JS, functions are objects. They may possess features and methods similar to other objects. They may be provided to other functions as parameters.
- Comprehends date and time.

- Performs Form Validation even if the forms are HTML-based.
- No compiler is essential.

Applications of JavaScript

Web Development
Adding functionality and interaction to static websites In 1995, JavaScript was created. Using AngularJS makes this incredibly simple to do.

Web Applications
With the advancement of technology, browsers have evolved to the point where a programming language is necessary to construct effective online apps. When using Google Maps to explore a map, we merely need to click and move the mouse. All detailed views are accessible with a single click, made possible via JavaScript. It employs Application Programming Interfaces (APIs) that enhance the functionality of the programming. Electron and React is beneficial in this field.

Server Applications
Node.js facilitated the transition of JavaScript from client to server, the most capable server-side language.

Games
Not only is JavaScript useful for websites, but also for designing recreational games. Combining JavaScript and HTML 5 increases JavaScript's popularity in game creation. It offers the EaseJS

Library, which offers methods for dealing with complex visuals.

Smartwatches
JavaScript is utilized in every device and application imaginable. It supplies the PebbleJS Library, which is used by wearable apps. This framework is compatible with apps that need internet connectivity to operate.

Art
JavaScript may be used to draw onto HTML 5 canvas, allowing artists and designers to construct whatever they can imagine. Additionally, the p5.js package can be used to enhance the sound quality of their creations.

Machine Learning
The JavaScript ml5.js library may be used for web development using machine learning.

Mobile Applications

JavaScript may be used to create applications for non-web environments as well. JavaScript's capabilities and applications make it an effective tool for developing mobile apps. It is a Framework to develop online and mobile applications using JavaScript. Thanks to React Native it's possible to create mobile apps for several operating systems. We are not required to create code for several platforms. Create once, and use everywhere!

Limitations of JavaScript

Security Risks

JavaScript may get data through AJAX or through manipulating data-loading elements such as <img>, <object>, and <script>. These are referred to as cross-site script assaults. They inject non-site-related JS into the visitor's browser, retrieving the information.

Performance

JavaScript does not give the same degree of speed as many classic programming languages; thus, a complicated JavaScript application would be quite sluggish. Speed is not a significant limitation as JavaScript is utilized to accomplish basic activities on a web browser.

Complexity

Programmers must fully understand all programming principles, fundamental language objects, and client and server-side objects to learn a scripting language; otherwise, building complex JavaScript scripts would be impossible.

Ineffective error handling and type checking

It is a language with weak typing since it is unnecessary to indicate the type of data variables. So incorrect type verification is not done by compile.

What makes JavaScript a lightweight programming language?

JavaScript is lightweight because it uses little CPU, is simple to implement, and has a limited syntax. Minimal syntax, in that it lacks data types. Here, everything is considered an item. Due to its syntactic similarity to C++ and Java, it is fairly straightforward to learn.

A lightweight programming language consumes little CPU resources. It does not place an excess burden on your RAM or CPU. Despite its complicated paradigms and logic, JavaScript operates on a web browser, using fewer resources than other languages. For instance, Node.js, a variant of JavaScript, not only executes calculations quicker than Dart or Java and utilizes fewer resources.

In contrast to other programming languages, it contains fewer built-in libraries and frameworks, contributing to its lightweight nature. Nonetheless, this necessitates the incorporation of other libraries and frameworks.

Is JavaScript interpreted, compiled, or both?

JavaScript is compiled as well as interpreted. In older versions of JavaScript, only the interpreter that processed code line by line and instantly displayed the output was employed. However, performance has become a problem since interpretation is extremely sluggish. Therefore, the JIT compiler was added to subsequent versions of JS, perhaps after V8, to optimize execution and show the output more rapidly. This JIT compiler creates substantially simpler-to-code bytecode. This bytecode is an instruction set that has been significantly optimized.

The V8 engine first interprets the code using an interpreter. On subsequent executions, a V8 engine compiles performance-enhancing patterns like frequently performed functions and commonly used variables.

JavaScript is often associated with web page creation, although utilized in several non-browser contexts. JavaScript can be learned from the ground up with our JavaScript Tutorial and JavaScript Examples.

Chapter 1: JavaScript Syntax and Data Types

Several data types can be used in a JavaScript application. For instance:
```
const x = 5;
const y = "Hello";
```
In this example, 5 and "Hello" are integer and string data types. JavaScript provides eight fundamental data types.

- String
- Number
- BigInt
- Boolean
- undefined
- null
- Symbol
- Object

String

In JavaScript, a string is a sequence of characters enclosed within single quotes (') or double quotes (""). Strings are one of the primary data types in the language and are typically used to represent text-based data. They allow you to store and manipulate text-based information such as names, messages, and any other form of textual content.

To create a string, simply enclose the desired text within quotes. For example:
```
let message = 'Hello, World!';
let name = "Mike Doe";
```
Strings in JavaScript are immutable, meaning that their values cannot be changed after they have been created. Nonetheless, they can be altered and new strings can be created by applying different operations to preexisting ones.

String concatenation is the process of joining two or more strings together to form a single string. This can be done using the plus (+) operator or the concatenation assignment operator (+=).

For example:
```
let firstName = "Mike";
```

```
let lastName = "Doe";
let fullName = firstName + " " + lastName; // "Mike Doe"

let greeting = "Hello, ";
greeting += fullName; // "Hello, Mike Doe"
```

Strings also have several built-in methods that allow you to manipulate and extract information from them. Some commonly used string methods include 'length,' 'toUpperCase()', 'toLowerCase(),' 'charAt(),' 'substring(),' 'split(),' and 'indexOf().' Here's an example of using some of these methods:

```
let message = "Hello, World!";
console.log(message.length); // 13
console.log(message.toUpperCase()); // "HELLO, WORLD!"
console.log(message.charAt(7)); // "W"
console.log(message.substring(7, 12)); // "World"
console.log(message.split(", ")); // ["Hello", "World!"]
console.log(message.indexOf("W")); // 7
```

Strings in JavaScript can also contain special characters and escape sequences. These allow you to include characters that are difficult to type directly or characters with special meaning, such as newline (\n) or tab (\t). For example:

```
let specialCharacters = "This string contains a
        newline:\nAnd a tab:\tEnd of string.";
console.log(specialCharacters);
```

Output

```
This string contains a newline:
And a tab:    End of string.
```

Working with strings and their manipulation is essential for handling textual data in JavaScript. They provide the foundation for tasks such as handling user input, manipulating strings in algorithms, and generating dynamic content in web applications.

Number

The number data type is used to represent numeric values. It encompasses both integer and floating-point numbers. Numbers can be positive, negative, or zero and can be expressed using decimal notation or scientific notation.

You can assign a number to a variable directly:

```
let age = 25;
let temperature = -10.5;
let pi = 3.14159;
```

A number type may be -Infinity, +Infinity, or NaN. (Not a Number). For instance,

```
const number1 = 3/0;
console.log(number1); // +Infinity
const number2 = -3/0;
console.log(number2); // -Infinity
// strings cannot be divided by numbers
const number3 = "abc"/3;
console.log(number3); // NaN
```

JavaScript uses a binary floating-point representation for numbers, which can lead to precision issues when performing certain calculations. To mitigate these issues, the language provides the 'toFixed()' method to control the decimal places when displaying or formatting numbers. Additionally, the 'Number' object provides various useful methods, such as 'parseInt()' and 'parseFloat(),' for converting strings to numbers.

BigInt

In JavaScript, the BigInt data type was introduced to address the limitation of the Number data type when dealing with large integers. The Number type in JavaScript has a maximum safe integer value, which is $2^{53}-1$, beyond which it loses precision. BigInt allows developers to work with arbitrarily large integers without losing accuracy.

You can use the BigInt() function or just attach the letter "n" to the end of an integer to create a BigInt. For example:

```
const bigNumber =
        12345678901234567890123456789012345678890n;
const convertedNumber =
        BigInt("9876543210987654321098765432109876543210");
```

BigInt values can be used in mathematical operations just like regular numbers. However, BigInts cannot be mixed directly with regular numbers, and explicit conversion is required. For instance:

```
const bigNumber =
        12345678901234567890123456789012345678890n;
const regularNumber = 42;

const sum = bigNumber + BigInt(regularNumber); // Valid
const multiplication = bigNumber * BigInt(regularNumber);
        // Valid

const invalid = bigNumber + regularNumber; // Invalid
```

Boolean

the Boolean data type represents a logical value that can be either true or false. Booleans are fundamental to decision-making and conditional logic in programming. They are used to evaluate conditions and control the flow of a program.

Boolean values can be assigned directly to variables or result from comparisons or logical operations. For example:

```
const isTrue = true;
const isFalse = false;

const num1 = 10;
const num2 = 5;
const greaterThan = num1 > num2; // true
const equalTo = num1 === num2; // false
const logicalAnd = greaterThan && equalTo; // false
const logicalOr = greaterThan || equalTo; // true
const logicalNot = !logicalAnd; // true
```

In the above example, 'isTrue' and 'isFalse' are variables directly assigned with Boolean values. The variables 'greaterThan' and 'equalTo' hold Boolean values resulting from the comparison operations. The variables 'logicalAnd,' 'logicalOr,' and 'logicalNot' demonstrate the use of logical operators (&&, ||, !) to perform logical operations and derive Boolean values.

Boolean values play a vital role in control structures such as if statements and loops (we will discuss this in detail in Chapters 3 and 4). For instance:

```
const isRaining = true;

if (isRaining) {
  console.log("Take an umbrella!");
} else {
  console.log("Enjoy the sunshine!");
}
```

Object

Objects in JavaScript are collections of key-value pairs where the keys are strings (or Symbols) and the values can be anything from numbers, strings, functions, or even other objects. These key-value pairs are known as properties of the object.

Objects can be created using the object literal syntax, which is a pair of curly braces '{}', or by using the new keyword followed by a constructor function or a class.

Here's an example of creating an object using the object literal syntax:

```
const person = {
  name: "Mike",
  age: 30,
```

```
    profession: "Engineer"
};
```

In the above example, 'person' is an object with three properties: 'name,' 'age,' and 'profession.' Every property has a key-value pair defined for it, with strings serving as the keys ("name," "age," and "profession") and any type of data as the values..

Properties in an object can be accessed using dot notation or bracket notation. For example:

```
console.log(person.name); // "Mike"
console.log(person["age"]); // 30
```

Properties can be added, modified, or removed after an object is created, making objects dynamic in nature.

Here's an example of modifying an object's property:

```
person.age = 35;
console.log(person.age); // 35
```

Overall, objects in JavaScript are powerful and versatile data structures that enable the organization and manipulation of data in key-value pairs. They provide a foundation for object-oriented programming in JavaScript and are extensively used in various aspects of web development, including managing state, modeling real-world entities, and interacting with the Document Object Model (DOM).

Symbol

The Symbol is a primitive data type used to create unique and immutable identifiers. Symbols are often used as keys in object properties to avoid naming conflicts and provide a level of privacy.

You can use the 'Symbol()' function for creating a symbol. Each symbol created using 'Symbol()' is unique, even if the description provided is the same. For example:

```
const symbol1 = Symbol();
const symbol2 = Symbol();

console.log(symbol1 === symbol2); // false
```

Symbols can also be created with an optional description, which is useful for debugging or providing additional information. The description does not affect the uniqueness of the symbol. For example:

```
const symbol3 = Symbol("symbolDescription");
const symbol4 = Symbol("symbolDescription");

console.log(symbol3 === symbol4); // false
```

Symbols are primarily used as keys in object properties. They help avoid unintentional name collisions when multiple parts of code use the same property names. Here's an example:

```
const id = Symbol("id");

const user = {
  name: "Mike",
  [id]: 123
};

console.log(user[id]); // 123
```

In the above example, the 'id' symbol is used as a property key in the 'user' object. The square bracket notation is used to access the property value using the symbol as the key.

You can explicitly retrieve symbols using the 'Object.getOwnPropertySymbols()' method. For example:

```
const id = Symbol("id");

const user = {
  name: "Mike",
  [id]: 123
};

const symbols = Object.getOwnPropertySymbols(user);
console.log(symbols); // [Symbol(id)]
console.log(user[symbols[0]]); // 123
```

Symbols also have built-in well-known symbols, such as 'Symbol.iterator' and 'Symbol.toStringTag,' which can be used to customize the behavior of objects or classes in JavaScript.

In summary, symbols in JavaScript are unique and immutable identifiers. They are often used as keys in object properties to ensure uniqueness and avoid naming conflicts. JavaScript objects and classes can be customized with unique behaviors using symbols, which offer a certain degree of privacy.

undefined

A variable or attribute that is either nonexistent or has not been given a value is represented by the value "undefined." It is one of JavaScript's basic data types and represents the absence of a relevant value.

When a variable is declared but not assigned a value, or if a property does not exist in an object, its value is automatically set to 'undefined.' For example:

```
let myVariable;
```

```
console.log(myVariable); // undefined

const myObject = {};
console.log(myObject.property); // undefined
```

In the above example, the variable 'myVariable' is declared but not assigned a value, so its value is 'undefined.' Similarly, the property key does not exist in the 'myObject' object, so accessing it returns 'undefined.'

It's important to note that 'undefined' is distinct from other values like 'null,' 'false,' or an empty string (""). It represents the absence of any value, whereas null is an explicitly assigned value that represents the absence of an object.

It's also possible to directly give the value undefined to a variable. For instance,

```
let name = undefined;
console.log(name); // undefined
```

It's a best practice to use 'null' to give a variable an "unknown" or "empty" value rather than assigning 'undefined' directly to a variable.

null

A unique basic data type called "null" denotes the intended lack of any object value. It is used to show that a property or variable has been specifically given the value "null," indicating that it is purposefully pointing to nothing.

When a variable or property is assigned the value 'null,' it signifies that there is an absence of a meaningful value or that it is explicitly set to indicate "no value." For example:

```
let myVariable = null;
console.log(myVariable); // null

const myObject = {
    property: null
};
console.log(myObject.property); // null
```

Output

null
null

The variable "myVariable" in the example above has the value "null," meaning that it represents nothing. Similarly, the 'property' key of the 'myObject' object is explicitly set to 'null.'

Unlike 'undefined,' which indicates that a variable or property has not been assigned a value, 'null' is a value that is deliberately assigned to represent the absence of an object or value. It can be used to indicate that a variable or property is intentionally devoid of any meaningful data.

When working with null, it's important to handle it appropriately in your code. If you encounter a variable or property with a value of null, you can check for it explicitly and handle it according to your application's logic.

typeof

The built-in unary operator called "typeof" lets you establish the data type of a given item or expression. It gives back a string that describes the operand's type.

The syntax for using the typeof operator is as follows:

```
typeof operand
```

Here, the 'operand' can be any value or expression that you want to evaluate the type of. The 'typeof' operator returns a string representing the data type of the operand.

Here are some examples of using the typeof operator:

```
console.log(typeof 42); // "number"
console.log(typeof "Hello"); // "string"
console.log(typeof true); // "boolean"
console.log(typeof undefined); // "undefined"
console.log(typeof null); // "object"
console.log(typeof Symbol("symbol")); // "symbol"
console.log(typeof BigInt(10)); // "bigint"
console.log(typeof [1, 2, 3]); // "object"
console.log(typeof { name: "Mike" }); // "object"
```

Note that this operator has some limits. For example, it treats 'null' as an object, which is a historical mistake in JavaScript.

The 'typeof' operator is often used in conditional statements, type checking, and debugging scenarios to perform specific actions based on the data type of a value.

JavaScript Data Types - Recap

The following table provides a recap of JavaScript data types:

Data Types	Description	Example
String	displays textual information	"Hello world!", 'hello'
Number	an integer or a floating-point value	3, 3.234, 3e-2, etc.
BigInt	a number with undetermined precision	9007199251247409999n, 1n
Boolean	either of the 2 values: true or false	true and false
Object	key-value pairs in a data collection	let student = { };
Symbol	data type with immutable, unique instances.	let value = Symbol('hello');
undefined	Uninitialized data type variable	let a;
null	represents a null value	let a = null;

The Object data type in the above table is not a primitive data type, but all other data types are primitive. The non-primitive Object data type may hold data collections, while primitive data types can only store a single piece of information.

Chapter 2: Variables and Operators

What is an operator?

The operator is a special symbol that executes operations on operands in JavaScript (values and variables). For instance,
```
2 + 3; // returns "5"
```
2 and 3 are operands, whereas + is the operator that executes addition.

The following operators are supported in JavaScript:

JavaScript Assignment Operators

We employ assignment operators to allocate values to variables. For instance,
```
const x = 5; // returns "5"
```
With the = operator, the value 5 is assigned to the variable x.

The following is a list of frequently used assignment operators:

Operator	Name	Example
=	Assignment operator	a=7; //returns "7."
+=	Addition assignment	a += 5; // a = a + 5
-=	Subtraction assignment	a -= 2; // a = a - 2
*=	Multiplication assignment	a *= 3; // a = a * 3
/=	Division assignment	a /= 2; // a = a / 2
%=	Remainder assignment	a %= 2; // a = a % 2
**=	Exponentiation assignment	a **= 2; // a = a**2

JavaScript Arithmetic Operators

Arithmetic computations are performed using arithmetic operators. For instance,

```
const number = 3 + 5; // returns "8"
```

Here, two operands are added using the + operator.

Operator	Name	Example
+	Addition	a + b
-	Subtraction	a - b
*	Multiplication	a * b
/	Division	a / b
%	Remainder	a % b
++	Increment (increments by 1)	++a or a++
--	Decrement (decrements by 1)	--a or a--
**	Exponentiation (Power)	a ** b

Example

```
let a = 5;
let b = 3;

// addition
console.log('a + b = ', a + b);   // returns "8"

// subtraction
console.log('a - b = ', a - b);   // returns "2"

// multiplication
console.log('a * b = ', a * b);   // returns "15"

// division
console.log('a / b = ', a / b);   // returns
      "1.6666666666666667"

// remainder
console.log('a % b = ', a % b);   // returns "2"

// increment
console.log('++a = ', ++a); // a is now 6
console.log('a++ = ', a++); // prints 6 and then it is
      increased to 7
```

```
console.log('a = ', a);        // returns "7"

// decrement
console.log('--a = ', --a); // a is now 6
console.log('a-- = ', a--); // prints 6 and then it is
        decreased to 5
console.log('a = ', a);        // returns "5"

//exponentiation
console.log('a ** b =', a ** b);
```

Output

```
a + b =  8
a - b =  2
a * b =  15
a / b =  1.6666666666666667
a % b =  2
++a =  6
a++ =  6
a =  7
--a =  6
a-- =  6
a =  5
a ** b = 125
```

Some browsers may not support the ** operator.

JavaScript Comparison Operators

Comparison operators compare 2 values and return either true or false as a Boolean value. For instance,

```
const a = 3, b = 2;
console.log(a > b);
```

Output

true

Here, comparison operator > is employed to determine if a is greater than b.

Operator	Description	Example
==	Equal to: If both the operands are equal, the expression returns true	a == b
!=	Not equal to: If the operands are not equal, returns true	a != b
===	Strict equal to: True if the operands are equal and of the same type	a === b
!==	Strict not equal to: If the operands are equal but of distinct types or not equal at all, this returns true	a !== b
>	Greater than: When the left operand is bigger, it returns true	a > b
>=	Greater than or equal to: When the left operand is equal to or larger, it returns true	a >= b
<	Less than: When the right operand is bigger, it returns true	a < b
<=	Less than or equal to: When the left operand is equal to or smaller, it returns true	a <= b

Example

```
// equal operator
```

```
console.log(2 == 2); // true
console.log(2 == '2'); // true
// not equal operator
console.log(3 != 2); // true
console.log('hello' != 'Hello'); // true
// strict equal operator
console.log(2 === 2); // true
console.log(2 === '2'); // false
// strict not equal operator
console.log(2 !== '2'); // true
console.log(2 !== 2); // false
```

Output

```
true
true
true
true
true
false
true
false
```

Operators are used to evaluating whether a condition is true or false within if/else statements or loops. We'll discuss in detail about these.

JavaScript Logical Operators

Logical operators execute logical operations and yield a true or false Boolean result. For instance,

```
const a = 5, b = 3;
(a < 6) && (b < 5); // returns "true"
```

Here, && represents the logical AND operator. Since a < 6 and b < 5 are both true, the outcome is also true.

Operator	Description	Example
&&	Logical AND: True if both operands are true or else false	a && b
||	Logical OR: True if either of the operands evaluates to true; false otherwise	a || b
!	Logical NOT: False if the operand is true and vice-versa.	!a

Example

```
// logical AND
console.log(true && true);
console.log(true && false);
// logical OR
console.log(true || false);
// logical NOT
console.log(!true);
```

Output

```
true
false
true
false
```

JavaScript Bitwise Operator

Operations upon binary representations of integers are carried out using bitwise operators.

Operator	Description
&	Bitwise AND
|	Bitwise OR
^	Bitwise XOR
~	Bitwise NOT
<<	Left shift
>>	Right shift with sign propagation
>>>	Right shift with zero-fill

JavaScript String Operators

The + operator may also be utilized to concatenate (join) 2 or more strings in JavaScript.

Example

```
// concatenation operator
console.log('hello' + 'world');
let x = 'JavaScript';
x += ' programming';   // x = x + ' tutorial';
console.log(x);
```

Output

```
helloworld
JavaScript programming
```

When + is applied to strings, concatenation occurs. When + is paired with numbers, though, it executes addition.

Chapter 3: Conditional Statements

If-Else

The if-else statement in JavaScript runs code if the condition is true or false. JavaScript has three versions of if statements:
1. If statement
2. If else statement
3. If else if statement

If statement

It only analyses the content if an expression evaluates to true. Here is the signature of the JavaScript if statement:

```
if(expression)
{
//content to be evaluated
}
```

Example

```
hour=20;
if (hour < 18)
{
    console.log("Good day");
}
```

JavaScript If else statement

It determines whether the condition is true or false. Here is the syntax of the JavaScript if-else expression:

```
if(expression)
{
//code to run if the condition is true
}
Else
{
//code to run if the condition is false
}
```

Example of an if-else statement in JavaScript to determine if a number is odd or even

```javascript
var num=20;
if(num%2==0){
console.log("num is even number");
}
else{
console.log("num is odd number");
}
```

Output

```
num is even number
```

JavaScript if else if statement

It examines the conditions only if several expressions evaluate to be true. Here is the signature of the JavaScript if else if statement:

```javascript
if(expression1)
{
//content to be evaluated if expression1 is true
}
else if(expression2)
{
//content to be evaluated if expression2 is true
}
else if(expression3)
{
//content to be evaluated if expression3 is true
}
else
{
//content to be evaluated if no expression is true
}
```

If else if statement example in JavaScript

```javascript
var num=20;
if(num==10){
console.log("num is equal to 10");
}
else if(num==15){
console.log("num is equal to 15");
}
else if(num==20){
console.log("num is equal to 20");
}
else{
```

```
console.log("num is not equal to 10, 15 or 20");
}
```

Output

```
num is equal to 20
```

Chapter 4: Loops

JavaScript iterates the code using while, for, do-while, or for-in loops. It makes the code more concise. It is often used in an array.

There are four different forms of JavaScript loops:

For loop

JavaScript For loop iterates through the specified number of items. It must be used if the number of iterations is known. The syntax for the for loop is shown below:

```
for (initialization; condition; increment) {
    code to be executed
}
```

JavaScript example of the For loop

```
for (i=1; i<=5; i++) {
  console.log(i + " ")
}
```

Output

1
2
3
4
5

While loop

The While loop in JavaScript iterates through the components an unlimited number of times. It must be used when the number of iterations is unknown. The while loop syntax is shown below:

```
while (condition)
{
     code to be executed
}
```

JavaScript While loop example

```
var i=11;
while (i<=15)
{
console.log(i + " ");
i++;
```

}

Output
```
11
12
13
14
15
```

Do-While loop

The Do-While loop iterates the items an unlimited number of times, similar to the while loop. Nonetheless, code is performed at least once regardless of the true condition. This is the syntax for the Do-While loop:

```
Do{
    code to be executed
}while (condition);
```

JavaScript example of the Do-While loop

```
var i=21;
do{
console.log(i + " ");
i++;
}while (i<=25);
```

Output
```
21
22
23
24
25
```

For-in loop

The For-in loop within JavaScript is employed to iterate through the attributes of an object. The for-in loop only iterates across keys of the object whose enumerable attribute is set to "true."

Syntax

```
for (let i in my_object)
{
    // Prints all the keys in my_object on the console
    console.log(i);
}
```

Example to illustrate the For-in loop

```
// An object with a few properties
```

```
var person = {"Name": "Clark", "Surname": "Kent", "Age":
    "36"};

//loop through all the attributes in the object
for(var prop in person) {
    console.log(" " + prop + " = " + person[prop] + " "); }
```

Output
```
Name = Clark
Surname = Kent
Age = 36
```

Chapter 5: Functions

Introduction to JavaScript Functions
While designing an application, repeating the same activity several times is often necessary. For instance, you might want to display a notice if an error occurs.

To prevent reusing the same code several times, you may wrap it in a function and reuse it.

Several built-in JavaScript methods exist, such as parseInt() and parseFloat().

Declare a Function
Utilize the function keyword, preceded by the function's name, a list of arguments, and the function body to define a function.

```
function functionName(parameters)
{
    // function body
}
```

The function must have a valid JavaScript identity as its name. By convention, function names begin with a verb, such as fetchContents(), getData(), and isValid().

A function may take zero, one, or more arguments. For numerous parameters, you must separate two parameters with a comma.

The following code defines a function without parameters called 'say()':

```
function say()
{

}
```

Below is a declaration of a method called square() that receives a single parameter:

```
function square(a)
{

}
```

And the following code defines an add() method that takes two parameters:

```
function add(a, b)
{

}
```

Inside the body of a function, you may write the code for implementing an action. For instance, the say() method below displays a message on the console:

```
function say(message)
{
    console.log(message);
}
```

In the say() function's body, we invoke the console. log() is used to send a message to the console.

Calling a Function

To execute a function, it must be called. Invoking a function is another term for calling a function. To invoke a function, you utilize the function's name followed by parenthesized parameters.

```
functionName(arguments);
```

On invoking a function, JavaScript runs the function body's code. The example below shows how to invoke the say() function:

```
say('Hello');
```

In this example, the speak() method is called with the literal text "Hello" as its argument.

Parameters vs Arguments

Parameters and arguments are frequently used interchangeably. Nonetheless, they are fundamentally distinct.

While defining a function, the arguments are specified. But, when invoking a function, you must supply the parameters' matching arguments.

In the say() method, for instance, the message is a parameter and the text 'Hello' is an argument that corresponds to a message parameter.

Returning a Value

Every method in JavaScript returns undefined unless a return value is explicitly specified. For instance:

```
function say(message)
{
    console.log(message);
}
let result = say('Hello');
console.log('Result:', result);
```

Output

```
Hello
```

```
Result: undefined
```

To provide a function's return value, we use the 'return' statement accompanied by a value or expression, as shown:

```
return expression;
```

The following add() method, for instance, computes and returns the sum of its two arguments. This also shows how to call the add() function:

```
function add(a, b)
{
    return a + b;
}
let sum = add(10, 20);
console.log('Sum:', sum);
```

Output

```
Sum: 30
```

The following example returns various values depending on circumstances using several return statements inside a function:

```
function compare(a, b)
{
    if (a > b) {
        return -1;
    } else if (a < b) {
        return 1;
    }
    return 0;
}

console.log(compare(7,12));
console.log(compare(23,5));
console.log(compare(18,18));
```

Output

```
1
-1
0
```

The method 'compare()' compares two values. It returns:

- -1 if the 1st argument exceeds the second argument
- 1 if the first parameter is smaller than the second
- 0 if the first and second arguments are equal

The function instantly terminates execution upon reaching the return statement. Hence, you can employ a return statement without the value to prematurely quit the function, as shown:

```
function say(message)
{
    // show nothing if the message is empty
    if (! message )
    {
        return;
    }
    console.log(message);
}
```

If a message is empty (or undefined) in this example, the say() method will display nothing.

The function may only return one value. If you want a function to return numerous values, you must wrap the values in an object or an array.

The arguments object

Within a function, you may access an entity called arguments, which represents the function's named parameters.

The arguments object acts as if it were an array even if it is not of type Array.

For instance, you may retrieve the arguments using the square bracket []: arguments[0] give the first parameter, arguments[1] returns the second, etc.

Moreover, you may determine the number of arguments by using the length attribute of the arguments object.

The example below defines a generic add() method that adds any number of parameters:

```
function add()
{
    let sum = 0;
    for (let i = 0; i < arguments.length; i++) {
        sum += arguments[i];
    }
    return sum;
}

// You can give any number of parameters as input to the
        add() method
console.log(add(1, 2));
console.log(add(1, 2, 3, 4, 5));
```

Output
3

15
Function Hoisting

You can use a function before defining it in JavaScript. This characteristic is known as *hoisting*. For instance:

```
showMe(); // an hoisting example
function showMe()
{
    console.log('an hoisting example');
}
```

Output

```
an hoisting example
```

The JavaScript engine uses function hoisting to physically relocate function declarations toward the top of the code before executing them.

The following demonstrates the copy of the code before its execution by the JavaScript engine:

```
function showMe(){
    console.log('a hoisting example');
}
showMe(); // a hoisting example
```

Output

```
a hoisting example
```

Chapter 6: Objects

Overview of Objects in JavaScript

Objects in JavaScript are fundamental data types that allow you to store and organize related information in a structured manner. An object is a collection of key-value pairs, where the values can be any kind of data, including other objects, and the keys act as distinct identifiers for each other. Through the definition of attributes and functions, objects offer a flexible means of representing concrete entities or abstract ideas. While methods are procedures attached to an object that allow it to carry out operations or tasks, properties are an object's qualities or attributes. Objects serve as containers that group related data and behavior together, allowing for better organization and management of complex data structures.

Objects play a vital role in programming for several reasons:

Modeling Complex Systems

Objects are a powerful tool for modeling complex systems, such as applications, websites, or simulations. They enable you to represent and simulate real-world entities or abstract concepts, providing a more intuitive and manageable way to structure your code.

Encapsulation of Data and Behavior

Objects enable the encapsulation of data and behavior, promoting the principle of encapsulation in Object-Oriented Programming (OOP). Encapsulation means bundling related data and functions together, allowing you to control access to the object's internal data and providing a clear interface for interacting with it. This improves code organization, readability, and maintenance.

Code Reusability and Modularity

Objects facilitate code reusability and modularity. An object can have several instances created once it has been defined, each with distinct data values but the same structure and behavior. This promotes code reuse, reduces redundancy, and makes your code more modular, leading to more efficient development and easier maintenance.

Object-Oriented Programming Principles

Objects are a fundamental aspect of OOP. Understanding and working with objects allows you to leverage key OOP principles, such as encapsulation, inheritance, and polymorphism, which are crucial for writing clean, scalable, and maintainable code.

By mastering objects in JavaScript, you gain a powerful toolset for organizing and manipulating data, modeling complex systems, and developing efficient and scalable applications.

Creating Objects

Object literals and their syntax

Object literals provide a straightforward way to create objects in JavaScript. They allow you to define an object and its properties directly within curly braces ({}) using a key-value pair syntax. The key represents the property name, followed by a colon (:), and the value represents the data associated with that property. Multiple properties can be defined within the object literal, separated by commas. For example:

```
const person = {
    name: 'Mike',
    age: 25,
    address: '123 Main St',
};
```

In addition to object literals, you can create objects using the "new" keyword and constructor functions. Constructors are regular functions used as templates to build new objects. They are defined using the function keyword and are usually named according to the accepted convention of the PascalCase. Using the "this" keyword, which refers to the object that is being formed, you can declare object properties inside the constructor function.

Here's an example:

```
function Person(name, age, address) {
    this.name = name;
    this.age = age;
    this.address = address;
}

const Mike = new Person('Mike', 25, '123 Main St');
```

Object properties and methods

Objects consist of properties and methods. Properties are variables that specify an object's characteristics and store values. You can use bracket notation or dot notation to access them. person.name or person['name'], for instance, can be used to access the "name" attribute of the "person" object that was previously constructed. On the other hand, functions connected to an object are called methods. They can be defined directly within the object literal or added dynamically to the object. Methods allow objects to perform actions or tasks. For example:

```
const person = {
```

```
    name: 'Mike',
    age: 25,
    greet: function() {
        console.log('Hello, I am ' + this.name);
    },
};
```

```
person.greet(); // Output: Hello, I am Mike
```

Understanding how to create objects, define properties, and add methods is essential for working effectively with objects in JavaScript. It allows you to create custom data structures and define behavior associated with those objects.

Accessing and Modifying Object Properties

As already mentioned, when accessing object properties, you have two options: dot notation and bracket notation. Dot notation is the most common and straightforward way to access properties. Simply use the dot operator followed by the property name. For example:

```
const person = {
    name: 'Mike',
    age: 25,
};
```

```
console.log(person.name); // Output: Mike
```

Bracket notation, on the other hand, uses square brackets and allows you to access properties dynamically or when the property name contains special characters or spaces. The property name is specified as a string within the brackets. For example:

```
const person = {
    name: 'Mike',
    age: 25,
};
```

```
console.log(person['name']); // Output: Mike
```

Nested object properties

Objects can have nested structures, meaning an object can contain properties that are also objects. You can use either bracket notation or chain dot notation to access properties within nested objects. For example:

```
const person = {
    name: 'Mike',
    age: 28,
    address: {
        street: '616 Burgess St',
```

```
        city: 'New Hampshire',
    },
};

console.log(person.address.street); //Output: 616 Burgess
    St
```

Modifying object properties

You can change an object's properties by giving them a new value. You can use either dot notation or bracket notation to modify properties. For example:

```
const person = {
    name: 'Mike',
    age: 28,
};

person.age = 32; // Modifying the 'age' property
console.log(person.age); // Output: 32

person['name'] = 'Jane'; // Modifying the 'name' property
console.log(person.name); // Output: Jane
```

It's important to note that when modifying object properties, the changes are reflected directly in the object itself.

Working with Object Methods

Object methods are functions that are linked to an object and that can be used to carry out certain tasks. Methods can be defined directly within the object literal or added dynamically to the object. To define a method, you assign a function as the value of a property. For example:

```
const person = {
   name: 'Mike',
   age: 25,
   greet: function() {
      console.log('Hello, my name is ' + this.name);
   },
};

person.greet(); // Output: Hello, my name is Mike
```

To invoke a method, you use dot notation and parentheses after the method name. In the example above, 'person.greet()' invokes the 'greet' method.

Accessing object properties within methods

Object methods have access to the object's properties through the **'this'** keyword. Within the method, you can access the properties of the current object instance by using the 'this' keyword. This allows the method to work with the data of that particular object. For example:

```
const person = {
    name: 'Mike',
    age: 25,
    introduce: function() {
        console.log('My name is ' + this.name + ' and I am '
            + this.age + ' years old.');
    },
};

person.introduce(); // Output: My name is Mike and I am 25
    years old.
```

'**this**' is an important keyword in object methods. It denotes the object on which the method is called and offers access to and manipulation of the object's properties along with access to other methods. The value of '**this**' is set dynamically at runtime based on how the method is called. This is the actual object when a method is called with dot notation, like 'object.method()'.

Working with object methods allows you to define reusable behavior associated with objects. Methods enable objects to perform specific actions, access and modify their own properties, and interact with other objects or the environment.

Object Iteration and Manipulation

Looping through object properties allows you to iterate over the properties of an object and perform operations on them. '**for...in**' loop and '**Object.keys()**' are two methods for object iteration in JavaScript. For example:

```
const person = {
    name: 'Mike',
    age: 25,
    occupation: 'Engineer'
};

// Using for...in loop
for (let key in person) {
    console.log(key + ': ' + person[key]);
}

// Using Object.keys()
const keys = Object.keys(person);
keys.forEach(key => {
    console.log(key + ': ' + person[key]);
```

});
Output
```
name: Mike
age: 25
occupation: Engineer
name: Mike
age: 25
occupation: Engineer
```

Object property enumeration

Object property enumeration refers to the process of listing all properties of an object. JavaScript provides methods like **'Object.keys()'**, **'Object.values()'**, and **'Object.entries()'** to extract specific information about an object's properties. For example:

```
const person = {
   name: 'Mike',
   age: 25,
   occupation: 'Engineer'
};

const keys = Object.keys(person);
const values = Object.values(person);
const entries = Object.entries(person);

console.log(keys);
console.log(values);
console.log(entries);
```

Output
```
[ 'name', 'age', 'occupation' ]
[ 'Mike', 25, 'Engineer' ]
[ [ 'name', ' Mike' ], [ 'age', 25 ], [ 'occupation',
      'Engineer' ] ]
```

These methods allow you to extract the keys, values, or entries of an object, providing flexibility in how you access and manipulate its properties.

Adding, removing, and modifying object properties dynamically

JavaScript allows you to dynamically add, remove, and modify object properties at runtime. You can add a new property by simply assigning a value to a new key, remove a property using the **'delete'** keyword, and modify an existing property by reassigning its value. For example:

```
const person = {
   name: 'Mike',
   age: 25
```

```
};

person.occupation = 'Engineer'; // Adding a new property
console.log(person); // Output: { name: 'Mike', age: 25,
        occupation: 'Engineer' }

delete person.age; // Removing a property
console.log(person); // Output: { name: 'Mike', occupation:
        'Engineer' }

person.name = 'Jane'; // Modifying an existing property
console.log(person); // Output: { name: 'Jane', occupation:
        'Engineer' }
```

Dynamically manipulating object properties allows you to adapt and update the object's data as needed during the execution of your program.

Working with Built-in Objects

JavaScript provides a set of built-in objects that offer a wide range of functionalities for performing common tasks. Some of the commonly used built-in objects include Math, Date, and Array.

Math Object

The Math object in JavaScript provides mathematical operations and functions. It allows you to perform operations like rounding numbers, generating random numbers, calculating trigonometric values, and more. The Math object does not require instantiation and can be accessed directly using the Math keyword.

Date Object

One particular point in time is represented by the Date object. It offers ways to retrieve and set the year, month, day, hours, minutes, and seconds, among other components of a date. With the Date object, you can perform operations like formatting dates, comparing dates, and performing calculations based on dates.

Array Object

Collections of elements are stored and managed using the Array object. It offers several methods to change, add, and remove elements from within an array le's scope by its location in th. Arrays can hold values of any data type, making them versatile for organizing and working with data.

Accessing and using methods and properties of built-in objects

To access the methods and properties of built-in objects, you use dot notation, which involves referencing the object name followed by a dot (.) and the method or property name.

```
// Example with Math object
const randomNumber = Math.random(); // Generates a random
        number between 0 and 1
const roundedNumber = Math.round(3.7); // Rounds the number
        to the nearest integer

// Example with Date object
const currentDate = new Date(); // Creates a new Date
        object representing the current date and time
const currentYear = currentDate.getFullYear(); // Retrieves
        the current year

// Example with Array object
const fruits = ['apple', 'banana', 'orange'];
const fruitCount = fruits.length; // Retrieves the number
        of elements in the array

// Using methods and properties of built-in objects
console.log(randomNumber);
console.log(roundedNumber);
console.log(currentYear);
console.log(fruitCount);
```

Output

```
0.6852906581451517
4
2023
3
```

Exercises

1. ## Create an object to represent a person
   - Define an object called **'person'** with properties such as **'name'**, **'age'**, and **'occupation'**.
   - Assign values to these properties to represent a specific person.
   - Access and display the values of the object properties using dot notation.

2. ## Create an object to represent a car
   - Define an object called **'car'** with properties such as **'make'**, **'model'**, and **'year'**.
   - Assign values to these properties to represent a specific car.
   - Access and display the values of the object properties using dot notation.

3. ## Create an object to represent a shopping cart
   - Define an object called **'cart'** with properties such as **'items'**, **'totalQuantity'**, and **'totalPrice'**.
   - Initialize the **'items'** property as an empty array.
   - Implement methods to add items to the cart, update the quantity of items, and calculate the total price.
   - Test the methods by adding items to the cart and displaying the updated quantity and total price.

4. ## Modify an object property
   - Take the previously defined **'person'** object and change the value of the **'occupation'** property to a new occupation.
   - Display the updated value of the **'occupation'** property.

5. ## Invoke an object method
   - Expand the **'cart'** object created earlier by adding a method called **'removeItem'** that takes an item name as a parameter and removes it from the **'items'** array.
   - Invoke the **'removeItem'** method to remove a specific item from the cart and display the updated **'items'** array.

6. ## Create a new object method
   - Add a method called **'getFullName'** to the **'person'** object that concatenates the **'name'** property with a greeting, such as "Hello, ".
   - Invoke the **'getFullName'** method and display the full name.

Chapter 7: Closures

What is a Closure in JavaScript?

In JavaScript, closure is a type of lexical scoping that enables variables from the outer scope of a function to be preserved within the inner scope of that function. Lexical scoping uses a variable's place in the source code to determine its scope.

All variables that are contained within a function that you define are only accessible from within the function. A scope error will occur if you try to access variables inside a function from outside; this is when closure comes in handy.

To better understand the concept of scope, consider the code example below that demonstrates variables declared in both global and local scopes.

```
let msg = 'Hi';

function Greeting() {
    let people = "World";
    console.log(msg + ' ' + people)
}

buildGreeting();
```

Output

```
Hello World
```

The example shows two scopes: the global scope containing the declaration of the variable "message" and the local scope of the function containing the declaration of the variable "audience". While the function can access the global variable "message", the local variable "audience" is restricted to the function's scope only. Attempting to access the function's local variable will result in a runtime error.

Understanding this concept is essential as it can aid in identifying and preventing errors in code, and it also sheds light on the functionality of lexical scoping. It's noteworthy that lexical scoping permits an internal scope to reach a variable in its encompassing function. To illustrate this, let's examine the code sample provided below.

A function stated at the global level is considered to be a nested scope. Every function declared in this range has its own level of accessibility and cannot be accessed from the global scope. Additionally, the scope of one function is not accessible from other functions. The following code block will illustrate this concept.

```
function buildGreeting() {
    let message = "Hello";
}

function greetUser() {
    let audience = "World";
    console.log(message)
}

greetUser();
```

Output
```
ERROR!
ReferenceError: message is not defined
```

If the greetUser() function is called, an error message will be displayed, causing the program to terminate. This design decision simplifies the debugging process by making it easier to identify the root cause of the error message.

JavaScript Closure

In JavaScript, a function has access to its local scope but not the global scope. This means the greetUser() function cannot be accessed from this global scope. However, it's worth noting that the greetUser() function can be accessed using the buildGreeting() function.

To make the greetUser() method accessible globally, we should return the greetUser() method from the buildGreeting() method and then assign the buildGreeting() method to a variable and invoke that variable like a method:

```
function buildGreeting(message) {
    return function(audience){
        return message + ' ' + audience;
    }
}

let greeting1 = buildGreeting('Hi');
let greeting2 = buildGreeting('Hello');

console.log(greeting1('User'));
console.log(greeting2('World'));
```

Output
```
Hi User
Hello World
```

This code example involves the creation of a function named buildGreeting(). The function returns another function that produces a string by combining two variables. These variables are passed in twice within the code. The first instance occurs when assigning the method to a variable, as demonstrated below.

```
let greeting1 = buildGreeting('Hi');
```

Following the assignment, the variable is invoked as a function with a specific value being passed in as an argument for your inner function. This function call is executed within a console log statement, which enables the user to view the string generated by the inner function.

JavaScript Closures and Loops

In JavaScript, implementing closure can be challenging when working with loops, as it can result in unintended consequences. This is demonstrated by the following function, which leverages a setTimeout function within a loop.

```
for(var id=0; id<3; id++){
    setTimeout(function(){
        console.log('seconds: ' + id);
    }, id*1000)
}
```

Output

```
seconds: 3
seconds: 3
seconds: 3
```

The code above utilizes a loop that executes three times. In each iteration, the setTimeout function waits for a designated moment to pass before executing the code within its scope. Based on the loop's current index value, one might anticipate the code to execute three times.

Nevertheless, the loops iterate and modify the id variable accordingly. The code executes from within the setTimeout function, which means that the id variable has already been incremented to the maximum value. Due to the shared scope of all 3 iterations of the loop, the setTimeout function generates a closure that each loop shares.

The implication of this fact is that the output displayed in the console log may not be the anticipated message. In reality, the log reflects the ultimate id value.

ES6 let Keyword

To resolve this problem, the JavaScript ES6 let keyword can be used to make sure that the code within this block runs as intended. With the let keyword, a new scope is created for every loop iteration, allowing the index value to be declared within the scope of the if block. The example below demonstrates how to use the let keyword to achieve this goal.

```
for(let id=0; id<3; id++){
    setTimeout(function(){
        console.log('seconds: ' + id);
    }, id*1000)
}
```

Output

```
seconds: 0
seconds: 1
seconds: 2
```

The provided code works as intended, with the setTimeout function executing during each iteration of the loop. This can be seen in the output below, where every iteration of the loop assigns a unique ID to the setTimeout function.

IIFE and Closures

To avoid the issue of closures in the loop, an alternative solution is to utilize the syntax for IIFE (Immediately Invoked Function Expression). This involves immediately invoking the setTimeout function as the loop begins to run rather than waiting for a loop to finish and then executing the code. By doing so, the setTimeout function behaves as intended. Below is an example of what the syntax for an IIFE looks like.

```
for(var id=1; id<=3; id++){
    (function(id){
        setTimeout(function(){
            console.log('seconds: ' + id);
        }, id * 1000);
    })(id)
}
```

Output

```
seconds: 1
seconds: 2
seconds: 3
```

The provided code runs loops that immediately invoke the function on each iteration. This results in the setTimeout function starting immediately and preserving the id's state for each iteration. It is important to acknowledge that the ES6 method is a more concise solution to this problem, but there may be instances where an IIFE is a better approach.

Moving Forward With JavaScript Closures

To progress in your understanding of closures in JavaScript, it is essential to practice the concepts you've learned. Since closures can be complex, it's especially critical to experiment with creating closures in various situations. Closures can be used to achieve a variety of tasks that would otherwise be challenging. Recognizing closures is the most excellent way to cement your understanding of how they work and how to implement them.

Chapter 8: Prototypes

Prototypes in JavaScript are a fundamental part of the language's object-oriented nature. Every object in JavaScript has a prototype, which is used as a guide or template when making new objects. An object that serves as the model for other objects' functions and properties is called a prototype.

JavaScript's approach to OOP heavily relies on prototypes. By enabling object inheritance, they make it possible for objects to reuse and share the attributes and functions specified in their prototypes.

When an object needs to access a property or method that it doesn't have, JavaScript searches the prototype chain to locate a property or method in its prototype and its prototype's prototype, and so on, until it reaches the top-level prototype.

Using prototypes in JavaScript offers several advantages:

Code reusability

Prototypes allow you to define properties and methods once in a prototype and have all instances of objects derived from that prototype share those properties and methods. This promotes code reusability and helps avoid duplication.

Dynamic property assignment

Prototypes allow you to add or modify properties and methods dynamically at runtime. This flexibility enables you to extend the functionality of objects even after they have been instantiated.

Memory efficiency

When multiple objects share the same prototype, they reference the prototype's properties and methods rather than duplicating them. This results in memory efficiency as the shared properties and methods are stored in a single location in memory.

Easy object modification

By modifying the properties and methods in a prototype, you can apply changes to all objects derived from that prototype. This simplifies the process of making modifications to object behavior and reduces the need for updating individual objects.

Prototype chaining and inheritance

Prototypes form a hierarchical chain known as the prototype chain. This enables objects to inherit properties and methods from their prototypes, allowing for the implementation of inheritance patterns and the creation of object hierarchies.

By leveraging prototypes, you can create more efficient and flexible code structures, improve code reuse, and take advantage of the dynamic nature of JavaScript to build powerful and scalable applications.

Prototype Chain

In JavaScript Objects can inherit properties and functions from their prototypes. Once an object is created, it is linked to a prototype object. If a property or method is not found on the object itself, JavaScript looks for it in the object's prototype. If it still doesn't find it, the search continues up the prototype chain until it hits the top-level prototype, **'Object.prototype'**. This chain of prototypes establishes the inheritance hierarchy in JavaScript.

For example, consider an object **'person'** created using the following code:

```
const person = {
  name: 'Mike',
  age: 30,
};
```

If you access **'person.name'**, JavaScript finds the **'name'** property directly on the **'person'** object. However, if you access 'person.toString()', JavaScript doesn't find the **'toString()'** method on person itself. It continues up the prototype chain and finds it in **'Object.prototype'**, which is inherited by all objects.

Prototypal inheritance

Prototypal inheritance is the mechanism by which objects inherit properties and methods from their prototypes.

Let's illustrate prototypal inheritance using constructor functions:

```
function Person(name, age) {
  this.name = name;
  this.age = age;
}

Person.prototype.sayHello = function() {
  console.log(`Hello, my name is ${this.name}.`);
};

const person1 = new Person('Mike', 30);
person1.sayHello(); // Output: Hello, my name is Mike.
```

In this example, **'Person.prototype'** contains the **'sayHello()'** method. When **'person1'** is created using the **'Person'** constructor, it inherits the 'sayHello()' method from 'Person.prototype'. Thus, 'person1' can access and invoke the 'sayHello()' method.

Creating and Using Prototypes

Prototypes in JavaScript are created through constructor functions. To distinguish constructor functions from normal functions, they are usually named with an uppercase letter at the beginning. When a constructor function is called with the **new** keyword, it generates a new object and assigns its prototype to the constructor's prototype property.

Let's see an example of creating a prototype for the object **Person** using a constructor function:

```
function Person(name, age) {
  this.name = name;
  this.age = age;
}
```

```
const personPrototype = new Person();
```

In this above example, the **Person** constructor function provides the name and age attributes. The **personPrototype** object is generated by using the **Person** constructor without specifying any parameters. It serves as a prototype for future objects generated using the **Person** constructor.

Once a prototype has been established, you may add attributes and methods to it. Any objects derived from the same prototype will inherit these attributes and methods.

Continuing with the **Person** example, let's add a **sayHello** method to the **personPrototype**:

```
personPrototype.sayHello = function() {
  console.log(`Hello, my name is ${this.name}.`);
};
```

Now, any objects created from the **personPrototype** will have the **sayHello** method available.

Instantiating objects from prototypes

To create new objects that inherit from a prototype, you can use the **Object.create()** method or the constructor function with the **new** keyword.

Using the **Object.create()** method:

```
const person1 = Object.create(personPrototype);
person1.name = "Mike";
person1.age = 30;
```

In this example, **person1** is created by using **Object.create()** and passing **personPrototype** as the prototype. The **name** and **age** properties are then added directly to **person1**.

Using the constructor function:

```
const person2 = new Person("Jane", 25);
```

The **Person** constructor is used to create **person2** with the **name** and **age** properties.

Person1 and **Person2** inherit the properties and methods provided in 'personPrototype'.

Chapter 9: The Document Object Model (DOM)

The Document Object Model (DOM) is an API for web documents that provides a programming interface. It models the webpage, enabling programs to modify the document's structure, style, and content. The DOM represents the document as a collection of nodes and objects, enabling developers to interact with and manipulate the webpage using JavaScript.

The Items have been arranged in a hierarchical fashion. When it comes to the organizing of items on a Web page, this hierarchical structure is the one to choose.

- The Window object - Represents the highest level in the hierarchy. The very last component of the object hierarchy is this very item.
- Document Object - Any HTML page that is imported into a window is converted into an object de-type document. The information that is on the page is included in the document.
- Form object - Anything that is included within the form>.../form> tags is considered to be part of the form object.
- Control elements - For the form The form object includes all of the components that have been specified for that object, including buttons, radio buttons, text fields, and checks.

There are a few different DOMs active in the world nowadays. In the next sections, each of these Document Object Models (DOMs) will have its own detailed explanation, as well as a description of how you may use it to access and alter document content.

When a web page loads, the browser creates a hierarchical tree-like structure, known as the DOM tree that represents the structure of the document. Each element in the HTML code is treated as a node in the tree. The top node in the tree is the document object, representing the entire web page.

JavaScript can be used to manipulate the DOM, allowing developers to modify the content, attributes, and styles of the webpage dynamically.

Developers can access elements in the DOM tree using a variety of methods, such as getElementById(), getElementsByTagName(), and getElementsByClassName(). Once the element is accessed, developers can modify its properties like innerHTML, textContent, style, and className.

The DOM also supports adding new elements, removing existing elements, and modifying existing elements, making it a powerful tool for creating dynamic and interactive web pages. Additionally, developers can use event listeners to detect user actions like clicks and keystrokes and respond appropriately, making web pages more engaging and responsive.

Example

When this page is loaded into a web browser, the browser creates a DOM tree, which represents the structure of the document. Each element in the HTML code becomes a node in the tree. The top node is the document object, which represents the entire web page.

```
<!DOCTYPE html>
<html>
  <head>
    <title>My Webpage</title>
  </head>
  <body>
    <h1>Welcome to my webpage!</h1>
    <p>This is a paragraph of text.</p>
  </body>
</html>
```

Output

⊕ My Webpage

Welcome to my webpage!

This is a paragraph of text.

Using JavaScript, we can manipulate the DOM to change the content of the web page.

Example

We can change the text of the <h1> element like this
```
document.getElementsByTagName("h1")[0].innerHTML = "Hello,
     world!";
```

The Original Legacy DOM

The Original Legacy DOM This is the model that was first implemented in the JavaScript language back when it was first released. It is fully supported by all browsers, although only some critical sections of documents, such as forms, form components, and pictures, are accessible via it. This model includes some characteristics that can only be read, such as the document's title, URL, and the time it was last modified. These attributes offer information about the document as a whole. Apart from that, this model offers a variety of methods that can be used to set or receive document property values. These methods are offered for your convenience.

Example

With HTML DOM, we are able to discover any HTML element included inside any HTML page. For instance, if a web page has a form element, we may refer to it using JavaScript as a document.forms[0] if the element is present in the document. In the event that your website document has two form elements, the first form will be referred to as document.forms[0], while the second form will be referred to as document.forms[1].

We can obtain the very first form element by utilizing the hierarchy and attributes that were shown before; specifically, document.forms[0].elements[0] will provide us access to the first form element, and so on.

An example of how to retrieve document properties using the Legacy DOM technique is provided here.

```
<html>

    <head>
        <title> Document Title </title>

        <script type = "text/JavaScript">
            <!--
                function myFunc() {
                    var ret = document.title;
                    alert("Document Title : " + ret );

                    var ret = document.URL;
                    alert("Document URL : " + ret );

                    var ret = document.forms[0];
                    alert("Document First Form : " + ret );

                    var ret = document.forms[0].elements[1];
                    alert("Second element : " + ret );
                }
            //-->
        </script>

    </head>
```

```
<body>
    <h1 id = "title">This is main title</h1>
    <p>Click the following to see the result:</p>

    <form name = "FirstForm">
       <input type = "button" value = "Click Me" onclick
       = "myFunc();" />
       <input type = "button" value="Cancel">
    </form>

    <form name = "SecondForm">
       <input type = "button" value = "Don't ClickMe"/>
    </form>

</body>
</html>
```

Output

This is main title

Click the following to see the result:

[Click Me] [Cancel]

[Don't ClickMe]

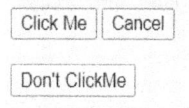

The W3C

The W3C, vast majority of today's browsers, are able to handle this paradigm. The majority of the historical DOM's functionalities are standardized inside the W3C Document Object Model (DOM), and more features have also been added. In addition to the support it provides for forms, images, and other array characteristics of the Document item, it also defines methods that enable scripts to manipulate and access any document element, not just elements with a specific purpose like shapes and images. These methods can be found in the element definitions.

Example

With W3C Document Object Model (DOM), it is relatively simple to modify (access and set) document elements. You are free to make use of any of the available methods, such as getElementsByName, getElementsByTagName, or getElementsById.

Accessing document properties with the W3C DOM technique is shown here with an example.

```html
<html>
   <head>
      <title> Document Title </title>
      <script type = "text/JavaScript">
         <!--
            function myFunc() {
               var ret =
         document.getElementsByTagName("title");
               alert("Document Title : " + ret[0].text );

               var ret =
         document.getElementById("heading");
               alert(ret.innerHTML );
            }
         //-->
      </script>
   </head>
   <body>
      <h1 id = "heading">This is main title</h1>
      <p>Click the following to see the result:</p>

      <form id = "form1" name = "FirstForm">
         <input type = "button" value = "Click Me" onclick = "myFunc();" />
         <input type = "button" value = "Cancel">
      </form>

      <form d = "form2" name = "SecondForm">
         <input type = "button" value = "Don't ClickMe"/>
      </form>
   </body>
</html>
```

Output
This is main title

Click the following to see the result:

[Click Me] [Cancel]

[Don't ClickMe]

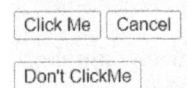

The IE4 DOM

The fourth version of Microsoft's browser for Internet Explorer included the introduction of this document object paradigm. Support for the majority of fundamental W3C DOM capabilities is included in Internet Explorer 5 and subsequent versions.

Example

The getElementById() function is not supported by the DOM in Internet Explorer version 4. Instead, it gives you the ability to seek any document components by their id attributes inside the all.array of the doc object. For example, the following will show you how to discover all of the li tags that are included within the first ul tag. It is crucial to maintain in mind that when utilizing the all.tags() function to access document attributes using the IE4 DOM approach.

```
var lists = document.all.tags("UL");
var items = lists[0].all.tags("LI");
```

The required HTML tag name must be specified in uppercase.

```
<html>
  <head>
    <title> Document Title </title>
    <script type = "text/JavaScript">
      <!--
        function myFunc() {
          var ret = document.all["heading"];
          alert("Document Heading : " + ret.innerHTML );
          var ret = document.all.tags("P");;
          alert("First Paragraph : " + ret[0].innerHTML);
        }
      //-->
    </script>
  </head>
  <body>
    <h1 id = "heading">This is main title</h1>
    <p>Click the following to see the result:</p>
    <form id = "form1" name = "FirstForm">
      <input type = "button" value = "Click Me" onclick = "myFunc();" />
      <input type = "button" value = "Cancel">
    </form>
    <form d = "form2" name = "SecondForm">
      <input type = "button" value = "Don't ClickMe"/>
    </form>
  </body>
</html>
```

Output

This is main title

Click the following to see the result:

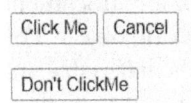

[Click Me] [Cancel]

[Don't ClickMe]

Chapter 10: Event Handling

An object's transition from one state to another is referred to as an Event. There are many different events in HTML, each of which represents a certain action that is carried out either by the user or by the browser. JS will respond to these events and enable the execution of the code when it is included in HTML as JavaScript. The act of responding to the occurrence of events is referred to as "Event Handling." As a result, jQuery is responsible for handling the events that are generated by HTML.

For instance, when a user clicks over the browser, JS code should be included. This code will then execute the job that has to be done on the event.

Click Event

Code

```html
<html>
<head> JavaScript Events </head>
<body>
<script language="JavaScript" type="text/JavaScript">
    <!--
    function clickevent()
    {
        document.write("This is JavaTpoint");
    }
    //-->
</script>
<form>
<input type="button" onclick="clickevent()" value="Who's
    this?"/>
</form>
</body>
</html>
```

Output

JavaScript Events

[Who's this?]

MouseOver Event

Code

```html
<html>
<head>
<h1> JavaScript Events </h1>
</head>
<body>
<script language="JavaScript" type="text/JavaScript">
    <!--
    function mouseoverevent()
    {
        alert("This is JavaTpoint");
    }
    //-->
</script>
<p onmouseover="mouseoverevent()"> Keep cursor over
    me</p>
</body>
</html>
```

Output

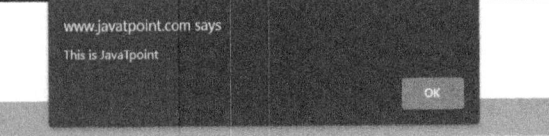

Javascript Events

Keep cursor over me

Focus Event

Code

```html
<html>
<head> JavaScript Events</head>
<body>
<h2> Enter something here</h2>
<input type="text" id="input1" onfocus="focusevent()"/>
<script>
<!--
    function focusevent()
    {
        document.getElementById("input1").style.background=
        " aqua";
    }
```

352

```
//-->
</script>
</body>
</html>
```

Output

Javascript Events

Enter something here

[heyy]

Keydown Event

Code
```
<html>
<head> JavaScript Events</head>
<body>
<h2> Enter something here</h2>
<input type="text" id="input1"
       onkeydown="keydownevent()"/>
<script>
<!--
    function keydownevent()
    {
        document.getElementById("input1");
        alert("Pressed a key");
    }
//-->
</script>
</body>
</html>
```

Output

www.javatpoint.com says
Pressed a key
                              OK

Javascript Events

Enter something here

Load Event

Code

```
<html>
<head>JavaScript Events</head>
</br>
<body onload="window.alert('Page successfully loaded');">
<script>
<!--
document.write("The page is loaded successfully");
//-->
</script>
</body>
</html>
```

Output

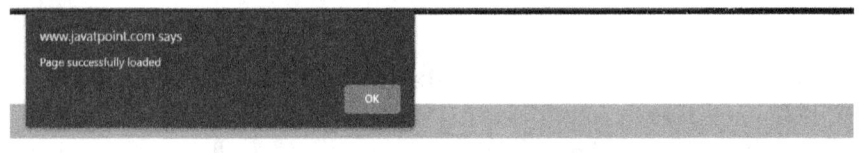

www.javatpoint.com says
Page successfully loaded
OK

Javascript Events
The page is loaded successfully

Chapter 11: Asynchronous Programming

Asynchronous vs. Synchronous communication

Before we get started, let's define these two terms: synchronous and asynchronous.

It is a synchronous, single-threaded language of programming by default. This indicates that instructions may only be executed sequentially, not concurrently. Consider the following code snippet:

```
let a = 1;
let b = 2;
let sum = a + b;
console.log(sum);
```

The given code sums two integers and then reports the result to the web console. The interpreter performs these instructions sequentially until they are completed.

Yet, there are several drawbacks to this strategy. Suppose we want to get a large quantity of data from a repository and present it on our UI. When the interpreter finds the instruction that retrieves this data, the remainder of the code is halted until the data is retrieved and returned. You can argue that the information to also be retrieved isn't that vast and won't take long. Assume you need to get data from numerous locations. This delay, when combined, does not seem like anything

people would want to encounter. Fortunately, the issues with synchronous JavaScript were solved with the introduction of asynchronous JavaScript.

Consider asynchronous programming to be code that may start now and end later. Because JavaScript runs asynchronously, the commands are not always performed sequentially, as we previously observed. There are a various of unique techniques that developers have tried throughout the years to appropriately handle this asynchronous behavior. Each solution improves on the one before it, making the code more efficient and simpler to comprehend if it becomes complicated.

To further comprehend JavaScript's asynchronous nature, we'll look at callback functions, promises, async and await.

What are JavaScript callbacks?

A callback is a procedure that is given within another function and then invoked to accomplish a job inside that function.

A console-logging software is above. It's new. The interpreter executes the first two instructions but skips the third and executes the last.

JavaScript's two-parameter setTimeout method. The first argument is yet another procedure, and the next is a millisecond timeout. Callbacks are now defined.

This setTimeout method must execute after 2 seconds (2000 milliseconds). Imagine it being taken away to be processed in a different browser section while the other

Code

```
console.log('fired first');
console.log('fired second');
setTimeout(()=>{
    console.log('fired third');
},2000);
console.log('fired last');
```

Output

```
fired first
fired second
fired last
fired third
```

Promises in JavaScript

Promises fixed callback functions. Promises to need two functions. Resolve and refuse. Resolve is a success, and reject is wrong.

Example

```
const getData = (dataEndpoint) => {
    return new Promise ((resolve, reject) => {
      //some request to the endpoint;

      if(request is successful){
        //do something;
        resolve();
      }
      else if(there is an error){
        reject();
      }

    });
```

```
};
```

A request to an endpoint encloses the promise above. As said, the promise requires resolution and rejection. If the endpoint call succeeds, we fulfil the promise and use the response. Errors invalidate promises. Promise chaining can solve callback issues. This approach successively retrieves data from numerous endpoints with much less code and simpler procedures.

JavaScript's Async/Await

Chaining promises like callbacks may become messy. Therefore, Async and Await.

Async Syntax

```
const asyncFunc = async() => {
}
```

Async functions always return Promises;

```
const test = asyncFunc();
console.log(test);
```

AsyncFunc delivers a promise in the browser console.

```
const asyncFunc = async () => {
    const response = await fetch(resource);
    const data = await response.json();
}
```

We may use await now to defer assigning till the .json method resolves.

Chapter 12: JavaScript Framework and Libraries

There is a notable difference between a programming framework and a library, even though they could seem to be the same thing or conceptually equivalent at first glance. It is necessary to consider the purposes for which they were designed.

Comparing Libraries and Frameworks

In computer programming, a "framework" is a collection of related "library" files to solve a certain problem. The key difference it offers is that the creator retains control over how it is used.

Library Definition

The library is a collection of code developers can include addressing a specific problem in their projects. For a library's code to be useful across various applications and scenarios, it has to be flexible and highly reusable. The timing of when the developer uses the library in their code is entirely up to them, and they are free to do so many times if they deem it essential.

Framework Definition

A Framework, in contrast, offers developers a more tightly organized code that they may insert their code at specified points of control. These points enable the developer to extend the framework's capabilities to meet their requirements. The framework is responsible for calling the developer-provided code when it considers it required.

The primary distinction is the developer's control over the code's application. Frameworks invoke the developer's code, which may then use Libraries to tackle common or difficult issues more readily.

As a real-world analogy, consider the bread-making process. Various stages must occur in a certain sequence for the production of bread. A framework for bread production can include, for instance:

```
// Make Bread Framework
function plantWheat() {
    // Put the code for Planting Wheat here
}
function millFlour() {
    // Put the code for Milling Flour here
}
```

```
function makeBread() {
    // Put the code for Making Bread here
}
function produceBread() {
    plantWheat();
    millFlour();
    makeBread();
}
```

No matter what occurs, makeBread() will always execute in the same manner. First, it will cultivate wheat, mill it into flour, and last, utilize the flour to produce the bread.

Yet, this framework provides the control plant points

Wheat(), millFlour(), and makeBread() let you describe the planting of wheat, milling of flour, and baking of bread. Depending on the inner workings of the control points, the bread you create might be vastly different, even though the foundation for their product remains the same.

Let's further specify this method by establishing these control points.

We wish to mill wheat into flour, eventually used to produce bread. Nevertheless, these processes might generate the desired result in drastically diverse ways. So, this is where the library comes in.

```
import * as farm from './modules/farm.js';
import * as windmill from './modules/windmill.js';
import * as bakery from './modules/bakery.js';
// Make Bread Framework
function plantWheat() {
    farm.plantWheat();
}
function millFlour() {
    getWheat();
    mill.millFlour();
}
function makeBread() {
    getFlour();
    bakery.makeBread();
}
function produceBread() {
    plantWheat();
    millFlour();
    makeBread();
}
```

Here, we use 3 libraries to separate the wheat-planting, flour-milling, and bread-making processes. These tasks are being delegated to a "farm" library, a "windmill" library, and a "bakery" library, in that order. Their inner workings remain a mystery to us. Yet, we are certain they will deliver what we need upon completing their procedures. Imagine if we have no access to windmills in the region. Yet, there is a nearby watermill which could mill flour for us. Our code may be modified to read:

```
import * as farm from './modules/farm.js';
import * as watermill from './modules/watermill.js';
import * as bakery from './modules/bakery.js';
// Make Bread Framework
function plantWheat() {
    farm.plantWheat();
}
function millFlour() {
    getWheat();
    watermill.millFlour();
}
function makeBread() {
    getFlour();
    bakery.makeBread();
}
function produceBread() {
    plantWheat();
    millFlour();
    makeBread();
}
```

We accomplished the same outcome with minor modifications by employing an alternative library. Even though we employed various libraries to produce bread for our needs, the production structure has not altered.

JavaScript Libraries

The following are examples of Libraries used in JavaScript projects.

jQuery

A popular library that offers, among other capabilities, HTML DOM navigation and manipulation, event management, and animation.

React

A library that enables components to be used to create interactive user interfaces.

Angular Material

A package that offers Angular web applications with several visual components that adhere to Google's Material Design.

Redux
A library that facilitates the implementation and management of your application's state in JavaScript applications. It is frequently used with other libraries to provide an interface atop its capabilities.

Three.js
A library for creating and displaying animated three-dimensional computer graphics inside a web browser. Compatible with the HTML5 canvas feature, SVG, and WebGL.

Lodash
A library includes a variety of utility functions for typical programming operations involving arrays, integers, strings, objects, and others.

JavaScript Frameworks
The following are examples of Frameworks utilized in JavaScript projects:

Angular
A framework for building web, mobile, and desktop apps from a single codebase.

Ember.js
A framework for developing web apps with sophisticated user interfaces.

Vue.js
A framework whose primary focus is the creation of user interfaces and single-page apps. Many officially supported libraries and packages are available for expansion.

Express
A lightweight framework for developing backends for Node.js web applications.

React
The creation of user interfaces may be facilitated with the help of the open-source JavaScript package known as React. Facebook first developed it, and web developers are using it all around the globe. By breaking down complex user interfaces into smaller, more manageable pieces that may be reused, the library's primary objective is to facilitate an easier development process. To update the user interface more efficiently, React uses a virtual Document Object Model (DOM), a lightweight version of the actual DOM.

Components

Components are the building blocks that make up the user interface in the React framework. A self-contained module that may be employed at any point in the program is referred to as a component. It's possible to think of components as custom HTML elements that can be rendered anywhere on the page. Functional components and class components are the two categories of components that may be found in React.

Creating a React Component

Creating components that can be reused is the primary focus of React. Getting started with constructing a component is the most effective method to learn React. The following is an example of how to construct a basic component:

```
import React from 'react';
class HelloWorld extends React.Component {
  render() {
    return (
      <div>
        <h1>Hello, World!</h1>
      </div>
    );
  }
}
```

In this demonstration, we will import React and then create a class derived from React.Component base class. The component's user interface (UI) is specified inside the render method.

React props

The data may be passed down from a parent to a child component using "props." As an illustration of how to send props to a component, consider the following example:

```
import React from 'react';
class Greeting extends React.Component {
  render() {
    return (
      <div>
        <h1>Hello, {this.props.name}!</h1>
      </div>
    );
  }
}
class App extends React.Component {
  render() {
```

```
      return (
        <div>
          <Greeting name="Alice" />
          <Greeting name="Bob" />
        </div>
      );
    }
}
```

In this demonstration, we have developed a Greeting component that can provide a custom-tailored greeting to the user. The Greeting component's parent, the App component, is the source of the name prop we supply.

React State

The state provides a mechanism for storing data that is subject to modification throughout time. The following is an illustration of one possible usage of state inside a component:

```
import React from 'react';
class Counter extends React.Component {
  constructor(props) {
    super(props);
    this.state = { count: 0 };
    this.handleClick = this.handleClick.bind(this);
  }
  handleClick() {
    this.setState({ count: this.state.count + 1 });
  }
  render() {
    return (
      <div>
        <p>Count: {this.state.count}</p>
        <button onClick={this.handleClick}>Click
        me</button>
      </div>
    );
  }
}
```

In this demonstration, we will construct a Counter component that will show a count and a button at the same time. We are using the state to keep track of the count, and each time the button is pressed, the count is brought up to date.

Functional Components

```
function Greeting(props) {
    return (
        <h1>Hello, {props.name}!</h1>
```

```
    );
}
```

```
ReactDOM.render(<Greeting name="Mike" />,
        document.getElementById('root'));
```

In this demonstration, we have created a Greeting functional component that takes a props object as its argument. This component may also return a greeting. Any attributes that are sent to the component when it is being rendered are stored in the props object. For the "name" property, we have decided to provide the value "Mike" in this scenario. The component will return a React element with a greeting and the name that was put in.

Class Components

It should be noted that the component is a JavaScript class that extends React.Component class. It is used when further control over the component's behaviour is desired, such as when handling events or maintaining a state. The following is an example of the component of class:

```
class Counter extends React.Component {
    constructor(props) {
      super(props);
      this.state = { count: 0 };
    }
    handleClick() {
      this.setState({ count: this.state.count + 1 });
    }
    render() {
      return (
        <div>
          <p>Count: {this.state.count}</p>
          <button onClick={() =>
          this.handleClick()}>Increment</button>
        </div>
      );
    }
}
```

```
ReactDOM.render(<Counter />,
        document.getElementById('root'));
```

In this demonstration, we have constructed the Counter class component responsible for controlling the count state. The count state is increased whenever the button is clicked, and the

component is re-rendered with the new count value when it has been updated.

JSX

JSX is an extension to the syntax of JavaScript that makes it possible to create code that is analogous to HTML while still working inside JavaScript. Inside React components, the user interface hierarchy may be defined with its help using this component. One example of JSX is as follows:

```
function Greeting(props) {
    return (
      <div>
        <h1>Hello, {props.name}!</h1>
        <p>Welcome to my website.</p>
      </div>
    );
}
ReactDOM.render(<Greeting name="Mike" />,
        document.getElementById('root'));
```

In this demonstration, we use JSX to construct a div element with a header and a paragraph. The name property is conveyed via the use of the props object.

Virtual DOM

The actual Document Object Model (DOM) is replicated in a manner heavier than in the virtual DOM. With React, the state of a component will cause the virtual DOM to be modified, at which point it will be compared to its previous state. The modifications between the two versions have been included in the Document Object Model (DOM). This strategy is more time and resource efficient than continuously updating the DOM.

The subsequent is an example that explains how the virtual DOM works:

```
// function to render time
function tick() {
    document.getElementById("root").innerHTML =
      "<div><h1>Hello, world! -- JS DOM
        Rendering</h1><h2>It is "
      + new Date().toLocaleTimeString()+
      ".</h2></div>";
}
setInterval(tick, 1000);
```

Angular

Google is responsible for developing the famous open-source web application framework known as Angular. It provides a complete collection of tools and capabilities to achieve its goal of making the process of developing web apps more straightforward. Angular is a web application framework created on top of TypeScript, a superset of JavaScript. It offers developers a strong set of capabilities with which they can construct online apps that are scalable, maintainable, and performant.

Angular Components

Components are the fundamental building blocks of an Angular application. Applications written in Angular are constructed of components that define the user interface (UI) and the application's behavior. A TypeScript class is used to define a component. An example of a component that is straightforward is as follows:

```
import { Component } from '@angular/core';
@Component({
  selector: 'app-hello',
  template: `<h1>Hello, {{name}}!</h1>`
})
export class HelloComponent {
  name = 'World';
}
```

In this demonstration, we will use a TypeScript class to create a component that we will refer to as the HelloComponent. The @Component decorator is responsible for providing information to Angular and instructing it on generating and utilizing components. The selector and template properties define the component's HTML content. The selector property is responsible for determining the name of the component's HTML element. The user's name will be shown whenever the name property is used.

Creating a new component that uses this one is required to include in an Angular application.

```
import { Component } from '@angular/core';
import { HelloComponent } from './hello.component';

@Component({
  selector: 'app-root',
  template: `<app-hello></app-hello>`
})
export class AppComponent {
}
```

In this demonstration, we will build a new component named 'AppComponent' and use the 'HelloComponent'. The HTML element representing the 'HelloComponent' is included in the 'template' that is part of the '@Component' decorator.

Angular Services

Angular Services provide the application with functionality that may be reused throughout. TypeScript classes are used to define services, often injected into the definitions of other components or services. One example of a straightforward service is as follows:

```
import { Injectable } from '@angular/core';
@Injectable({
  providedIn: 'root'
})
export class DataService {
  getData(): string {
    return 'Hello, World!';
  }
}
```

In the following example, we will use a TypeScript class to define a service named 'DataService'. The '@Injectable' decorator is responsible for providing information to Angular and instructing it on establishing and using the service. The 'providedIn' property is responsible for determining the scope of the service, which in this instance, refers to the application as a whole. The 'getData' function produces a string that is usable by other components or services and may be passed along to them.

For a component to make use of this service, we may inject it into the function Object() { [native code] } of the component:

```
import { Component } from '@angular/core';
import { DataService } from './data.service';
@Component({
  selector: 'app-hello',
  template: `<h1>{{message}}</h1>`
})
export class HelloComponent {
  message: string;
  constructor(private dataService: DataService) {
    this.message = dataService.getData();
  }
}
```

In this demonstration, we are going to use the function Object() { [native code] } of the 'HelloComponent' to inject the 'DataService' into it. The output of the 'DataService's' 'getData' function is used to populate the value of the 'message' property of the component.

Angular Routing

Inside an Angular application, the process of navigating between the various views and pages is handled by Angular Routing. To provide a smooth transition from one page to the next for the user, it is frequently implemented in single-page applications (SPAs). Angular has its built-in routing module, which may be used to allow Angular apps to implement Routing. The following is an example of how to implement Angular Routing in a simple application:

```
import { NgModule } from '@angular/core';
```

Node.js

Node.js is a robust JavaScript runtime that provides developers with the ability to create applications that are both scalable and high performing. Since Node.js is built on top of the Google V8 JavaScript engine and uses an event-driven, non-blocking I/O architecture, it is well suited for constructing real-time web applications.

Node.js Modules

Modules written with Node.js are self-contained functionality that may be used in various applications. A JavaScript file is used to create a module in Node.js. This file may export functions, objects, or variables other modules can utilize. The following is a demonstration of a basic Node.js module:

```
// module.js
module.exports = {
    sayHello: function() {
      return "Hello, World!";
    }
};
```

In this demonstration, we will construct a Node.js module that will send out an object with a sayHello function attached to it.

The need function will allow us to include this module in another file if we so choose:

```
// app.js
const myModule = require('./module.js');
console.log(myModule.sayHello()); // Output "Hello, World!"
```

In this demonstration, we need the module.js file and print a message to the console using the sayHello function exported from the module.

Node.js HTTP Server

Building web servers that can handle HTTP requests and answers may be accomplished with the help of Node.js. The HTTP module in Node.js allows users to establish an HTTP server capable of monitoring incoming requests and responding appropriately. The following is an example of how to establish a basic HTTP server by using Node.js:

```
// server.js
const http = require('http');
const server = http.createServer((request, response) => {
    response.writeHead(200, {'Content-Type': 'text/plain'});
```

```
    response.end('Hello, World!');
});
server.listen(3000, () => {
    console.log('Server running at http://localhost:3000/');
});
```

Using the createServer method available in the http module, we will now construct an HTTP server for this demonstration. The server is configured to accept incoming requests and respond with a plain text message that reads "Hello, World!" when it receives one. The listen function must first be called to start the server and monitor port 3000 for incoming requests.

Node.js NPM

Node Package Manager, sometimes known as NPM, is a package manager for Node.js that makes it simple for developers to install and manage the packages and dependencies necessary for their projects. Applications written in Node.js may add more functionality by using the packages and modules that can be obtained via the NPM package manager. To demonstrate how to use NPM to install and make use of a package in a Node.js application, consider the following example:

```
// app.js
const moment = require('moment');

console.log(moment().format('MMMM Do YYYY, h:mm:ss a')); //
        Output "February 21st 2023, 10:23:35 am"
```

We use the moment package to demonstrate how to format the current date and time. The need and format functions are used to import the moment package. The require function is used to import the moment package, while the format function is used to format the date and time in a certain manner.

Node.js Express

Express is a well-known web framework for Node.js that offers features and tools to develop online applications. Express is a web server framework built on top of the Node.js http module and offers a simpler and more user-friendly application programming interface (API). The following is an example of how to use Express to develop a basic web server:

```
// server.js
const express = require('express');
const app = express();
app.get('/', (req, res) => {
    res.send('Hello, World!');
});
app.listen(3000, () => {
    console.log('Server running at http://localhost:3000/');
});
```

NPM

Node.js utilizes Node Package Manager, often NPM, as its default package management. It is a sophisticated tool that gives developers a platform to exchange and reuse code with one another. NPM is now an indispensable component of the Node.js ecosystem, with over 1.3 million available packages. In this post, we will investigate the fundamentals of NPM, including its installation, management of packages, and management of dependencies.

What is NPM?

Node.js relies on package management called NPM. It offers a method for installing, managing, and sharing packages with other users. Packages are reusable units of code that may be implemented in a variety of different kinds of applications. NPM simplifies the management of these packages, ensuring that they are installed, updated, and uninstalled appropriately.

Installing NPM

If you have Node.js installed on your computer, you also have NPM installed since the two programs are distributed together. Execute the command below in your terminal to see whether or not NPM is already installed:

```
npm -v
```

This command will output the NPM version number if the NPM package is installed. You may install NPM if it is not already on your computer by installing Node.js. Downloads of Node.js are available on the website that is officially associated with the software. As soon as the installation is complete, NPM will be accessible through the command line.

Using NPM

The primary purpose of NPM is to manage the dependencies involved in Node.js applications. The proper operation of your project relies on several external modules, which are called dependencies. For instance, if you are developing a web application, you may want a module that gives you access to an HTTP server. This module is not pre-installed with Node.js; it is available for installation using the NPM package manager. Your project may use the module to offer an HTTP server when installed.

Just enter the following command into your terminal to install a package using NPM:

```
npm install <package-name>
```

For instance, the following command has to be executed to install the Express web framework:

```
npm install express
```

When you execute this command, the Express package will be downloaded and installed in your project. When the package has been installed, you may utilize it in your project by requiring its inclusion in the code:

const express = require('express');

Moreover, NPM will generate a node modules directory inside your project. This directory will house all of the packages that were installed. Since NPM may create this directory at any moment, it must not be included in the version control system and must not be checked in.

In addition to this, NPM gives you the ability to control the dependencies that are involved in your project. When you use NPM to install a package, it automatically installs any dependencies the package needs. For instance, when you install

the Express package, NPM will also install any other packages that Express needs to operate as intended. The package.json file, which may be found in your project's top-level directory, declares these dependencies.

The information for your project, such as the name, version, and dependencies, are all defined in the package.json file, which is why it is so important. The following is an example of a file named package.json:

```
{
    "name": "my-project",
    "version": "1.0.0",
    "dependencies": {
      "express": "^4.17.1",
      "body-parser": "^1.19.0"
    }
}
```

This file specifies the name and version of your project, in addition to the dependencies necessary for your project to function properly. The dependencies section contains key-value pairs that relate the names of packages to the respective

versions of those packages. A particular version number, a range of version numbers, or a semantic versioning expression may be used as the version number.

Semantic Versioning

A standard for versioning software packages inside the Node.js environment, Semantic Versioning (SemVer) is sometimes shortened as "SemVer." It makes it simpler for developers to manage dependencies and assure compatibility across multiple versions of a package when it is used to design a set of rules for versioning Node.js packages that are explicit and predictable. This is done with the help of this tool.

The SemVer standard includes a version number that is composed of three components, which are denoted as follows: MAJOR.MINOR.PATCH. These components, each of which has its unique meaning, are assembled into a whole that communicates the extent to which a product has been modified.

MAJOR version

This number is increased by one if a change in the package's application programming interface (API) breaks existing functionality. Because of this, it is possible that the code that was functional with an earlier version of the package will not be compatible with the current version. A function signature change or removing a public function, both examples of breaking changes, would fall into this category.

MINOR version

This number increases when new features are introduced to the package; nevertheless, the application programming interface (API) is compatible with earlier versions. This indicates that the code functional with the earlier package version should also continue to function with the updated version. One example of a modification that is deemed to be small is the introduction of a brand-new public function or the enhancement of the performance of an existing function.

PATCH version

This number is increased whenever problems are addressed or modest modifications are made to the package that does not impact the API. PATCH versions are available for download from the project's GitHub repository. This indicates that the code functional with the earlier package version should also continue to function with the updated version. A patch could consist of, for instance, correcting a misspelt word in the documentation or bringing an existing dependency up to date.

SemVer permits the inclusion of pre-release versions and builds information to the version number, in addition to the standard three-part format for the version number. Pre-release versions are indicated by adding a hyphen and a string, such as 1.0.0-alpha.1, and signify that the version has not yet reached a stable state or may still be subject to modifications. Build metadata is indicated by inserting a plus sign and a string, such as 1.0.0+build.1, and is used to identify the particular build or commit from which the version was created. For example, 1.0.0+build.1 is an example of build metadata.

Developers have a much simpler time managing dependencies when they adhere to the SemVer standard, which also helps them verify that their code is compatible with various versions of their packages. The development of Node.js apps may now be executed in a way that is both more efficient and dependable.

Webpack

Webpack is a bundler for JavaScript applications' modules that enables developers to bundle their code and assets into a single efficient package. Webpack is designed specifically for use with JavaScript applications. It is a widely used utility within the JavaScript ecosystem, and a significant number of large-scale applications make use of it. In this post, we will investigate the process of using Webpack to bundle a simple application written in JavaScript.

Getting Started

To begin working with Webpack, we must install it using the npm package manager. Using the following command on our terminal will allow us to do this:

```
npm install webpack webpack-cli --save-dev
```

The most recent version of Webpack and its command-line interface will be installed due to this (CLI). Using the command line, Webpack is executed via the command line interface (CLI).

When Webpack has been installed, all required to bundle our application is a simple JavaScript file and some CSS. For the demonstration, we will construct a simple web page with a button that allows us to alter the colour of the page's backdrop.

```
// index.js
import './style.css';
document.querySelector('button').addEventListener('click',
    () => {
  document.body.style.backgroundColor = 'red';
});
/* style.css */
button {
    background-color: blue;
}
```

With a simple HTML file, we will be able to execute this code in the browser:

```
<!doctype html>
<html>
  <head>
    <title>Webpack Example</title>
  </head>
  <body>
    <h1>Webpack Example</h1>
    <button>Change Color</button>
    <script src="index.js"></script>
```

```
      </body>
</html>
```

Now that we have Webpack, we can combine JavaScript and CSS into a single file using that tool. To do this, a Webpack

configuration file has to be created. In the directory that is the base of our project, we may create a file with the name webpack.config.js and fill it with the following contents:

```
const path = require('path');
module.exports = {
  entry: './index.js',
  Output {
    filename: 'bundle.js',
    path: path.resolve(__dirname, 'dist'),
  },
  module: {
    rules: [
      {
        test: /\.css$/i,
        use: ['style-loader', 'css-loader'],
      },
    ],
  },
};
```

This configuration file instructs Webpack to use index.js as the entry point for our application and to output the bundled code to a file named bundle.js in a new directory named dist. It also tells Webpack to output the bundled code to a file named bundle.js in the application's root directory.

Also, a module rule is specified to manage CSS files using the style-loader and the CSS-loader. Whereas the css-loader is responsible for interpreting the CSS and resolving any dependencies, the style loader injects it into the HTML content during runtime.

Now that everything is set up, we can execute Webpack from the command line by using the following command:

`npm webpack`

This will start Webpack and create a new file in the dist directory called bundle.js. Now that we have this new file, we can change our HTML file to incorporate it:

```
<!doctype html>
<html>
  <head>
    <title>Webpack Example</title>
  </head>
  <body>
```

```html
    <h1>Webpack Example</h1>
    <button>Change Color</button>
    <script src="dist/bundle.js"></script>
  </body>
</html>
```

When we load up this file in a browser, we will see that the website's background color is altered when we click our button.

One of the most useful tools for current web development is Webpack since it bundles and optimizes assets. Because of its adaptability and extensibility, it can be set up to support a wide variety of development workflows and can be combined with a wide variety of plugins to improve the efficiency of the build process further. Both of these features allow it to be utilized in several different contexts. Developers can enhance the functionality of their web apps and provide their customers with a more satisfying experience by using the usage of Webpack.

Babel

Babel is a popular JavaScript compiler that enables developers to write code in the most recent version of JavaScript (ES6/ES2015 and beyond) and convert it into backwards-compatible versions that can run on older browsers or environments that do not yet support the most recent syntax or features. Babel also allows developers to write code in a language beyond the most recent version of JavaScript. In the present world of web development, where new features and syntax are being released quickly, Babel is a crucial tool. This is because developers want to use these new capabilities while keeping backward compatibility with older browsers.

Babel's ability to enable developers to employ new language capabilities that are not yet widely supported by browsers is one of the most significant advantages offered by the platform. For instance, earlier browsers did not support the arrow functions and template literals introduced in ES6. These functions were introduced in ES6. Babel may convert this code into an equivalent version that will operate with browsers of a previous generation.

Babel has the additional benefit of being compatible with various tools and frameworks, such as webpack, gulp, and rollup. This is just another one of its many benefits. Moreover, well-known frameworks like React, Vue, and Angular may be used with Babel.

The following is a selection of examples demonstrating how Babel may be used to convert code written in ES6 to code written in ES5:

Arrow Functions

The arrow function syntax was first introduced in ES6, enabling developers to construct more succinct functions. On the other hand, older browsers do not allow arrow functions. Babel can translate the syntax of arrow functions into code that is equivalent and will operate in earlier browsers as follows:

```
// ES6 arrow function
const add = (a, b) => a + b;
// Transpiled ES5 code
var add = function add(a, b) {
  return a + b;
};
```

Template literals

In addition, ES6 introduces template literals, which make it possible for programmers to include expressions in string literals. Template literals are not supported in browsers of the previous generation. Babel may transform template literals into comparable code that is compatible with older browsers in the following ways:

```
// ES6 template literal
const name = 'Mike';
const message = `Hello, ${name}!`;
// Transpiled ES5 code
var name = 'Mike';
var message = 'Hello, ' + name + '!';
```

Destructuring assignment

The destructuring assignment was another feature introduced with ES6, and it gives programmers the ability to pull values out of arrays or objects and assign them to variables. Older browsers do not support the destructuring assignment programming construct. Babel can convert destructuring assignments into comparable code that is compatible with earlier browsers, including the following:

```
// ES6 destructuring assignment
const person = { name: 'Mike', age: 30 };
const { name, age } = person;
// Transpiled ES5 code
var person = { name: 'Mike', age: 30 };
var name = person.name;
var age = person.age;
```

Babel is an important piece of software for contemporary web development since it enables developers to use the most recent features and syntax while preserving compatibility with older web browsers. Using Babel, developers can write code in the most recent version of JavaScript and then have it automatically transpire into earlier versions. These older versions of JavaScript can operate on older browsers or environments that do not yet support the most recent capabilities.

Conclusion

We have covered a wide range of topics, starting from the fundamentals of JavaScript syntax and data types to advanced concepts like closures, prototypes, and asynchronous programming. This book serves as a comprehensive guide for beginners who want to learn JavaScript and gain a solid foundation in web development.

Throughout the chapters, we explored various aspects of JavaScript, including variables and operators, conditional statements, loops, functions, objects, the Document Object Model (DOM), event handling, and asynchronous programming. By understanding these core concepts, readers have gained the necessary skills to create dynamic and interactive web pages.

We delved into the importance of JavaScript in web development and learned about its versatility and wide range of applications. JavaScript is not only limited to the client-side; we also discussed its usage in frameworks and libraries like React, Angular, and Node.js. These tools empower developers to build powerful and scalable applications.

Additionally, we covered essential topics like the JavaScript type system, working with strings, numbers, and other data types, and explored how to manipulate them using operators. We also introduced the concept of functions, which are the building blocks of reusable code, and examined objects and prototypes, which play a crucial role in JavaScript's object-oriented nature.

Understanding the Document Object Model (DOM) and event handling are essential for creating dynamic web pages, and we explored how JavaScript interacts with the DOM and responds to user actions. We also discussed asynchronous programming techniques, such as callbacks, promises, and the newer async/await syntax, which enable us to handle time-consuming operations without blocking the user interface.

As we conclude this book, it's important to emphasize that learning JavaScript is just the beginning of your journey as a web developer. The language is constantly evolving, and new frameworks, libraries, and tools emerge regularly. However, with a strong understanding of the fundamentals provided in this book, you have laid a solid foundation for further exploration and growth in the JavaScript ecosystem.

Remember, practice is key. The more you code and experiment with JavaScript, the better you will become. Embrace challenges and keep building projects to apply what you have learned. The online community is a valuable resource, so don't hesitate to seek help or collaborate with others.

Congratulations on completing this book! With your newfound knowledge, you are well-equipped to start your journey into the world of web development. Happy coding!

Made in the USA
Las Vegas, NV
21 May 2024